ITALIAN
LAKES

Produced by AA Publishing

European Regional Guide

CREDITS

2

Written by Richard Sale

Copy editor: Christopher Catling

Edited, designed and produced by AA Publishing. Maps © The Automobile Association 1993.

Distributed in the United Kingdom by AA Publishing, Fanum House, Basingstoke, Hampshire, RG21 2EA.

The contents of this publication are believed correct at the time of printing. Nevertheless, the publishers cannot accept responsibility for errors or omissions, or for changes in details given. We have tried to ensure accuracy in this guide, but things do change and we would be grateful if readers would advise us of any inaccuracies they may encounter.

© The Automobile Association 1993.

A CIP catalogue record for this book is available from the British Library.

ISBN 0 7495 0583 4

Published by The Automobile Association.

Colour separation: Daylight Colour Art Pte, Singapore

Printed by Printers Trento S.R.L., Italy

Cover picture: **Lake Maggiore**
Opposite: **Lake Garda**
Page 4-5: Cadenabbia, **Lake Como**

The main entries in this book are cross-referenced to the regional map on pages 110-111. All heights on maps are in metres.

·INTRODUCTION·

This guide reveals the true character and flavour of the Italian Lakes, its people, legends and traditions, with detailed information and special features, illustrated throughout in full colour.

Specially drawn, easy-to-follow maps accompany over 25 walks and tours which take you out and about into the countryside as well as round the most popular towns and cities.

With practical information and a glossary of useful words and phrases, this is an invaluable guide to visiting this fascinating region of Italy.

·GEOGRAPHY·

Between the Alps, forming the border between Italy and Switzerland, and the Apennines, the ridge of peaks that forms the bone in Italy's leg, there lies a broad, flat plain. This extremely fertile land is usually known as the Lombardy Plain though, in deference to the other regions of Italy through which its primary river flows, it is sometimes also called the Po Plain.

During the Pleistocene period of geological time – the earliest part of the Quaternary Era, starting around 2 million years ago – the rivers that flowed into the Po from the Alps and the Apennines carried down vast quantities of silt. This was deposited on the plain, adding to the sediment left behind when the earlier Pliocene sea had retreated. These deposits proved remarkably fertile, one of the reasons why Lombardy was so highly prized and saw so many battles over its long history.

Today seasonal flooding – itself a link with ancient history since the Po routinely burst its banks when spring floods poured down from the hills – provides irrigation for one of Europe's leading centres for rice production. Though better land drainage techniques have extended the range of crops grown on the plain, rice is still of great economic importance and is the main ingredient of many characteristic regional dishes.

The Pleistocene period included several phases of glaciation; the final phase is known as the Quaternary Ice Age – because the Pleistocene period had by then been replaced by the Holocene period – and it ended around 11,000 years ago. Although all

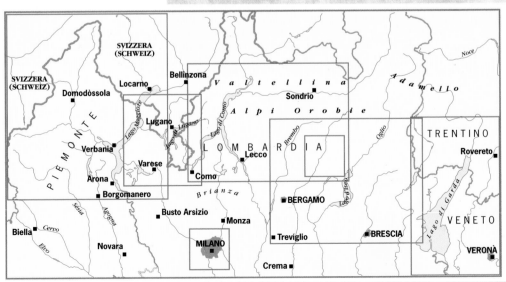

these periods of glaciation were important in shaping the land mass of northern Italy, it was this final Ice Age which created much of what we see today. Prior to the Ice Age there were three broad valleys where we now see lakes.

With the coming of the Ice Age the rivers in these valleys were replaced by glaciers. The glaciers were still confined by the ridges of hard rock that defined the river valleys – even though most of those ridges lay beneath an ice sheet – and as they flowed they gouged out the valley bottoms. This resulted in a phenomenon known as over-deepening, that is the creation of a basin in which the deepest point is lower than the exit point. Over-deepening was once the cause of great controversy in geological circles and many eminent scientists maintained that the phenomenon was impossible because it required ice to flow uphill. When boulders were discovered in Norway that could only have come from Sweden by being carried over the intervening 1,500m peaks, the concept of uphill flow was fully established. Today it is recognised that, provided the surface slope of a glacier is maintained, over-deepening is feasible and ice will flow up and over the basin lip.

Such over-deepening can occur along the length of the glacier, creating a series of long, narrow ribbon lakes, the correct geological name for the great lakes of northern Italy. The name is apt when you consider that Lake Maggiore, for instance, is over 10 times longer than it is broad. Staggering depths are achieved by the process: Lake Como is 410m at its deepest, that point lying 300m below sea level.

When the glaciers retreated at the end of the Ice Age the basins they had carved out filled with water to form the lakes. As they filled, the shaping of the land by the glaciers created some odd effects. In the Adda valley the glacier had been split into two by the hard upland of the High Brianza so that two over-deepened valleys were created. Today the Lecco arm of Lake Como is emptied by the Adda, but the Como arm has no outflow. When heavy rain raises the lake level the flow in the Adda increases, but not quickly enough to drain the excess water. This backs up in the long Como arm and overflows to flood Piazza Cavour and the lakeside roads of Como city. Lake Orta is also unusual since its waters drain northwards into Lake Maggiore, this 'uphill' drainage pattern having been superimposed by the glacial effects.

The retreating glaciers also left behind substantial amounts of debris which they had carried down from the mountains, a paste of ground up rock debris and boulders. The moraine, as the debris is termed, was laid down at the glacier's tip – terminal moraine – and its sides – lateral moraine. So enormous were the glaciers and their debris burden that this effect added substantially to the depths of the lakes: Lake Garda is 346m at its deepest point, the moraine thickness adding 149m – that is 43 per cent – to the depth.

Garda differs from the other lakes in several respects. It was created by a 'piedmont' glacier, one that thickened at its tip, a feature that explains the broad southern end of the lake. The glacier also penetrated much further into the plain than those that created Como and Maggiore. As a result, Lake Garda continues far beyond its retaining ridges, its southern end being formed by a morainic dam. In sharp contrast to this 'swimming pool' edge of southern Garda is the northern end of Lake Como, where the V-notch carved through the mountain gives the lake an almost fjord-like character.

After the final retreat of the glaciers the rivers that flowed into the lakes carried a heavy burden of silt. The deposition of this silt created Lake Mergozzo, which was once a continuation of Lake Maggiore, by forming a dam across the lake. It also helped in the creation of Lake Garlate and Lake Olginate on the Adda south of Lecco, though here there was assistance from the uneven deposition of terminal moraine.

The mountains that define the lakes change as we travel from east to west. In the west the rock is formed of calcium carbonate, or limestone. Dolomite, a specialised form of limestone – that is synonymous with northern Italy – is found in the Brenta Dolomite north of Lake Garda, though there is also a dolomite-like outcrop in the Grigna massif beside Lake Como. The high Alps of the Adamello and the Orobie are formed of hard, granitic hills whose resistance to erosion means that there is no great lake in the long gap between Garda and Como. Westward again, the intrusions of crystalline rock (schists and gneisses) become more pronounced as Lake Maggiore is approached.

Left: the peak of Griga towers above Lecco (Lake Como). Above: this traditional fishing boat symbolises the tranquillity of the lakes area

·HISTORY·

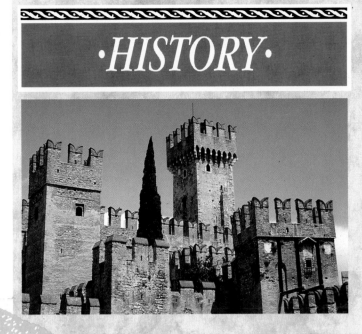

The fertility of the Po Plain was recognised by the earliest settlers who moved north into the region, in the wake of the retreating ice, about 11,000 years ago. These earliest folk were hunter-gatherers, living off the wildlife and plants of the area. The people of the Remedello culture, named after a site near Brescia, were among the first to exploit the area's agricultural potential.

GREGORIVS·III·PAPA·SYRVS.

A little later, at the transition from the Bronze Age to the Iron Age, the folk of the Golasecca culture, living near Lake Maggiore's southern tip, were erecting their burial tombs – built of serpentine rock slabs – and fashioning their funerary urns. The Golasecca folk, and the very similar Comacine peoples of Lake Como, had an agriculturally based lifestyle, supplemented by hunting and fishing – and, probably, by the occasional raid on nearby tribes, as there is significant evidence of a warrior class.

Gradually these early Iron Age tribes were displaced by the Celts, a sophisticated, but warlike, people who spread out from central Europe to take over most of the continent. In northern Italy the Celts were not totally dominant since the area formed the meeting point between themselves and the Etruscans. The origin of the Etruscans is still a hotly debated issue in academic circles: they may have migrated to Italy from Asia Minor, bringing Greek influences with them or they may have been a native Italian people who absorbed Celtic and Greek influences into their culture. All that can be said with certainty is that they controlled much of northern Italy until the coming of the Romans.

Rome was founded by Romulus

in 753BC, or so the legend has it. Soon Rome was spreading its sphere of control, expanding southwards to Sicily and North Africa and northwards to the Alps. The Roman advance was not inexorable and continuous, however. In the 4th century BC the Gauls of Switzerland and Austria swarmed over the Alps, sacking Rome in 390BC and forming Cisalpine Gaul – Gaul beyond the Alps. Not for another century was the whole of northern Italy finally brought under Roman control.

The Romans resisted the rise of Christianity that spread from its colonies in Asia Minor in the 1st century AD. The Emperor Nero presided over the first persecution of the Christians in AD64 but, despite a further 250 years of repression, Christianity maintained its impetus. Under the Edict of Milan of AD313 Constantine the Great granted freedom of worship to Christians, and in AD391 Theodosius made it the state religion.

It is an irony that the two emperors associated with the rise of Christianity also ensured the fall of Rome. In AD330 Constantine moved the capital of the Empire to Byzantium, renaming it Constantinopolis. Then, in AD393, Theodosius split the Empire into two halves – the eastern, centred

LOGIE STEADING
FORRES

Café • Antique Country Furniture

Contemporary Art • Secondhand Books

River Findhorn Walk & Heritage Centre

| **Walled Garden** | **Adventure Playground** |
| **Dressmaker** | **Plant Shop** |

OPEN
Mid March
to
Christmas
7 days a week
10.30am to 5.00pm
Established in 1992

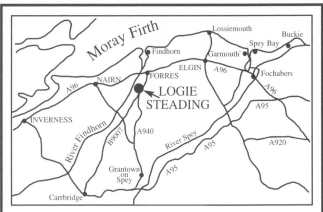

Logie Steading is in the beautiful
Findhorn Valley 6 miles south of Forres
on the B9007 signed off the A940.
Close to 'Randolph's Leap' on the
River Findhorn.

*Within the converted sandstone farm
buildings you will find
Fresh Coffee & Teas
Lunches, Homemade Cakes and Scones
at the Café.*

*Secondhand Books
Antique Country & Folk Art Furniture
Hardy perennials and shrubs
Contemporary Scottish Art
Gardens Open
Dressmaker - Alterations and Made-To-Measure
and other creative businesses.*

*Adventure Playground
River Findhorn Walk & Heritage Centre
giving an insight into River Findhorn life.*

LOGIE STEADING VISITOR CENTRE

Forres, Moray IV36 2QN
Tel: 01309 611378
Fax: 01309 611300
panny@logie.co.uk
www.logie.co.uk

DEESIDE BOOKS

a good selection of

SCOTTISH

MILITARY

FISHING

TRAVEL

SHOP OPEN

Monday ~ Saturday
10 - 5

Sunday
12-5

November ~ February
hours are variable depending
on weather condition
so please phone for details

Books bought & sold

Home visits & free valuations

No obligation booksearch available
for tracing out of print books

on Constantinopolis, and the western, centred on Rome. This weakening of the Empire allowed the early loss of the western part to the warlike tribes of central Europe, the Huns and the Vandals – names synonymous with violence and tyranny.

When the western Empire fell, the lakes area was occupied by the Lombards, a Teutonic tribe. Legend has it that their invasion was sparked off by a petty act in Constantinople. A senior official there, the eunuch Narses, was deeply offended when the Emperor's wife suggested that he should join the women, rather than the force preparing to defend the city. The outraged Narses sent Alboin, King of the Lombards, a crate of wine from northern Italy, and instructions on how to invade the poorly protected country.

The Lombards were converted to Christianity by Theodolinda, the daughter of a Bavarian duke who married a Lombardic king. For this she was given a True Nail from the Cross of Christ by Pope Gregory III. The nail was incorporated into the iron crown used at the coronation of Lombardic kings and for the coronation of Charlemagne – 1,000 years and 40 kings later it was also used to crown Napoleon. It is now held in the Treasury of Monza Cathedral, near Milan.

Charlemagne defeated the Lombards to create a Frankish state in northern Italy in the 8th century. Frankish rule was followed by 300 years of German rule after Otto I, the German Emperor, invaded the country (see the Rocca at Garda, page 93). Eventually the cities of the north united to form the Lombard League, threw off the German yoke by defeating Barbarossa, and gained control of the whole of northern Italy.

The subsequent emergence of the City States (see page 78) gave rise to the finest period of Italian culture, though their fragmented nature made the country vulnerable, and ultimately they were swept aside by bigger and better organised countries. First Spain, then the Austrian Habsburgs, dominated northern Italy. This situation was briefly interrupted when Napoleon invaded the country and had himself crowned king, though the north returned to Austrian rule following his defeat.

In the early 19th century the Italians, particularly those of the north under Austrian rule and the 'free' Italians of the neighbouring kingdom of Piedmont, began to yearn for an Italy free of foreign influence. A real voice was given to this movement in 1842 when a newspaper called *Il Risorgimento* (*The Awakening*) was published. An unlikely group of partisans was formed – King Carlo Alberto of Piedmont, Count Camillo Cavour, his Prime Minister, Giuseppe Mazzini, an anti-monarchist from Genoa, and Giuseppe Garibaldi, a flamboyant adventurer from Nice (see page 53). A rising in the north in 1848 failed but a second, in 1859, succeeded, with French help, in driving the Austrians out of Lombardy after the appalling Battle of Solferino (see page 94). Garibaldi invaded Sicily and soon most of Italy was united under King Vittorio Emanuele II, Carlo Alberto's son. The war between the new Italy and the Austrians resulted in the incorporation of the Veneto into Italy and the country was finally unified with the capture of Rome in 1870.

As a result of the treaty concluded at the end of World War I, Italy – one of the Allies – gained the South Tyrol and Istria, but lost the city of Fiume. Gabriele d'Annunzio (see page 97) occupied the city, and though this

action failed it allowed Mussolini to call for the return of Italia Irredenta (Unrecovered Italy) which led to the invasion of Abyssinia and, ultimately, to the 'Pact of Steel' with Hitler's Germany. When the Allies invaded Italy in 1943 Mussolini set up the Saló Republic in the north (see page 101) but defeat and Mussolini's death were inevitable. In the subsequent Treaty of Paris Italy lost Istria to Yugoslavia.

In 1946 King Vittorio Emanuele III abdicated and a national referendum abolished the monarchy. Today, with its past troubles behind it, the Italian Republic is a respected member of both the European Community and NATO.

Left: Gregory III, whose gift of a nail from the Cross of Christ was incorporated into the Lombardic crown, used at the coronations of Charlemagne and Napoleon. Above: Charlemagne crosses the Alps to subdue the Lombards

PEOPLE, CUSTOMS AND CLIMATE

Centuries of foreign domination left the emergent Italy of the 20th century with enormous problems. These problems were exacerbated by Italy's tragic involvement in World War II, a war which left the country ravaged and its people battered. It is estimated that 80 per cent of the houses in Milan were hit by bombs or incendiaries, with more than a third of all homes being destroyed. Though the damage was less appalling away from the main industrial centres the whole infrastructure of Italy had been severely damaged.

People

From those ashes Italy rose with a remarkable assuredness. Utilising its large manpower resource the economy was soon growing as fast as any in the world. Though the recovery was led by Fiat and its subsidiaries, the industrial base was actually very wide so that Italy was able to take advantage of most new developments, playing a leading part in industries as diverse as electronics and ship building. In addition, government involvement in many of the leading companies allowed profits to be drawn off to rebuild the infrastructure. New roads, were built which involved staggering feats of engineering – with tunnels bored though mountains and viaducts crossing valleys – the railway network was consolidated and an efficient power industry was created.

The power base of the new Italy was the north, with Milan its undoubted capital. Indeed, Milan has a cultural heritage and a sophistication comparable with, and in many cases superior to, that of many European capitals. In Milan, and throughout the north, the economic miracle allowed the people to create and sustain an elegant lifestyle that is the envy of many visitors.

Of course, Italy is still a country of staggering contrasts, the sophistication and elegance of the north being at odds with the grinding poverty of the south. The reasons for the differences are both historical and geographical. The City States and the proximity of northern Europe offered advantages that the more introverted southern kingdoms could not match, and the heat and dryness of the south means that the agricultural base will always be poorer, while those living off the land will always have to work harder to achieve less, with consequent knock-on disadvantages for urban dwellers.

Customs

Italian society is said to be dominated by the three Ms – Madonna, Mamma and Mangiare. This is an exaggeration but, like all good generalisations, it contains several grains of truth. The Italians are certainly a religious people, as the number and splendour of their churches testifies. Even quite small villages may have several churches and Sunday morning brings out scores of people, many in family groups, walking their way to mass. Most Italians devote the afternoon to play. For many this means walking or climbing, both very

Farmers help each other in everyday rural tasks

popular sports. As the Sunday driver will find, many go cycling, Italy sharing with France a national passion for the sport.

Whether Italian society is matriarchal depends on who you ask. It is certainly true that, until a very few years ago, Italian life was family orientated, and children were the focus of the social unit. Mothers were therefore of prime importance, caring for the children and ensuring that their needs were satisfied. The system created a good number of spoilt children, but adult Italians seem none the worse for the experience – unless fanatical support for football and 'artistic' driving methods can be put down to a reaction against a sheltered upbringing. Today, northern Italy seems to have a more liberal attitude towards the role of women.

The final M is Mangiare, eating. This really is an important feature and Italians enjoy both the eating and its social side. For the visitor this can only be good news; the enthusiasm that Italians bring to the table ensures that all eating establishments, from the humblest *pizzeria* to the grandest *ristorante,* serve well-prepared food in good surroundings.

Italians are also very fond of coffee breaks and have turned them into a highly sociable activity. Many workers, particularly shop and office workers, stop at a bar on their way to work for a coffee and breakfast – which never amounts to much more than a pastry – and then go out again for another in the midddle of the morning. Long lunch hours mean that many can be found in the bars again in the early afternoon, and there is another collecting time at the end of the working day.

The standard bar fare is *liscio,* a thick black coffee served in small cups, usually heaped with sugar and drunk standing up. It is lethal in quantity, and many visitors might prefer *caffé lungo,* with added hot water, or *caffé macchiato,* with a little milk. *Cappuccino,* served with frothed milk and, usually, a shake of ground chocolate, is only drunk at breakfast. At other times, particularly if they are male, *cappuccino* drinkers receive glances that assess their virility.

Climate

The lakes hold such vast quantities of water that they distort the local climate, making winters warmer, by acting as giant storage radiators, and taking the edge off summer's searing heat. The result is a Mediterranean-type climate, with dry hot summers, but not stickily humid, and cool, usually rainy, winters. The average monthly temperatures for the area are given below. Lakes Como and Maggiore are so close that a combined figure is given. Lake Garda, being further to the east, has a different temperature profile. In practice there is also a difference between Maggiore and Como, the former being closer to the Piedmont Alps. Thus, on average, temperatures in the Lake Maggiore resorts are about 1°C (1.5°F) lower than those in spring, autumn and winter. In summer the temperature of the two lakes is the same.

A similar table of comparitive rainfalls is given below. In this case the large differences between Lake Maggiore and Lake Como mean that separate figures must be given.

Lake Garda's apparently heavy summer rainfall is not as bad as the raw figure suggests since much of the rain falls in short torrential bursts from thunderstorms brewed up in the neighbouring peaks. Such storms also affect the other lakes, but are less pronounced as the visitor moves westwards.

The lakes are swept by winds funnelled down, or up, the valleys of the inflowing rivers. These winds blow more or less steadily, making the lakes a paradise for sailors, especially those new to the sport who do not have to worry about sudden gusts. As a general rule the winds blow from the north (down the lakes) in the mornings, and to the north (up the lakes) in the afternoons. The winds are stronger at the northern end of the lakes. Strangely these winds rarely affect the beaches.

Average temperatures	Lakes Como and Maggiore	Lake Garda
January	6°C (43°F)	4°C (40°F)
February	7°C (45°F)	6°C (43°F)
March	10°C (50°F)	9°C (48°F)
April	13°C (55°F)	13°C (55°F)
May	18°C (64°F)	19°C (66°F)
June	21°C (70°F)	22°C (72°F)
July	24°C (76°F)	25°C (77°F)
August	22°C (72°F)	24°C (76°F)
September	18°C (64°F)	20°C (68°F)
October	12°C (54°F)	16°C (61°F)
November	10°C (50°F)	11°C (52°F)
December	8°C (46°F)	7°C (45°F)

Rainfall	Lake Maggiore	Lake Como	Lake Garda
January	90mm	75mm	30mm
April	60mm	50mm	60mm
July	20mm	12mm	70mm
October	20mm	20mm	90mm

11

MAGGIORE AND ORTA

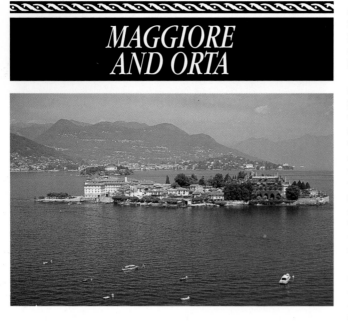

By comparison with the lakes to its east, Lake Orta is a mere splash of water, 13.5km long and only 2.5km wide at its broadest point. Orta is, however, a very beautiful lake, its waters filling a cauldron ringed by mountains high above Lake Maggiore. Orta drains into the bigger lake some 100m below but – unusually – the outflowing river, the Torrente Nigoglia, flows north, towards the Alps, rather than south, before emptying into the River Strona. The direction of the flow was imposed by the glacial action that created the lake but the inhabitants of the Orta valley see it as striking a blow against conformity; they have maintained a tradition of independence, yet are very friendly to visitors.

The Romans called Lake Orta *Cusius,* and Cusio is the name still given to that part of Piedmont's Novara province in which the lake is located. In early medieval times, the lake was called San Giulio, after the saint who brought Christianity to the area and after whom its island and prettiest town are named. The island is the most impressive of all those on the great lakes, for although it does not have Isola Madre's quiet beauty or Isola Pescatori's charm (both of which are found on Lake Maggiore), it has an extraordinary sense of history, a calm dignity and compelling prospects across the lake to a background of fine hills.

The island also looks good from the shore, especially if you are lucky enough to be in Orta San Giulio when the lake is flat calm and a gentle mist is rising from the water; the mist obscures the hills of the western shore and softens the focus of Isola San Giulio, so that the island and its churches seem to float between heaven and earth, as though unsure of their true position. At such moments the island really does appear to be a magical place.

By contrast, Lake Maggiore seems more worldly. It is busier, more accessible and so big that its northern tip lies in a different country – Switzerland. Yet for all that it is a beautiful lake. In 1800 the young Henri Marie Beyle arrived on Maggiore's shores in the wake of Napoleon's Italian campaign. The young man was to go on to achieve considerable fame as a writer, better known to the world by his pseudonym of Stendhal. Under that name he wrote of his first sighting of the lake. He was entranced: 'When one, by chance, has a heart and a shirt, one should sell one's shirt to see the surroundings of Lake Maggiore', he wrote.

The Romans called the lake *Verbanus,* a name still remembered in the town of Verbania on the western shore, a town that forms part of the urban

Above: the boat-shaped outcrop of Isola Bella. Below: the church-filled isle of Isola San Giùlio

complex of Intra, terminus for the lake's car ferry. Maggiore's present name is unromantic: it just means 'greater'. As well as lacking romance, the name is untrue; Lake Garda is a bigger lake than Maggiore, in terms of surface area, though Maggiore is the longer of the two, measured from tip to tip. Lake Maggiore covers 215 square km and is 65km long; it is 2km wide on average – though about twice that width near Luino, and much wider if measured into the further recess of the Borromean Bay (between Verbania and Baveno). At one time the lake was even wider, but silt brought down by the inflowing River Toce dammed off the extremity of the Borromean Bay to create Lake Mergozzo.

The Borromean Bay, where the lake is at its deepest (over 370m) deep, is studded by the three Borromean Islands, which represent one of the highlights of a visit. Isola Bella's palace and gardens are a riot of baroque architecture, Isola Pescatori is one of the last places on the lake

where characteristic fishing boats can still be seen, while the quiet and beautiful Isola Madre has one of the lake's finest gardens. Elsewhere there is much to see, including Angera castle, with its

Isola San Giùlio's church complex, once a hermit's cell

collection of dolls, elegant Stresa and the huge bronze statue of San Carlo Borromeo at Arona.

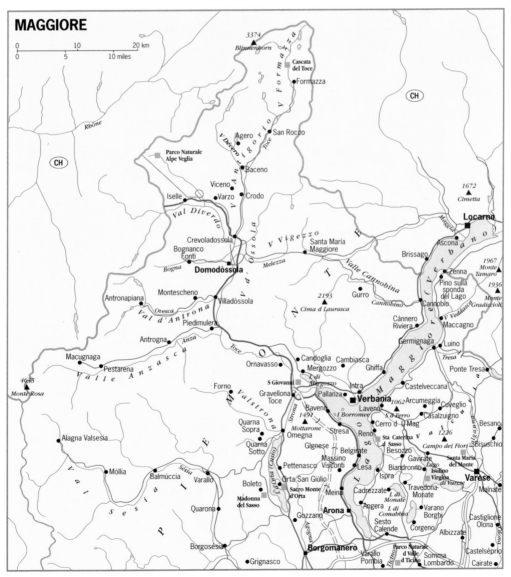

ANGERA
MAP REF: 110 B3

Angera was the birthplace of Pietro Martire, the chief contemporary chronicler of Columbus's expedition to America. This is one of the items of local history covered in the museum in Via Marconi. Elsewhere, be sure to walk along the lakeside in the shade of the double row of chestnut trees.

For most visitors the castle (see page 102) is the main draw. This houses a superb doll museum and hosts summer exhibitions featuring the work of local artists. There are fine views from the castle across the lake to Arona and the statue of San Carlo Borromeo. In summer the castle is floodlit and is quite magnificent when viewed from Arona.

ARONA
MAP REF: 110 B3

Arona, once a Roman village and probably first settled even earlier, is the largest town on the Piedmontese shore of Lake Maggiore. Arona owes its size and prosperity to its position at the point where the railway from Switzerland – coming through the Simplon tunnel and down the Ossola valley to the lake – joins the line from Turin to Milan. Prosperity has resulted in much recent building which has not added substantially to the town's elegance. Behind the newer buildings of the wide lake-front road you will find the older parts of the town. The Palazzo de Filippi houses the Museo Civico (Civic Museum), with an interesting collection on the town's history and the mineralogy of the area. The main church, Santa Maria in Via San Carlo, has a fine painting of the Nativity by Gaudenzio Ferrari. Further north, in the Piazza del Popolo beside the river, is the old Borromeo Palace of Justice, a fine building with its arches and pillars. Close by is Madonna di Piazza, a church designed by Pellegrini.

North again is the *rocca* (castle), a natural fortress – making an elegant backdrop to harbour views – topped by the ruins of a medieval Borromeo family castle. The history of the Borromeo family is closely linked to Arona – and to Angera just across this narrow section of the lake – the family having succeeded the Visconti to the lordship of the town in the late 15th century. The Borromeo family produced many great men including one saint

whose huge statue stands north of Arona, back from the lake.

The statue of San Carlo Borromeo (see opposite) was erected in 1679 by Federico Borromeo, Archbishop of Milan, a later member of the family. A marble statue, surrounded by 15 chapels, was originally planned. In the event, the statue was made of bronze and there are three chapels, only one of which was ever completed.

The statue is certainly not great art – though it is certainly high art, being 23.5m tall and standing on a granite plinth 12m high. The statistics are more impressive than the statue's historical or artistic importance. The circumference of the thumb is 1m while the forefinger is 1.95m long – twice the length of the nose. For a fee you can climb the plinth for a close encounter with the saint and, for another fee, you can enter the statue and climb precariously up into the head – though be warned that, in summer, this becomes as hot as a roasting oven.

ASCONA
MAP REF: 110 B4

Ascona is the second Swiss town on the lake, smaller than Locarno, but with a more pleasant position, being sheltered from north winds and set in an excellent small bay. The old fishing harbour is delightful. The town is modern, elegantly Swiss and has several fine museums. The Modern Art Museum in Via Borgo has works

Spring in flower-filled Baveno

by Klee and Utrillo, among others, a tribute to the town's artistic past, the setting having long attracted painters. The Ignatz Museum in Via Albarelle has a collection of puppets, while the Museum Casa Anatta is claimed to be the oldest 'original' wooden house in Switzerland.

BAVENO
MAP REF: 110 A3

Baveno nestles below a mountain of beautiful pink granite. Quarrying helped the town prosper, though today it is almost purely a tourist village, with a line of villas opposite the excellent lakeside flower gardens. Queen Victoria once stayed at the pink Castello Branca, set on the hillside in the southern part of the village; Wagner came here too, and Winston and Clementine Churchill honeymooned in Baveno.

Close to Castello Branca is Casa Morandi, an Italian National Monument and the most photographed spot in Baveno. It is a delightful four-storey building, the floors being reached by interwoven outside stairways. The church is also worth visiting. It is set a little aloof from the village and has a fine 12th-century Romanesque facade and campanile, the rest being 17th-century baroque. Alongside the church is an octagonal baptistery, its domed ceilings decorated by superb 15th-century frescos.

SAN CARLO BORROMEO

Carlo Borromeo was born in Arona's *rocca* on 2 October 1538. He was a cardinal at 22 and Archbishop of Milan by 26, though these appointments owed more to the fact that his uncle was Pope Pius IV than to any personal qualities. From the time he arrived in Milan, however, he became a devout and hard-working Christian. Later in life it was claimed that Carlo was too ugly to be anything but a saint; all portraits show extraordinarily large ears and an even bigger nose – and they are likely to be flattering.

Carlo was a staunch defender of the faith, once complaining that far too few heretics were being executed. In late 16th-century Italy such an attitude made the archbishop a true soldier of Christ. Carlo died on 3 November 1584 and his body is preserved in Milan's Duomo, laid out in his archbishop's robes, his skeletal face covered by a silver mask. Only 26 years later Carlo was canonised, and shortly after plans were laid for the awful statue outside Arona

ANGERA'S DOLL MUSEUM

The Borromeo Castle at Angera is largely unfurnished, the austerity of the rooms reflecting its early history as a military stronghold. Some of the rooms, however, are used to house what is, arguably, the finest collection of dolls in Italy, and one of the most interesting in Europe. The dolls are all European – French, German and Italian in the main – and date from the middle of the 19th century through to the early years of this century. Most of the dolls are of porcelain, dressed in their original period costumes.

The castle also houses a separate display of LENCI dolls; the curious name derives from the initial letters of the company's Latin motto insisting that play is the doll-making company's aim. LENCI was founded in Turin in 1919 with the aim of producing an all-fabric doll that could withstand rough handling. A special technique was used to form a seamless head, whose life-like features were painted by hand; every doll is thus unique.

Doll Museum

The waterside villas and gardens of Bavena below misty granite peaks

BOLETO
MAP REF: 110 A3

High on the western ridge of the mountains that enfold Lake Orta is Boleto, a pleasant village that was once the capital of a local 'free state', remarkable for its progressive policy of having women on its ruling council. On a hilltop nearby is the church of Madonna del Sasso, built like a small village in pale stone and set on an outcrop of bare grey rock. The church is both beautiful and beautifully sited; the view to the lake is exquisite and there are some fine 18th-century frescos inside as well as a superb 17th-century wooden crucifix.

CÁNNERO
MAP REF: 110 B4

Cánnero was once described as the 'Genoese Riviera in miniature...a pearl in a bracelet of vineyards and villas'. The vineyards have largely gone, though the villas remain - Garibaldi stayed at one of them, the Villa Sabbioncella, after the battle at Luino. The town now

styles itself Cánnero Riviera, claiming the title of the 'Nice of Maggiore' because of its mild winter climate.

Even so, the town is quiet, with a feeling of being a little off the beaten track. Like its neighbour, Cannobio, it has a fine collection of old houses in narrow streets, and an even more striking harbour. Again, like Cannobio, there is also a beautiful gorge, that of the Torrente Cánnero, which comes into the town under a picturesque old bridge.

Lying offshore are the two Cánnero, or Malpaga, castles, each standing on an island and originally connected by a drawbridge. The castles were built in the 12th century but did not enter history forcibly until the early 15th century when they were taken over by the five Mazzarditi brothers who used them as a base for terrorising both lake travellers and unfortunate lakeside dwellers.

The Mazzarditi were notorious for the viciousness of their piratical exploits. One of the brothers once murdered a monk and used his habit to enter a

Tranquil today, Cerro del Lago Maggiore's fine beach once saw the execution of a notorious 15th-century pirate

convent where he raped a nun. When news of this crime reached the local ruling family, the Visconti, an army was formed which marched to Cánnero, in 1414, to bring the brothers to justice. Even then it took a six-month siege, so impregnable were the castles.

Not surprisingly the Visconti had the castles destroyed; today the remains consist largely of the ruins of a later fortified villa. Visitors are not allowed to land on the islands, but boat trips around them are available from Cánnero.

CANNOBIO
MAP REF: 110 B4

The first town in Italy, for those driving southwards along the lake shore, is also one of the best Maggiore towns, being far enough up the western shore to be left quieter than the towns closer to the Lombardy Plain. A stone at the edge of the town records that the

**Shady waterfront colonnades lead
to the site of the Cannobio Miracle**

townsfolk played their part in the
Italian War of Independence by
attacking an Austrian fleet on the
lake in 1859. The town is
unfortunately split by the main
road, which makes it seem
fragmented, but the old quarter,
with its narrow winding streets, is
delightful and deserves a visit.

In that section of the town, away
from the lake, look for the Palazzo
della Ragione, the old council hall,
which was built in the 12th
century to a glorious design, with
porticoes and pillars. The building,
also known as the Palazzo
Paradiso, an immodest little title,
houses a small museum of local
history. Nearby is the church,
which is much more recent than
its 12th-century campanile. On the
lake side of the road is the
Santuario della Pietà, the site of
the Cannobio miracle (see right).
The chapel was built by Pellegrini
on the instructions of San Carlo
Borromeo; in addition to the
miraculous painting itself, the
church has several other works –
mostly based on the miracle –
worthy of note. The nearby
harbour is excellent and the site of
a Sunday market.

From Cannobio a road heads up
the Valle Cannobina reaching,
after about 2.5km, the *orrido*
(gorge) of Santa Anna, with a
church dedicated to the same saint
alongside. Here the valley's
stream, the Torrente Cannobino,
passes through a tight gorge to
emerge into a wide, calm pool.
The spectacular gorge can be
viewed from either of two bridges
(one that is Roman, according to
local tradition) or from a boat.

CERRO DEL LAGO MAGGIORE

MAP REF: 110 B3

Cerro has a fine beach and the
village was beloved of the writer
Manzoni who frequently stayed
here. From the headland close to
the village there are especially
good views across the lake
towards the Borromean Islands. It
is doubtful whether a 15th-century
pirate called Polidoro would have
agreed. Captured after a reign of
terror, both on and off the lake, he
was sentenced to be hanged on
the beach near the headland.
When given the chance of a last
request he asked for a glass of
wine; on being told that the town
had no inns he screwed up his
face in disgust and turned to the
executioner saying 'Better hell
than this town of abstainers'.

THE CANNOBIO MIRACLE

Tommaso Zaccheo, a Cannobio
innkeeper, had a painting in his
house, a Pietà, depicting the
dead Christ removed from the
cross between the Virgin Mary
and St John. On 8 January 1522
real blood was seen to emerge
from the painted Christ's
wounds. As if this event were
not miraculous enough,
Cannobio then escaped
completely unscathed from a
plague that devastated the
surrounding area.

Other miracles followed and
Tommaso's house was
demolished to make way for a
chapel soley constructed to
house the painting. History
does not record how Tommaso
felt about this. About 50 years
after the initial miracle San
Carlo Borromeo decreed that a
new church should be built to
house the painting, which was
given a silver frame. Almost
immediately after the painting
was rehung Cannobio was
spared when plague again
devastated the area. The
painting still hangs in its ornate
frame in that church, the
Santuario della Pietà.

COUNTRY WALK

This 6.5km walk links Cánnero to
Cannobio, two of the finest
Maggiore lake villages, and takes
approximately two hours. The
walk can be extended by taking
the lake steamer from Luino across
to Cánnero, and then walking to
Cannobio. At the end of the walk
the return journey can be made by

steamer from Cannobio to Luino.

Leave Cánnero along the
Cannobio road; after 400m take
the mule track to the left that leads
to Carmine Superiore.

Carmine Superiore is a very old
and pretty village with a 14th-
century Romanesque church
decorated with 15th-century
frescos.

Leave the village along the well-
defined mule track, ignoring the
track that leads to the lower
village of Carmine Inferiore. The
track rises in a series of big bends
to reach Molineggi.

From the tiny village of
Molineggi there are beautiful
views of the lake and several old
mills that once made the
community prosperous.

The same mule track continues
from the mills and leads easily
down to Cannobio. To return to
Cánnero you can take a bus or the
lake steamer.

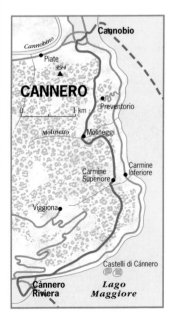

17

GIGNESE
MAP REF: 110 A3

Gignese stands on the road that crosses the high ridge separating Lake Maggiore from Lake Orta. The name of the village is said to derive from a former landowner who gave refuge to three girls when they fled a cruel master. The girls brought their umbrellas with them, causing a stir since umbrellas had never been seen in the village before. The sons of the landowner married the three girls, copied the umbrellas and began a local trade whose fascinating history is explained in the village museum (see opposite).

GOZZANO
MAP REF: 110 A3

Gozzano is a light-industrial town with a complex of older buildings. The church of San Lorenzo, in baroque style, houses a Roman marble font and a sarcophagus, said to be the tomb of San Giuliano, brother of San Giulio who founded the monastery on the island in Lake Orta. The Palazzo Vescovile (Bishop's Palace), beside the church, dates to the 13th century. The town is overlooked by the Lombardic Buccione Tower.

Approaching the garden isle of Isola Bella by boat

GRAVELLONA TOCE
MAP REF: 110 A3

This small industrial town grew up at the mouth of the Ossola valley, where the Strona river from Lake Orta meets the Toce river which drains the Val d'Ossola into Lake Maggiore. The site has always been an important one and the town museum holds many treasures from local sites, dating from the late Bronze Age through to the time when Imperial Rome was at its height.

ISPRA
MAP REF: 110 B3

Although it sounds a most unlikely mix, this fine town manages to combine the atmosphere of a small fishing village with cosmopolitan sophistication, thanks to the prosperity generated by the nearby Euratom research complex.

CYCLE TOUR

This cycle tour covers the southern end of Lake Maggiore, where good views and the most interesting sites are concentrated.

Leave Stresa, going south on the lake road. Soon you will pass the entrance to the Villa Pallavicini Giardino Botanico.

Villa Pallavicini
This elegant mid-19th-century villa, set in one of the most desirable positions on Lake Maggiore, is privately owned and sadly not open to the public, but the 16ha parkland surrounding the villa can be visited. The parkland and formal gardens are exquisite, the more so for being the home to many free-roaming animals, such as deer, wallabies, llamas and birds. The facilities include a restaurant, a good coffee/snack

bar and an excellent children's playground.

Continue along the lakeside road, with fine views across the water to the church of Santa Caterina del Sasso set into the cliffs. At this point you should look back for good views towards the Borromean Islands, though better views await as Belgirate is reached.

Belgirate

Here you will find a delightful mix of old lakeside fishing port and elegant 19th-century villas. The old part of the town is grouped close to the church with its 12th-century campanile, the villas stretching away along the lake. The Villa Bono Cairoli once belonged to the Cairoli family, famous for their role in the history of Italian independence. Garibaldi frequently stayed here as their guest. When the poet Manzoni stayed at nearby Lesa he would walk to Belgirate, claiming that the town's shoemaker was the only one who could make shoes that fit him correctly.

Before the Ice Age gouged out the valley to create Lake Maggiore, the River Ticino looped right below Belgirate to go around Monte San Quirico. The headland of that peak now causes the lake to narrow; we follow the lake road sweeping in a gentle arc to Meina.

Meina

This is another village of elegant villas, one of which, the Villa Farraggiana, has a beautiful neo-classical façade, sited between the blue of the lake and the green of the lush hillside.

Continue into Arona and take the lake steamer to Angera (cycles are not allowed on the aliscafo (hydrofoil) boats). From Angera the lake road cuts straight through Monte San Quirico to reach Ispra. From there it hugs the shore again before rising to reach the road for Santa Caterina del Sasso and the village of Reno. Continue past Cerro before the final free-wheeling descent into Laveno. From Laveno you can take the car ferry across to Intra/ Verbania and change boats there to return to Stresa. Energetic cyclists could return from Intra to Stresa along the lake road, but be warned that this particular section of the lake is a little dull and the road traffic is much busier.

BOAT TRIP

This tour covers the southern end of Lake Maggiore. You can join it at several points along the lake but Arona is the main terminus for the Maggiore lake steamer and by starting there you can have the pick of seats. Sitting outside is preferable but, depending on the weather, you may want to take a warm coat. You may also want to pack some snacks, especially if you are travelling with children; the boats do have snack bars but it will be several hours before Intra is reached. Do check beforehand that your boat will dock at Santa Caterina del Sasso.

From Arona the boat does the short crossing to Angera, whose castle dominates the skyline and looks more impressive the closer the boat is to the village. On the reverse crossing towards Meina the statue of San Carlo Borromeo looms ahead, but the view improves when Meina itself, with its backdrop of fine hills, comes into view. A tantalising glimpse along the lake is to be had when the boat clears the headland of Monte San Quirico, but the best view northward is not obtained until the quaint old harbour of Lesa is approached.

The next stop is Belgirate, the boat offering a fine view of the elegant villas of the 'new' part of the village. Ahead now, as the boat approaches Santa Caterina del Sasso, is one of the highlights of the trip and one of the finest views on Lake Maggiore; the chapel of Santa Caterina apparently clinging limpet-like to a sheer cliff.

Recrossing the lake the boat heads for Stresa. On this leg of the journey try to be on the right-hand (starboard) side of the boat when the first view to the extreme north end of the lake is obtained, looking up to the high peaks of the Swiss Ticino, which make a wonderful backdrop to the water. Stresa looks beautiful from the lake, the elegant hotels nestling below the Mottarone, but the view to the Borromean Islands is even better.

Isola Bella is the first you will approach – its boat-like prow being more obvious from the water than from either the mainland or the island itself. The approach to Isola Pescatori is prettier, the old harbour being more peaceful than bustling Bella.

Next comes Baveno, before the isolated Isola Madre is reached. The quay on Madre always seems full of people waiting to leave, having toured the island's only

attractions, its magnificent villa and gardens.

Beyond Isola Madre some boats go to Villa Taranto, though little enough is visible from the water, before docking at Intra/Verbania where the town offers shops, cafés and restaurants in plenty.

THE UMBRELLAS OF GIGNESE

The area around Gignese was once famous for its umbrellas and parasols, which were exported all over the world. The local umbrella-makers were themselves in demand and migrated to start industries in many other countries. Queen Victoria and the other crowned heads of Europe once boasted a Gignese umbrella. Today the trade has declined, partly because the fashion for parasols has all but disappeared. The great days of the trade are recalled in the village by one of Italy's most curious and fascinating museums. The museum explores the history of the umbrella as a useful accessory and a fashion essential from the earliest known examples – painted on Greco-Roman pottery – to modern times. Many of the best exhibits date from the Golden Age of both the umbrella and the Gignese umbrella-makers, the late 19th century. Some of these, with their carved handles and elaborate canopies, are pure works of art.

THE PIEDMONT ALPS

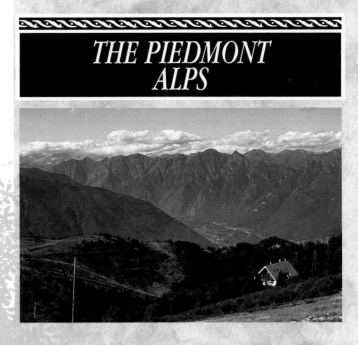

Lake Orta and the Italian part of the western shore of Lake Maggiore both lie in the province of Piedmont. The name of the province derives from its position, at the foot of mountains. The mountains in question are the high Alpine peaks that form the border between Switzerland and Italy. The peaks of the Piedmont Alps are approached by several beautiful valleys that lie close to Lakes Orta and Maggiore.

The high Alpine peaks (above) shelter flowery valley meadows (below)

The Valle Anzasca

The closest valley to the lakes is the Valle Anzasca, reached by driving up the Ossola valley, passing the Candoglia marble quarries on the right (see opposite), and turning off westward after the main road crosses the River Toce via Ponte della Masone. The Anzasca valley is about 30km long and over this distance the road climbs by over 1,100m.

Antrogna is famous for its military processions, the village folk dressing up in August each year to parade in braided red coats and white trousers. Traditionally the costumes are called Napoleonic, though in reality both the parade and the costumes are much older, probably dating from around 1600.

Parades are also held in the villages of Bannio, Calasca and Anzino and they may date from the time of border troubles between the Italian-speaking villagers of the lower valley and the Walser villagers of the upper valley. Today that border is crossed close to Pestarena, traditional Walser costumes being seen occasionally here and in the higher villages.

At the head of the valley is Macugnaga, famous as a centre for winter sports and summer mountaineering. From the village itself, or from the top of the nearby cable cars, the view of Monte Rosa, the second highest mountain in Europe, is awesome.

The Val d'Antrona

A little way north of the Valle Anzasca, Val d'Antrona also heads west towards the high Alps. Antrona is rarely visited and is more beautiful, if less rugged, than Anzasca. Many of the valley's womenfolk still wear the traditional costume of a black jacket decorated with an embroidered front (*puncett*) and Venetian lace collar.

The Val di Bognanco

Two valleys lead off from Domodóssola. The Val Vigezzo, to the east, is worth exploring in detail (see page 27). To the west lies the Val di Bognanco, a valley more famous for its thermal springs than for its spectacular scenery. The main centre is Bognanco Fonti, a small village with a bottling plant where the hot mineral waters are used for the treatment of intestinal disorders.

The Valle Antigorio and the Val Formazza

A little way north of Domodòssola the long valleys of Antigorio and Formazza follow the Toce river back to its source near the Swiss border. At Baceno, the Valle Dévero (see below) leads off westward.

Beyond, a scenic drive leads to the valley's most famous attraction, the Cascata del Toce, one of the loveliest waterfalls in Europe. The falls drop 143m but are often dry since the Toce is normally diverted to drive a hydro-electric power station. The falls usually run as Nature intended on Sundays, public holidays and during the first fortnight in August. Beyond the falls the road rises to the Passodi San Giacomo (San Giacomo Pass) before descending into Switzerland.

The Valle Dévero

The tiny Dévero valley, which leaves the Valle Antigorio at Baceno, is little visited and very unspoilt, particularly at its upper end where there are fine lakes. The last village, Agero, can only be reached by a 3km walk through a tunnel.

The Val Divedro

This final valley is a continuation of the Val d'Ossola, taking the main road over the Simplon Pass and into Switzerland. The valley also sees the re-emergence of the railway that crosses from Switzerland by way of the Simplon rail tunnel, a monumental work that took eight years to complete and cost 67 men their lives. In its day the 19.8km tunnel was the world's longest. Leading off the Val Divedro is a side valley to the Alpe Veglia where a park has been set up to protect the plant and animal life and the natural scenery. Here are the finest marmitte dei giganti (giant's bowls) in Italy. The bowls are smoothed hollows in the rock caused by centuries of water flow.

ALPINE FLOWERS

Whenever you see a small cluster of alpine flowers it always comes as a surprise that anything so fragile could survive such a harsh environment. The high ground surrounding the lakes is a favourite hunting ground for the flower lover, many of the choicest alpine species being found on the ridges, or on the flanks of the valleys of the Piedmont Alps.

If you want to learn how to identify the various plants you should first visit the Giardino Alpino, the Alpine Gardens, at Alpino above Stresa. Here you can admire hellebores and orchids, alpine chrysanthemums, the parasitic lousewort, alpine toadflax, alpine bistort, monkey flower, the stemless carline thistle, rock roses and saxifrages and, best of all, the fabulous Pyrenéean and martagon (Turk's-cap) lilies.

THE CANDOGLIA MARBLE QUARRY

Milan's cathedral – Il Duomo, the world's third largest cathedral – is built almost entirely of a pinkish-white marble from the quarries at Candoglia, on the flank of Monte Faïe, the peak that rises above Lake Mergozzo in the Val d'Ossola. In the 14th century, when the decision was made to build the cathedral, the quarry was owned by Duke Visconti who negotiated a contract for the stone that freed it of all taxes when it was moved into the city. To ensure that only stone bound for the cathedral was exempt, blocks were stamped AUF, short for *Ad Usum Fabricae*, 'for building use'. Later, *auf* became a Milanese expression for a long wait, or working for nothing.

The stone was loaded on to barges at Candoglia, and taken down the River Toce, then across Lake Maggiore and down the River Ticino. Close to Magenta the barges transferred to the Naviglio Grande, the Great Canal, which linked the river with the Milanese canal system. The blocks were unloaded at the Laghetto and transferred by land to the cathedral site. Today the Candoglia quarries are still in use, extracting marble for repairing buildings in Milan.

Cornflower (*Centaurea montana*) contrasts with mustard (*Brassica nigra*)

LAVENO

MAP REF: 110 B3

This compact lakeside town lies at the point where the Torrente Boesio reaches Lake Maggiore. It is occasionally called Laveno Mombello, though strictly Mombello is the nearby industrial town whilst Laveno is the tourist resort and the terminus of Lake Maggiore's only car ferry (from Intra/Verbania). It is said that Laveno is named after a Roman general, Titus Labienus, who fought a critical battle here. Another important battle took place here many centuries later when Garibaldi's troops fought the Austrians who controlled the town castle. What remained of the castle after this conflict can be seen in the park laid out on the Punta San Michele, the northern headland of the small bay in which Laveno lies. A memorial to those who died in the battle can also be seen at the lakeside.

The car ferry makes Laveno a busy place in summer, but there always seems to be a spare place at one of the numerous good cafés which are one of the better features of the town. Another is the huge church of Santi Giacomo e Filippo, built in the 1930s, decorated outside with statues by Casarotti and inside with paintings by Salvini.

About 3km north of the town look out for the rock tower of Sasso Galletto, which rises out of the lake. Viewed from a certain angle the tower is said to resemble a praying nun and it is finished off with a statue. North again is the Rocca di Calde, a huge limestone outcrop once topped by a 9th-century castle that was

successfully defended when Otto I came this way, but was destroyed by the Swiss in 1513. Close by is Castelvecanna: the church here has a rare marble altar and a fine, sharply pointed campanile.

LESA

MAP REF: 110 B3

Lesa was Manzoni's favourite spot on Lake Maggiore, the novelist and poet staying at the Palazzo Stampa. To commemorate the great man's visits the town has a small museum of Manzoni memorabilia. The village has long been famous for its peach orchards – there is a painting in the church entitled *Jesus in the Orchard* which gives some idea of the significance of the crop to the town's prosperity. A professor once wrote a whole book in praise of Lesa's fruit – and a stroll along the lake front should definitely be accompanied by the consumption of a peach or two.

LOCARNO

MAP REF: 110 B4

Locarno is the largest town of the Swiss Maggiore, a colourful place with several parks and gardens. The best of these are the Giardini Pubblici – the Public Gardens – which form the southern edge of the main square. In summer, when the flowers are all in bloom, this is one of the most pleasant spots of any town on Lake Maggiore. On the north side of the square a row of arcaded shops welcomes those who have finished their garden stroll. The fine old town of Locarno lies inland from the gardens, grouped around the old Visconti castle, little of which survives. Part of the castle now

Laveno, terminus of Lake Maggiore's only car ferry, is dominated by its 1930s church

houses the town museum which concentrates on local history, though it also has a small collection of contemporary art.

North of the Public Gardens a rack railway takes visitors to the church of Madonna del Sasso. The church is reached by a series of descending steps and ramps, which offer a superb view both of the church itself and of the lake. The church, built in the 15th century, is somewhat over decorated but it contains an important Bramantino altarpiece of the Flight into Egypt.

Beyond the top station of the railway a short walk leads to a cable car that rises to the Cardada. From there a chair lift rises higher still to the top of Cimetta (1,672m) from where there is a fabulous view of the Swiss mountains and of the lake.

LUINO

MAP REF: 110 B4

Luino, located in Lombardy, is the main town of Maggiore's eastern shore, a light-industrial town with a large railway complex. The town is thought to have been the birthplace of the Renaissance artist Bernardino Luini and one of his works, *The Adoration of the Magi*, can be seen in the church of San Pietro, situated in the eastern, uphill, section of town. The church of Madonna del Carmine, by the lakeside, has several frescos that are also attributed to Luini.

Luino has a better defined shopping centre than any other Maggiore town. The shops cluster round Piazza Garibaldi, a large, rambling square marred by streams of homicidal drivers. Wednesday is the best day to be in the square, for then the weekly market adds colour to the town and keeps the drivers at bay. The monument to Garibaldi in the square was the first to be erected in Italy in honour of the hero of the Risorgimento; after his defeat at Custozza, Garibaldi raised a small army in Luino to continue the struggle against Austria.

To find the better parts of Luino head north from the main square, past the elegant palazzo that houses the town hall, and then turn left off the main road into a maze of steep and narrow streets alive with interesting buildings and shops.

MOUNTAIN WALK

Allow at least an hour for this 1.5km climb from Laveno to the summit of Sasso del Ferro. Make for the bottom station of Laveno's *funivia*, or cable car.

The Laveno *funivia* is one of the great adventures of Lake Maggiore. Passengers stand in two-person buckets that finish at waist level so as to ensure that there is no interruption to the view. This is especially good over the town and over the lake to Monte Rosa, visible beyond the Mottarone. You can also look straight down, if you

Locarno's public gardens, ablaze with rhododendron blooms, provide a quiet retreat from the bustle of this busy town

have a head for heights, to see the entertaining butterflies that congregate along the corridor cleared through the woodland beneath the *funivia*. More panoramic views are to be had from the top station (Poggio San Elsa), located at 974m.

From the top station take the track that climbs to the top of Sasso del Ferro (1,062 m).

From the summit Monte Rosa dominates the view, but there are also good views inland towards the valleys around Varese and of the lake, particularly the northern section, hemmed in by the mountains of Switzerland.

After admiring the extensive views you can either return to the funivia *top station or take the track that runs east, then north and downhill towards the village of Casere. This path is occasionally waymarked with a number 8, but the signposting is erratic and cannot be relied upon. When a track is reached, turn left and left again after 400m on to a path (marked with an 8) that leads back to the* funivia *top station.*

THE LAVENO SCULPTOR

Sergio Tapia Radic was born in Puerto Natales in Chile in 1938 and studied at the University of Santiago School of Art before working on commissions from Chile, Brazil, Europe and the USA. One of his best-known works of this era was a bust of the assassinated US president, John Kennedy. In the early 1970s he left Chile for Italy and settled in Laveno. For several years he has had a permanent summer exhibition in Angera Castle.

Sergio's commissioned work is chiefly devotional and includes a superb bronze in Luino church. The non-commissioned works reveal a love of elegance; horses and ballerinas figuring prominently in the subject matter.

Technically Sergio is a superb artist, having once sculpted a woman holding a child, the pair being held aloft by a man, all out of a single matchstick! His relief panels also display a rare talent – so much so that some critics have found similarities between his work and that of the Renaissance genius, Michelangelo.

In Laveno, Sergio's studio can be found at 177/181 Via Labiena, the road leading inland from the town centre. If you are really lucky the master will be at work and, being a gracious man, he will no doubt be willing to share his love of art with the visitor.

24

MACCAGNO

MAP REF: 110 B4

Maccagno has one of the best campsites on the lake, a well-tended park with its own café and private beach. The village behind the site is just as good, with its old square and the steep, but pretty, section near the church. From the village the beautiful Val Veddasca can be reached. A turn off from this valley leads to Lake Delio, whose dark waters, so the legend has it, cover a town drowned for losing its faith.

North of Maccagno is the village of Pino sulla Sponda del Lago Maggiore, which has the longest placename in Italy, and Zenna – the last village before Lake Maggiore becomes Swiss.

MASSINO VISCONTI

MAP REF: 110 A3

Close to this tiny and beautifully rustic village is a castle which was built in the 12th century, dismantled a century later, and then restored. The castle was owned by the family whose name is now attached to the village of Massino, a family that gave Milan their mightiest lords and whose name is encountered all over Lombardy. It is remarkable to think that so powerful a family should evolve from such a modest, though delightful, place.

MERGOZZO

MAP REF: 110 A4

Mergozzo and its lake are rarely visited because they are bypassed by the main road to the Val d'Ossola and by the road that links Intra to Baveno. Both the lake, nestling below Monte Faïe, and

Ochre-coloured walls and sub-tropical palms in old Maccagno

the village, with its medieval towers, are very attractive and well worth seeking out. Mergozzo was both a Celtic and a Roman village and the local museum has many interesting local finds.

Close to Mergozzo is the village of Mont'Orfano, below the mountain of the same name. Here stands the church of San Giovanni, one of the best examples of Lombardic Romanesque architecture in the area.

OMEGNA

MAP REF: 110 A3

Omegna is a small industrial town made interesting by surviving stretches of its medieval walls and the ruins of an old bridge – some experts say Roman in date, others medieval – that once spanned the river. The town's old quarter, particularly the part close to the lake, has some beautiful old houses with balconies, outside staircases and wrought ironwork. Two streams flow through the town, the Strona, which flows down the Valstrona, and La Nigoglia, Lake Orta's outflow, which joins the Strona just beyond the town. La Nigoglia flows the wrong way – that is northwards, towards the mountains instead of southwards, and the folk of Omegna have a saying that 'La Nigoglia goes up, and we make the laws'.

MOTOR TOUR

This 72km tour, lasting $1^3/_4$ hours, takes in several characterful villages occupying the hinterland between the region's two main lakes, Orta and Maggiore.

Leave Omegna, travelling south along the eastern shore of Lake Orta. The road hugs the lake, with views across to the hills of

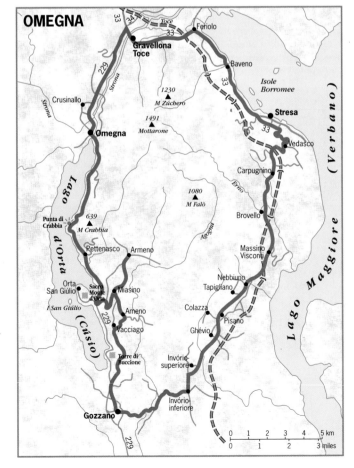

the western ridge, and leads to Punta di Crabbia.

Punta di Crabbia
This viewpoint on the right-hand (lake) side of the road is named after the conical peak that rises to the left, Monte Crabbia. Views stretch almost the whole length of the lake.

Ahead now the road leaves the lake to pass along Pettenasco's main street, regaining the lake shore to head towards San Giúlio. At the crossroads for San Giúlio, turn left for Miasino, first passing through the village of Legro.

Miasino
This village is positioned on the side of a hill and offers splendid views over Lake Orta and the hill of the San Giúlio Sacro Monte. The 17th-century church of San Rocco was built in baroque style by Richini and is stocked with works of art from the same period, so many in fact that it is more remminiscent of a gallery than a church. The village also has some very fine villas set in pretty gardens. Perhaps the most attractive house is Casa Nigra, with its Renaissance façade, galleries and orangery.

Close to Miasino, but requiring an out-and-back detour, is Armeno, whose fine church is decorated with very old frescos.

From Miasino take the road south to Ameno - not to be confused with Armeno.

Ameno
The village is huddled around a fine Romanesque campanile and has several fine baroque churches. Look out for Villa Monte Oro with its huge garden of very rare plants.

From Ameno drive to the nearby village of Vacciago.

Vacciago
Though a tiny village, little more than a straggling collection of houses, Vacciago has one of the region's most interesting art galleries. The Calderara Foundation is housed in a magnificent 16th-century villa with a three-storey arcade and an elegant courtyard. The collection centres around the work of Antonio Calderara himself, a local painter whose misty, stylised works capture the essence of Lake Orta in autumn. The collection also includes works by over 100 other artists from all around the world.

From Vacciago take the road for Gozzano, passing below the Torre di Buccione to reach the town. Go left in the centre of Gozzano, on the road for Arona, driving as far as Invório.

Invório
Like several other towns in the region, Invório is divided into two halves. The lower town (Invório Inferiore) has the remnants of a 15th-century Visconti castle, the upper town (Invório Superiore) being undistinguished.

Turn left in Invório Inferiore following the signs for Invório Superiore and Pisano, but bypassing the upper town by taking the Pisano road. Go through Pisano and on to Nebbiuno.

Nebbiuno
Between Invório and Pisano our route switched from Lake Orta to Lake Maggiore. Nebbiuno completes the transfer, offering a panoramic view of Maggiore.

Continue to Massino Visconti from where the road goes due north, cutting off lake views until it drops into Stresa. Turn left along the Maggiore shore road, with the Borromean Islands to the right, going through Baveno to Feriolo. Here bear left with the road into Gravellona Toce, and turn left there, with the River Strona on your left, to return to Omegna.

COUNTRY WALK

This walk links the villages of Curiglia and Monteviasco. Curiglia is located in Valle Veddasca, one of the thickly forested valleys that lie between the northeastern shore of Lake Maggiore and the Swiss border. The valley is reached from Luino by way of Dumenza. Beyond Dumenza the valley road is narrow and twisting, an exacting piece of driving. It is best to travel on Sundays, because that is the only day that the local bus - driven with great enthusiasm and total disregard for all other traffic does not run.

Curiglia is a delightful place, surprisingly remote, although Monteviasco, the village at the end of the walk, is even more isolated. Monteviasco can only be reached on foot or by cable car. It is said to be a journey of a 1,000 steps, but you would be wise to allow approximately 2 hours for the 7km round trip.

From Curiglia follow the Valle Veddasca road to the point where it ends at the Ponte di Piero. From the bridge a mule track rises sharply to Monteviasco, about 150m above. Follow the mule track all the way to the village.

Monteviasco is a picturesque little village once occupied by almost 400 hardy souls. Today most of the houses have been turned into holiday homes, the permanent population numbering only about 20. The cable car on the walk is a relatively new innovation - until very recently the villagers' only connection to the outside world was the footpath from Curiglia. Monteviasco's houses are built of dry-stone walls and each has a *lobbie*, a balcony, not only for taking advantage of the fabulous views, but also serving as an outside passage linking the rooms of the house. The roofs are covered by *piode*, flat stone slabs skilfully cut to bed with each other.

To return to Curiglia, you can either retrace your steps or continue up the steep valley of the Torrente Viascola; the mule track leading up and out of the village leads towards Switzerland and crosses the head of the valley before descending into Curiglia. The latter is a fine walk, but will take a strong walker 4 hours.

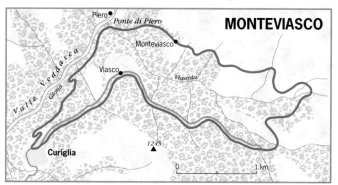

ORTA SAN GIULIO

MAP REF: 110 A3

In the 4th century AD two brothers, called Giulio and Giuliano, left Rome to spread the word of Christianity. Giuliano stopped off at Gozzano. His brother pressed on to the shores of Lake Orta where the locals told him that the offshore island was occupied by dragons. Giulio flung his cloak on the water, stepped upon it and, to the amazement of the locals, drifted across the lake to the island. The dragons, fled in disarray and Giulio built himself a hermit's cell from which he converted the lake folk to Christianity.

Today the Basilica di San Giulio, built in the 9th century, stands on the site of the hermit's cell and is the most important Romanesque church in Novara province. The church is a real treasure house of artwork: look especially for the 11th-century ambo, or pulpit, in black Oira marble and the painted wooden sculptures. The 'dragon's bone' actually comes from a 19th-century whale rather than from a 4th-century monster.

The island is reached from Orta San Giulio, a very pretty town with good restaurants and a wonderfully airy lakeside square. Some of the town's houses are frescoed externally, which makes a walk around the steep streets a real delight.

Orta's treasure is Sacro Monte, situated on the hill above the town. Here a path threads through woodland, passing 21 chapels containing a total of 376 lifesize terracotta statues illustrating incidents from the life of St Francis of Assisi. The chapels and statues date from the 17th century to modern times and expert opinion suggests that chapels 11 and 16 are the best.

PALLANZA, INTRA AND VERBANIA

MAP REF: 110 B3, B4, B3

These three villages have now virtually met to form one large complex, though differences are still discernible. Just offshore at Pallanza there is a row of fountains; these are floodlit at night, offering one of Maggiore's most memorable night-time views. On shore, old Pallanza has a maze of narrow streets leading to the Palazzo Dugnani. This houses the Museo del Paesaggio, the Landscape Museum, a collection of items from local Celtic and Roman sites, and an art collection that includes many works by the Intran

A lifesize terracotta scene taken from the life of St Francis, Orta San Giulio

sculptor Paul Troubetzkoy.

Verbania's most remarkable building is the Villa Taranto, standing on the village headland. Beyond is Intra, named for its position between two streams and the most industrialised town on the lake. It is not without merit, however; the Basilica di San Vittore is a good church and there are many excellent lakeside villas set among the chestnut trees and the oleanders.

PETTENASCO

MAP REF: 110 A3

Pettenasco has a pretty lake front and a much less pretty, but very impressive, viaduct which takes the railway over the Torrente Pescone. The village church has a fine Romanesque campanile, but the remainder of the building dates from a 17th-century rebuild.

QUARNA

MAP REF: 110 A3

The two villages of Quarna Sotto and Quarna Sopra are beautifully positioned among chestnut woods high above Lake Orta. The lower village, Quarna Sotto, has an interesting museum of musical instruments.

MOTOR TOUR

This 140km tour, lasting $3^1/_2$ hours, takes in a number of beautiful valleys celebrated in art, including Val Vigezzo.

From Intra/Verbania take the lakeside road northwards to Ghiffa.

Ghiffa

This charming village is famous for hat-making and has an array of fine villas grouped around the remains of an old castle. On the hill above the village is Ronco, where a butcher called Mazzarditi once lived, the father of the five brothers who once terrorised the neighbourhood from the Malpága islands (see Cánnero, page 16). Ronco has an interesting church, the Santuario della Trinita, made up of several linked chapels with some fine decorations.

Continue along the lake road through Cánnero and into Cannobio. Now turn left to follow the Valle Cannobina, passing the Orrido di Sant'Anna (see Cannobio, page 17) on the right.

The Valle Cannobina

Following the Battle of Pavia in 1525 some Scottish mercenaries, serving with the French army that was defeated by the Spanish, fled to this remote and beautiful valley. With hope of a return to their native land all but gone, the soldiers settled down in countryside reminiscent of the Highlands, married local girls and farmed the mountains. Today the museum in Gurro, just off our route, shows the Scottish influence, including a hint of tartan in the old costumes of the valley dwellers.

Continue along the Valle Cannobina, whose landscape is justly popular with artists, to reach the Val Vigezzo between the villages of Santa María Maggiore and Re.

Santa María Maggiore
The village is famous for its artists' school where some of Italy's most prominent painters have studied. There is also a curious little museum to the art and history of chimney sweeping, though this is only occasionally open. Just north of the village a cable car transports the visitor up to Piana di Vigezzo where there is excellent walking and fine views. Re is a smaller village, with a quite magnificent church.

After visiting the two villages, head down the Val Vigezzo towards the town of Domodòssola.

The Val Vigezzo
This wide, sunny and beautiful valley has been popular with artists since the 18th century when the various shades of green,

brown and grey and the pure quality of the light were first noticed.

Another claim to fame, though one that is hotly disputed, is that the type of perfume known as eau-de-Cologne was first invented here.

When the valley joins the Val d'Ossola take the left turn into Domodòssola.

Domodòssola
This is the largest town in the Val d'Ossola, a valley of some significance because it ends with the impressive Simplon Pass into Switzerland. The route over the Pass was built by Napoleon in 1805, the railway tunnel being completed a century later, in 1905. The tunnel, at a length of 19.8km, was the longest in the world at the time.

Another first is recorded by the memorial to Georges Chavez in Domodòssola's Piazza Liberazione. Chavez, a Peruvian, was the first man to fly over the Alps, on 29 September 1910, but sadly the successful flight ended when he crashed near the town and was killed.

From Domodòssola, drive down the Val d'Ossola valley, looking out for the famous Candoglia marble quarries on the left (see page 21) before turning left into Mergozzo. Go straight through the village and past Lake Maggiore to rejoin the main lakeside road. Turn left to return to Intra/Verbania.

(see page 21)

THE VILLA TARANTO
The Villa Taranto, near Pallanza on the shores of Lake Maggiore, is renowned for its superb garden, created this century by Neil McEacharn, a Scottish gentleman. When McEacharn bought the villa he named it after one of his ancestors who became a marshal in Napoleon's army and was created Duke of Taranto for his services in the Emperor's cause.

The 16-hectare gardens are criss-crossed by 8km of paths so that every corner can be explored. Visitors can see 20,000 varieties of trees, shrubs and flowers, some found nowhere else in Europe.

To create the gardens McEacharn landscaped what had been an area of unruly wood, producing a valley, formal areas with ponds and gently sloped areas for trees and shrubs. Water for the gardens is drawn from Lake Maggiore.

The whole garden is magnificent, but the 'Victoria Amazonica' greenhouse, which contains rainforest plants, is particularly compelling: the huge pads of the giant water lilies look strong enough to walk on. Elsewhere there are several hundred varieties of rhododendron and azaleas. One of the highlights of the year is Tulip Week – in late April or early May – when some, 80,000 tulips are in bloom.

QUARNA

27

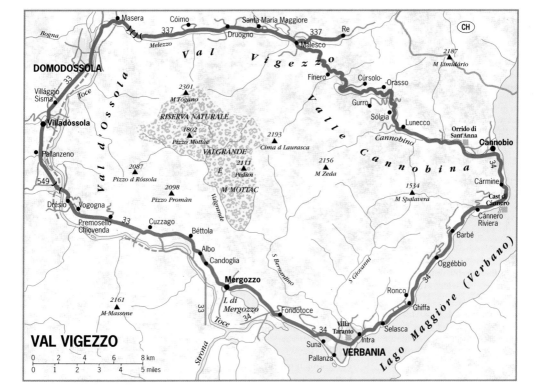

VAL VIGEZZO

0   2   4   6   8 km
0   1   2   3   4   5 miles

THE BORROMEAN ISLANDS

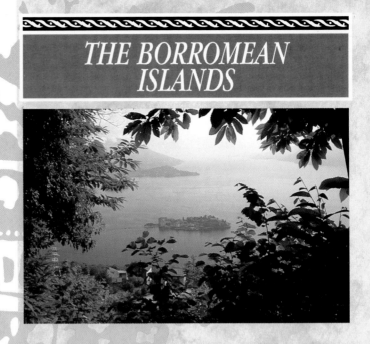

Where the River Toce reaches Lake Maggiore a deep inlet cuts into the western shore of the lake, a legacy of the Ice Age when the Toce valley was filled by a glacier rather than a river. The inlet is called the Borromean Bay, named after the noble Borromeo family. From their castles at Arona and Angera, this family gave Italy a host of great men, including several archbishops and one saint, San Carlo Borromeo, whose colossal statue stands close to Arona. The Borromeo name is attached to the Bay because Isola Bella and Isola Madre, two of the three islands, have long been owned by the family. Even though the family has never owned the third island, Isola Pescatori, the group as a whole is known as the Borromean Islands. All three can be reached by ferries from Stresa.

Top: Isola Bella, transformed into the shape of a palatial boat. Above: part of the same island's terraced gardens

ISOLA BELLA
MAP REF: 110 B3

The island closest to the mainland was a rocky outcrop occupied by a couple of fishing families when Count Carlo III Borromeo decided to transform it into a garden for his wife, Isabella, in the early years of the 17th century. The Count started the transformation by removing the families and then shipping out huge quantities of earth for his architect, Angelo Crivelli, to fashion. Early on a decision was made to transform the island into the shape of a palatial ship 'moored' off Stresa, with its prow pointing down the lake. At the same time the Count renamed the island after his wife though Isola Isabella was rapidly shortened to Isola Bella.

Crivelli piled the new earth 40m high and created 10 terraces for the gardens that would complement the Count's palazzo. The palace itself is in baroque style and stretches the full width, and more, of the island's northern end.

Externally the building is simple and plain, a sharp contrast to the interior. On the ground floor is the Arms Room, with the Borromean family coat of arms. On the first floor the Medals Room is named after a series of 10 medallions decorated with a variety of scenes. The Great Hall is beautiful, its lack of decoration complementing its height and lightness and the delicate china blue of the walls. Notice too the elegant Murano glass chandeliers.

The Music Room has a collection of old instruments and walls full of paintings. The Napoleon Room, where Napoleon and Josephine stayed in August 1797, is elegant, as is the Luca Giordano Room, which has three paintings by the late 17th-century master. The terraced gardens of the island are reached from the Tapestry Room, hung with 10th-century Flemish tapestries in silk and gold thread, depicting fantastic animals.

Before going out into the gardens, however, the visitor should go down to the grottoes, six cool rooms decorated with light and dark stones to give them a sea-cave appearance. The grottoes contain some curious items: the puppet theatre is full of fascinating grotesques – a mummy coming out of its tomb and a sedan chair turning into an old woman.

In the gardens of Isola Bella pure white peacocks strut amongst a rippling sensation of azaleas, rhodondendrons, camellias, citrus trees and many other shrubs, including some rarities – tea bushes and coffee trees – set among beautiful stone staircases and balustrades. The shrubberies are beautiful and the island's terracing has been cleverly filled with plants to create a botanical whole, but there is also evidence of the same tasteless extravagance that permeated parts of the palace. The terraces are dotted with fairly ordinary statuary and, at the head of the most formal section of garden, the visitor is suddenly confronted by a three-tier folly whose façade is covered with shells, niches, statues and porticoes; the whole confection is topped by two dreadful Muses flanking a rearing unicorn with a child on its back. Stairs lead up the sides of this mass to a flagged piazza offering superb views of Stresa, the Mottarone and the most southerly part of the gardens – the Garden of Love, with its intricate hedging designs and central pond.

ISOLA PESCATORI
MAP REF: 110 B3

The Fishermen's Isle contrasts starkly with Isola Bella. Happily there are a few souvenir and postcard sellers and traditional *lucia* boats are drawn up on the stone beach of the little quay, their nets draped over the breakwater walls to dry. The island's single village consists of close-packed houses lining narrow streets, those nearest to the harbour having elegant arcades and balconies. On all sides the warm waters of the lake gently lap the stones of the tree-sheltered shore.

In ancient times the island was held by the Archbishops of Vercelli and Novara, which is why the Borromeo family were never able to claim it; now it forms an outlier to the village of Baveno. At the island's heart is the church of San Vittore with its tall white campanile finished off by a short conical spire. The church is 11th century but has been remodelled several times. Inside it has several good pieces of artwork, including two 17th-century paintings.

ISOLA MADRE
MAP REF: 110 B3

Isola Madre, the Mother Island, is

the most isolated of the three Borromean Islands. It is also the largest of the islands but is occupied by a single villa and its surrounding parkland. The 18th-century villa stands beside a small chapel containing the tombs of members of the Borromeo family. The villa is worth visiting but the grounds are the major attraction. The island has been landscaped to form five terraces – though only near the villa is this actually apparent – and planted with a profusion of trees and shrubs from around the world.

In front of the villa is a superb Kashmir cypress, the finest specimen in Europe, and elsewhere there are Egyptian papyrus plants and a huge Chilean palm tree that produces 300 coconuts each year. The greenhouse is used to grow the Tahitian hibiscus whose flowers last only one day and are seen gracing the hair of Tahitian girls in Gauguin's paintings. The nearby pond is full of fine lilies and delightful green frogs.

On Isola Pescatori (Fishermen's Isle) gaily coloured boats of traditional design can still be seen on the stony harbour beach, backed by houses with elegant balconies (above) while calm reigns in its narrow streets (below)

RENO

MAP REF: 110 B3

Reno is a beautiful village set on a small bay formed by the headlands of Santa Caterina and Cerro. The hermitage here is the most beautifully sited of all Maggiore's churches, as well as being one of the most interesting. The story of the hermitage began in the 12th century. One Alberto, a man from the nearby village of Besozzo, was notorious locally as a thief, usurer and smuggler. One day Alberto was out on the lake when a sudden storm capsized his boat. As he clung to a piece of wreckage Alberto promised God that if his life was spared he would renounce his evil ways and devote the remainder of his life to prayer and penance. Miraculously a huge wave threw Alberto on to a ledge half way up a steep cliff where he landed unharmed.

On this ledge Alberto spent the rest of his life, almost 40 years according to the story, kept alive by the local folk, who put food in a basket for him to raise, and by water from a spring. When plague swept through the area Alberto prayed to Santa Caterina on behalf of the locals and they were spared. They showed their gratitude by building a chapel to the saint on the hermit's ledge. There, after his

death, Alberto was buried. In the 14th century the Dominicans added a monastery to the chapel. Later, in the mid-17th century, huge rocks fell from the cliff above the church but they were prevented from crushing the hermit's tomb by three bricks; these had jammed in such a way that they supported the huge weight of the numerous boulders, which took years to remove.

Today the church is reached by a steep flight of downward steps – and the only way back is to go up the same steps – while the visitor is accompanied by scores of scuttling lizards. The church is exquisite, despite damp-damaged frescos on the walls, and it has superb views to the lake. Alberto's basket winch can still be seen and, most remarkable of all, so can Alberto, his naturally mummified body lying in a glass-topped tomb.

SESTO CALENDE

MAP REF: 110 B3

When you drive down Maggiore's western shore you will leave Piedmont for Lombardy when you cross the Ticino river which drains the lake into the River Po. The first town in Lombardy is Sesto Calende. The town's name is thought to date to Roman times when the town had a market on

Clinging tenaciously to the cliff-face, the hermitage of Santa Caterina at Reno

the sixth (*sesto*) day after *kalends* (the first day of a new month). Even in Roman times the town was already ancient; in the Bronze Age the region was occupied by people of the Golasecca culture, named after a village a little way south of Sesto Calende. Many finds from their sites can be seen in the town museum in Piazza Mazzini.

STRESA

MAP REF: 110 B3

Stresa is, without doubt, Maggiorie's capital of fashion and elegance – a small town but with the best of the region's hotels and the longest list of social functions. The lakeside road, with its fine gardens and hotels, is the epitome of prosperity. The Grand Hotel et des Iles Borromées is one of two luxury class hotels in the lakes area – the other being Cernobbio's Villa d'Este – and is a sumptuous building both inside and out. This hotel, and many of the others, are often used for conferences and conventions and from late August to September they are filled with visitors who have come to enjoy Stresa's International Music

Festival.

Stresa is also a fine centre for excursions: the cable car to Monte Mottarone leaves from nearby Carciano and the Borromean Islands are most conveniently visited from here. At the heart of the old town is a delightful central square, Piazza Cadorna, where the pavement cafés offer a rest from shopping and lakeside walking.

MOUNTAIN WALK

It is possible to walk all the way from Stresa to the top of Monte Mottarone, a fine walk, which goes past the Giardino Alpino (Alpine Gardens - see page 21), through the village of Levo then across high alpine meadows through scented pine forests. For many visitors the time required for such a walk - around 3 hours - is too long. This shorter version, covering a distance of 2.5km and lasting an hour, starts from the cable car (*funivia*) station in Carciano, a little way north of Stresa.

Seven lakes are visible from the summit of Monte Mottarone and on a clear day views extend as far as Milan and Switzerland

Take the cable car to the top station, go up the road, then break left on to high meadow, following the scarred path upward. The top of Monte Mottarone is soon reached.

The Mottarone has one of the best viewpoints of any in the lakes region. To the east no less than seven lakes are visible backed by the mountains of the Adamello and Ortler Alps. Westward, the high peaks of the Piedmontese Alps are visible, though the eye is naturally drawn to Monte Rosa, a huge wall of a mountain, with the second highest summit in Europe, which sits on the border between Italy and Switzerland. To the south, on a very clear day, Milan's Duomo (cathedral) is visible. On such clear days it is difficult to imagine why John Ruskin, a fine British writer, felt that the Mottarone was the 'stupidest of mountains, grass all the way, no rocks, no interest, and the dullest view of the Alps'. How could he be so wrong ?

From the summit, somewhat spoiled by the high-tech paraphernalia, descend to the unmissable wooden chalet. This is a very good café, where you can enjoy coffee and views from

the terrace seats. To return to the funivia top station, either retrace the outward route or descend along the road from the café - heading south along what is actually a toll road - to reach a well-defined track to the left after about 400m. Take this track, which leads under the cable way, to return to the top station.

PARCO NATURALE DELLA VALLE DEL TICINO

The Ticino Nature Park, close to Angera and Sesto Calende, was set up to protect the beautiful countryside and wildlife that abounds on the banks of the Ticino river. The park extends well south of Lake Maggiore; for the most rewarding area go to Pombia, about 20km south of Sesto Calende and close to Malpensa airport, where a walk has been laid out. You can start the 2km walk from either Pombia or Varallo Pombia. Depending on the season, you are likely to see many butterflies - including the magnificent southern festoon - and insects - including the praying mantis - as well as flowers and trees almost without number. The trees cover a very wide range, from riverside willows through to southern deciduous species. The birdlife includes many ducks and river birds - such as the darting kingfisher, the elegant night heron and little egrets - as well as some local species, such as the southern sub-species of the long-tailed tit. You may be fortunate enough to catch sight of elusive foxes, dormice and hares, but some of the reptiles, including water snakes and green lizard, are more easily seen.

Best of all are the flowers, with orchids, gentians, and irises topping the list. Look out too for the martagon (Turk's cap) lily, one of Europe's most beautiful flowers, and keep a nostril alert for the scent of wild honeysuckle.

MONTE MOTTARONE

Lago Maggiore

Carciano

Someraro

Stresa

1491 ▲ *Monte Mottarone*

Rif Omegna

976 ▲ *M Croce della Tola*

Levo

Molino

Atrolo

Vla.Cristalli

0   1 km

LAGO DI LUGANO (LAKE LUGANO)

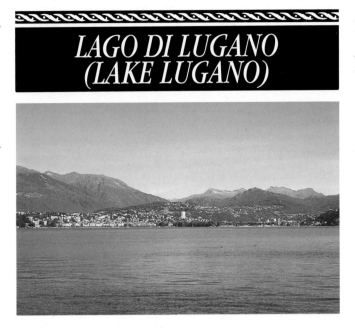

Lake Lugano is a curiously shaped piece of water. On the map it looks like a crudely drawn cartoon animal with its nose at Ponte Tresa, ears at Agno, paws at Porto Cerésio and Capolago and a huge bushy tail spreading back towards Lake Como. From the tip of the nose to the tip of the tail, at Porlezza, the lake measures 36km, though on average it is less than 2km wide. Partly as a result of this narrowness Lugano is the only lake which is bridged; Melide and Bisonne, on the western and eastern shores, are linked by a road, rail and autostrada crossing.

Campione d'Italia, is situated on the eastern shore to the north of the bridge, and is a geographical freak, an Italian town completely surrounded by Swiss territory. A few years ago there was a plan to build a cable car from Campione to Sighignola – a spot known as the 'Balcony of Italy' because of its superb views of Lake Lugano and the Swiss Alps. The cable car would have allowed direct access to the town from Italy, but money and enthusiasm ran out. Today, visitors to the Balcony must walk a few paces to avoid the concrete blocks and rusting steel bars of the abandoned cable car which would otherwise form the foreground of their view. And below, the Italian enclave of Campione can still only be reached by passing through Swiss territory.

Most of Lake Lugano itself lies in Switzerland. Lugano, the only city on the lake – and one of the most important cities in Switzerland's Italian-speaking canton of Ticino – was once part of the Duchy of Milan. The Swiss took the city and the surrounding area in 1512, but at the time of the Risorgimento, Italy claimed only that territory held by the Austrians, leaving most of Lake Lugano in Swiss hands. Thus, apart from Campione, only a small section of the lake's westernmost end lies in Italy, a 12km section running from Ponte Tresa to Porto Cerésio. The latter village derives its name from *Ceresio*, the Roman name for the lake. Italians still occasionally refer to the lake by this antique name – Lago di Ceresio.

At its eastern end the lake is wholly Italian. Italy thus claims the deepest waters – at approximately 290m – and the superb valleys of Cavargna to the north and Intelvi to the south. Each of these valleys is well worth exploring, their tiny mountain villages giving a flavour of an older, more hardy way of life. By stark contrast, Lugano is a very modern city with numerous shops, restaurants, nightclubs and hotels of the highest quality, and many of the villages of Swiss Lugano have developed into high-class resorts.

Southwest of the lake, Varese is, like Lugano, a modern city, often called 'the Garden City' because of its delightful parks and its position, close to the mouths of several lush, green valleys. Varese also stands at the foot of Monte Campo dei Fiori, so named because of its flower meadows, one of the foremost pilgrimage sites in northern Italy. The pilgrims journey to this spot to follow the steep Via Crucis (Way of the Cross) up the southern slope, called Sacro Monte, to a church that holds a greatly revered statue of the Virgin Mary once owned, according to legend, by the Apostle Luke.

Above: the city of Lugano viewed from across Lake Lugano. Below: Lugano's Piazza Riforma

Close to Varese are three small lakes – Commabio, Monate and Varese. Presently these are subject to a reclamation programme, local pollution having destroyed their potential as tourist centres. Good progress is being made and it is hoped that soon the lakes will be able to support both fish and swimming visitors. These three lakes will then be a fine addition to the local amenities, particularly as Isolino Virginia, the little island on Lake Varese, is such an important historical site.

Two valleys converge on Varese: these are the Valganna and the Valcuvia. The Valganna is a beautiful valley whose roadsides are dotted with stalls selling peaches and melons in summer, and with the occasional mossy enclave where water drips from caves into lush hollows. The Valcuvia is short and airy, and from it the visitor can reach Arcumeggia, one of the most fascinating villages in the western lakes area principally because of its external murals, frescoed by leading artists.

Panoramic views extending over a small section Lake Lugano towards the city of Lugano, from the top of Monte San Salvatore

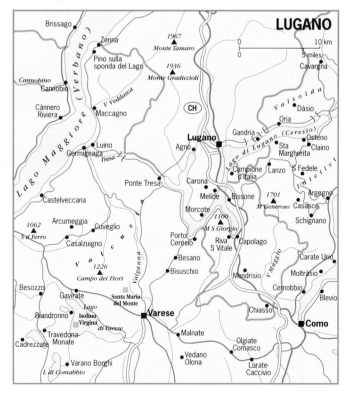

BISUSCHIO

MAP REF: 110 B3

This pleasant little village is notable for the Villa Cicogna Mozzoni, a beautiful 16th-century building containing superb frescos and rare furnishings surrounded by fine gardens in Italian style.

Close to Bisuschio is Besano, a small town of no great merit except for the Triassic era fossils that are found in (relative) abundance locally and displayed in the small museum. The church of San Giovanni is also worthy of note for its frescos and fine views over Lake Lugano.

CAMPIONE D'ITALIA

MAP REF: 110 B4

Campione is an Italian enclave entirely surrounded by Swiss territory. This unusual situation arose in the 8th century when the local lord gave the site to the church of San Ambrogio in Milan. Since that time Campione has shared the same fate as the rest of Italy, including annexation by the Austrians and fighting for independence during the Risorgimento. Switzerland, having no quarrel with Italy, allowed the town to remain Italian during the whole of that period. Today the town is still proudly Italian, though it uses the Swiss postal service and currency.

From the entrance to the town,

The Italian enclave of Campione, surrounded by Swiss territory, announces itself with style

The stately Villa Cicogna Mozzoni, at Bisuschio

with its splendid arch and boisterous fountain, it is clear that Campione is a prosperous place. There are still the typically Italian alleyways, a little dark and narrow and always interesting, but there is also a more sophisticated side, most obviously at the Casino, set right by the lake shore with a fine view to the city of Lugano.

In medieval times the town was home to the Maestri Campione, master builders who formed part of the more famous group known as the Maestri Comacina. The Maestri were architects, builders and sculptors, the Campione group being most renowned for their work on Modena's cathedral and San Ambrogio in Milan. Within the town their work is best seen in the early 14th-century church of San Pietro.

CAPOLAGO

MAP REF: 110 B3

This old fishing village would barely be recognisable to its former inhabitants, the old centre having been demolished to make way for the new town that serves as the terminus for the Monte Generoso cog railway. The nearby village of Riva San Vitale is worth a visit to see the 5th-century octagonal baptistery and the church of Santo Croce, reckoned

to be the finest Renaissance church in Switzerland.

CARONA

MAP REF: 110 B4

Carona, reached by *funivia* from Melide is a delightful village with excellent views towards the lake and the Alps. The village also has a fine park with an excellent collection of trees and shrubs.

CASALZUIGNO

MAP REF: 110 B3

Between Varese and Laveno lies the Valcuvia, one of the greenest and least spoilt valleys near any of the large lakes. Though only 12km long, it is well worth visiting. Casalzuigno is one of the better Valcuvian villages, the Villa Bozzolo having fine gardens that are open to the public. Nearby is Arcumeggia (see page 45).

CASTIGLIONE OLONA

MAP REF: 110 B3

The beauty of this village is enhanced by the early 15th-century religious complex built by Cardinal Branda Castiglioni. This consists of the Cardinal's own palazzo, a house built for his parents, a beautiful church, a superbly frescoed baptistery and a collegiate church with equally good frescos. There is also a small museum with exhibits on the complex and on the life of the Cardinal. The village centre hosts the Fiera del Cardinale (Cardinal's Fair), a second-hand and antique fair, on the first Sunday of every month. Close to Castiglione Olona is Castelséprio, originally a Roman fortress town, then a Lombardic stronghold and finally destroyed by the Visconti in 1287. Today designated an Archaeological Zone the site includes the remains of town houses, castle walls and a medieval monastery.

CLAINO-OSTENO

MAP REF: 110 B4

The pretty twin villages of Claino and Osteno, on the southern shore of Lake Lugano, guard an entrance to the Intelvi valley and are the only inhabited places of any note between Porlezza and Campione. Osteno was the birthplace of the Bregni, sculptors renowned for their work in Venice. Andrea Bregno has left us a astounding marble *Madonna and Child* in Osteno's church of Santi Pietro e Paolo.

There is also a fine gorge near Osteno, one best viewed by boat.

MOUNTAIN WALK

This 8km walk of Monte Generoso (allow 2 $^1/_4$ hours) starts and ends in Switzerland, but the great majority of it lies in Italy. Be sure to carry your passport: the border guards can be just as scrupulous on this high peak as they are on the *autostrada* crossing points.

Start in Capolago, taking the Monte Generoso cog railway to the Albergo Vetta.

The railway is now over 100 years old. The hotel at its upper terminus, the Albergo Vetta, is located 100m below the summit of Monte Generoso and has rooms for those who fancy something different in terms of a breakfast view, plus a bar and a self-service restaurant - just the place to end a good walk.

At the top station there is also a small chapel; go to the side of this to reach a path that passes below the summit of Monte Generoso (a short detour to the top can be made at this point) and then passes below the rocky towers of Baraghetto.

In springtime the mountain here is a sea of purple and yellow *Primula auricula* flowers. The English name for the flower is

The high ridge of Monte Generoso is renowned for the colourful gentians and oxlips that splatter its Alpine slopes

Auricula Cowslip, but the common Italian name is much more poetic: *orecchia d'orso*, the bear's ear.

Continue along the path - here bordered by shrubby green alder - heading northeast with some spectacular views. The path passes a bolla, *a trough-like rainwater tank used by the farm animals of the alpine slopes. It then passes along the edge of the wooded Alpi di Gotta, before bearing east to the farmhouse of Cascina di Boll.*

In summer the alpine slope here is covered with yellow laburnum and purple willow gentian. From the Cascina the view extends to the Denti della Vecchia (the Old Woman's Teeth) across Lake Lugano and beyond to the peaks of the Valsolda and the Engadine Alps.

From Cascina, go east to Alpe d'Orimento, a little group of houses and farms huddled around a tiny church, looking out for a track to the right on the way (we will take this track later).

In summer there is a restaurant at Alpe d'Orimento, and on Pizzo Croce, just a short distance away, there are the remains of trenches dug, but never used in anger, during World War I. From Pizzo Croce a whole array of Italian peaks can be seen – Monte Disgrazia (3,678m), Monte Legnone (2,610m), the Bisbino (1,325m), the Galbiga (1,697m)

and, above Lake Como, Sasso di Gordone (1,409m).

Retrace your steps towards Cascina di Boll, taking the path to the left that we noted on the outward journey. The new path crosses the Breggia Alp, meandering between low green alder and the occasional sycamore tree.

The crude shelters that you will pass are called *baitocchi* – temporary bivouacs built by hunters at the start of each season. As the deserted buildings of Alpe Pesciò are reached the alder and sycamore give way to cherry and maple, the trees standing among yellow oxlip and deep violet, but poisonous, monkshood.

Follow the path ahead, which runs along the Swiss border, return to the Generoso railway station.

THE INTELVI VALLEY
MAP REF: 110 B3/4

The Val d'Intelvi is actually a series of sunny valleys with numerous delightful villages, many with superb churches by the Maestri Comacini, famous medieval builders and sculptors, some of whom lived in the valley. The Val d'Intelvi has always been an important link between lakes Lugano and Como and was heavily fortified in medieval times. Later, during the Risorgimento, it was a centre for resistance against the Austrian occupiers.

From Argegno, on Lake Como, two roads start up the valley cut by the Telo river. The southern road climbs up the valley side to Schignano, a picturesque village providing magnificent views of the lake. From here the road drops back into the valley, going through Cerano with its fine 11th-century campanile. A road now leads off to Casasco d'Intelvi, where the church has 17th-century frescos by valley artists, and on to Erbonne where the old communal wash-house is still used by the village womenfolk.

In the main valley the first village is Castiglione d'Intelvi where the remains of an old tower and some very interesting old houses can be seen. Just beyond the village a road off to the right leads to Pigra from where, many claim, there is the finest view of the lake.

Another way to reach the village is by *funivia* (cable car) from the station a little way north of Argo.

San Fedele d'Intelvi is one of the foremost tourist centres in the valley, a lovely village whose church has one of the best doorways constructed by the local Maestri Comacini. Pellio d'Intelvi is divided into an upper and a lower part, each having a church built and decorated by valley craftsmen, while nearby Laino has the finest of all valley churches. Originally Romanesque, the church was rebuilt in the 16th century and has some beautiful paintings and a fine baroque altar.

From Laino the road continues to tiny Ponna, a village split into two hamlets. Ponna Superiore, the upper hamlet, has a museum furnished in the style of the 19th century and lighting that dates from 1910, the time of the first valley electricity supply.

Another museum, dedicated to the history of the valley and its art, can be seen at Scaria. Beyond is Lanzo d'Intelvi, popular with summer visitors and, increasingly, with winter sports enthusiasts. Lanzo has a fine central square and fountain and several interesting houses; one, in Via Mascheroni, has an 18th-century external fresco.

Two excursions can be made from Lanzo to outstanding viewpoints. Sighignola, known as the 'Balcony of Italy', has a fine

The view from Sighignola, justly called the 'Balcony of Italy'

view of Lake Lugano. The ironmongery is all that remains of a projected cableway from the enclave of Campione, which can be seen below. The better viewpoint is the belvedere to the northeast of Lanzo. From here most of Lake Lugano can be seen, together with Monte Rosa, the Matterhorn and the peaks of the Bernese Oberland. From the viewpoint a cable car descends to Santa Margherita, a lakeside village that cannot be reached by road.

LAGO DI COMABBIO
MAP REF: 110 B3

Lake Comabbio is a beautiful emerald green but swimming is not allowed because of pollution. Varano Borghi is small and industrial, though the splendid Villa Borghi is worth a look, while there is a horse riding centre near Corgeno

LAGO DI MONATE
MAP REF: 110 B3

Lake Monate is the smallest of the Varese lakes, about 2km long and 1km wide. At Cadrezzate there are fine views across this lake and towards Lake Maggiore. At the northern end, Travedona's 13th-century Romanesque church has good frescos. At the double village

of Cocquio-Trevisago there is a museum dedicated to the work of the Impressionist artist Innocente Salvini.

LAGO DI VARESE
MAP REF: 110 B3

Heading west from Varese on the road to Gavirate the visitor soon reaches Lake Varese. On the way to the lake the road passes the Luvinate golf course whose clubhouse is converted from an 11th-century Benedictine monastery. Beyond is Comerio a centre for exploring the caves that riddle Monte Campo dei Fiori.

Gavirate is the largest town on the lake, a neat place whose museum, in Via Volterro, celebrates the local pipe-making industry. At one time the town was a centre for fishing but, sadly, the lake became very polluted; the clarity of the water reflects an absence of life rather than the opposite but, thankfully, a rescue operation has now been put into effect.

From Biandronno, on the southern shore of the lake, boats cross to Isolino Virginia, an Italian National Monument because of its neolithic and Bronze Age remains. The natural island was extended on wooden piles to support the lake dwellings of early fisherfolk. Many of the items found on the island can be seen in the museum in Varese. Anyone interested in

visiting the island should enquire at the same museum, or in the Varese Tourist Office, for details of the guided tours which take place on Saturday and Sunday afternoons in summer.

LUGANO
MAP REF: 110 B4

The city that shares the name of the lake is one of the most important in the Swiss canton of Ticino. It stands at the foot of Monte San Salvatore in a small, sheltered bay – a delightful site for an elegant city that vies with Como as being the finest of all the lake cities. Lugano has something for all tastes. The cathedral of San Lorenzo has a fine façade and some excellent 14th-century frescos, while the simple 15th-century church of Santa Maria degli Angeli, in Piazza Bernardino Luini, is famous for its Luini frescos. Luini was Leonardo da Vinci's best student, and the *Passion* at this church is thought to be his masterpiece.

The whole lake front, from the aptly named Paradiso – just beyond Luini's church – to the Parco Civico, is ideal for a leisurely stroll. The tree-shaded front has several beautiful flower gardens – notably the Parco Civico itself and those surrounding the Villa Ciani and the Palazzo dei Congressi.

A little east of Lugano is Gandria, the last Swiss village on Lake Lugano's eastern arm. The village is steep, the alleys narrow and characterful. The local fish restaurants are excellent and there

is an interesting Customs Museum. This has to be reached by boat as it is on the south side of the lake – a great adventure in itself. The museum deals with the time when Gandria was a centre for smuggling, keeping the local customs officers very busy.

THE VILLA FAVORITA

The Villa Favorita is located on the edge of the lake at Castagnol, a pleasant surbub a little way to the east of Lugano. The 17th-century mansion houses what is widely regarded as the finest private art collection in the world. This was built up over several generations by the Thyssen-Bornemisza family of Germany, whose fortune was based on the manufacture of steel.

Around 250 major European artists are represented. The earliest works include a diptych by Van Eyck and Memling's *Portrait of a Young Man*. One of the most famous works is the younger Holbein's portrait of Henry VIII. From a century later comes Caravaggio's marvellous *St Catherine of Alexandria*, the beautiful, but enigmatic, saint depicted beside the wheel that now bears her name. From the same period are Palma's portrait of a Venetian courtesan, and several fine El Grecos. Other works include a superb Rembrandt self-portrait and canvases by Canaletto, Fragonard. Bellini, Titian, Uccello, Velasquez, Vermeer and Veronese.

Lugano, below Monte San Salvatore

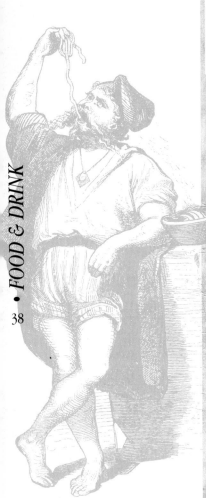
·FOOD & DRINK·

In Italy there are several sorts of restaurant and, though the names of these have been adopted in other parts of the world, their true meaning has often been left behind so that visitors may not find what they are expecting.

The bar is the place to go for tea and coffee, together with a limited range of snacks, sandwiches and pastries, as well as alcoholic drinks. Italians visit the bar for breakfast or for their mid-morning and mid-afternoon breaks. The *pizzerie* specialises in serving pizza but most of them also serve a (sometimes limited) pasta range and have a grill bar. Next up the scale is the *trattoria*, an inexpensive eating house where the menu will be short and the food basic. This does not mean that it will also be of a poor standard. All Italian restaurants serve very high quality food.

Finally there is the *ristorante*. These vary from relatively inexpensive establishments to those where the bill could come as an unpleasant shock. However, by law all restaurants must display a menu outside so you can read and walk on if you do not like what you see, either in the choice of food or the price. The only other establishment that might tempt the visitor is the *gelateria*, an ice-cream restaurant. In the lakes area, most of these are now attached to bars and will serve ice-cream cones as well as the more exotic dishes that require a seat – and an afternoon's strenuous walking to burn off the calories.

Summer's heat has persuaded the Italians that it is preferable to take several hours off work in the middle of the day, when the sun is at its highest. In the countryside

working folk usually go home at noon, but in towns and cities this is less easy, so restaurant lunches are popular. Restaurant clients have a couple of hours to kill so they are in no hurry. The same is true in the evenings; Italians make eating out a social occasion that is to be enjoyed, not hurried. As a result, the service in restaurants may be slower than in some other European countries. Finally, when you sit down you will be given a basket of bread. The price of this is added to the bill. It is listed as *coperto e pane*, literally 'cover and bread', though this is usually shortened to *coperto*.'It is worth remembering this because if you eat your 'free' bread and the basket is replenished, then the bill will also rise.

Food

It will come as no surprise to discover that the lakes area specialises in fish dishes. The main lake fish is perch, usually grilled in breadcrumbs and served with rice. The little perch fillets are barely two mouthfuls in size, but many will be served to you if that is your chosen dish. In taste perch is more like white fish than trout, but the similarity does not extend to the price, perch being more expensive than trout despite its apparent abundance. For something a little different, try *missoltini*, sun-dried fish. Trout is the other speciality, usually grilled but also baked with herbs and served with rice.

The promise of traditional food

This preference for rice is also not surprising since Lombardy is Europe's foremost rice-producing area. Another dish based on rice is *risotto alla Milanese*, a broth of rice and saffron. This dish was once unique to Milan, but it has spread throughout Lombardy. Another Milanese speciality that is now found on menus all over the lakes area is *cotoletta alla Milanese*, breaded veal cutlets. In view of the Austrian domination of Lombardy, which ended only a century or so ago, it is best not to refer to this as Wiener schnitzel!

The most unusual meat dishes tend to be found in the mountain areas rather than around the lakes where the restaurants are too cosmopolitan to have maintained a specific regional menu. In the Lake Orta area some menus may still offer *asino*, donkey. If your sentiment does not get the better of you, try it stewed. Moving to the north of Lake Maggiore, the Ossola valley is famous for *viulin*, salted leg of goat. The goat in question could be chamois, the small mountain goat. Nearby, Val Vegezzo is well known for its smoked ham. On the northern end of Como, wild rabbit is often served in the small villages. It is best when wrapped in cooking foil and baked on a charcoal fire. The Valtellina specialises in *bresaola* (dried salt beef). The very best varieties are those that have been dried in cool mountain caves – or so it is said. Further east, *cassoela* is a stew of pork and cabbage, while *ossi buco* is knuckle of veal and rice.

Pasta in the lakes area is much as elsewhere in Italy, but several local specialities are worth trying. *Pizzocheri* is a Valtellina speciality. It is a curious looking dish, being a fat spaghetti made from black flour served hot with melting butter. Polenta is fatter still, a sausage-shaped pasta made with maize flour. It is served with the standard pasta sauces, tomato or meat (except near Lake Orto where it is often served with a cheese sauce); it is heavy going and sticky, but excellent ballast. *Agnolotti* is another local pasta; it is similar to ravioli, but stuffed with beef and spinach.

Sometimes, especially in the mountain areas, pasta is served with *funghi*. The Italians are very adventurous in the range of fungi they will eat, and a basket of frightening looking toadstools will often greet the diner. Do try some – they are much better than they look (but they can be expensive).

The local mountain cheese specialities are made with the milk of sheep or goats as well as the more usual cow's milk. The most famous is Taleggio which comes from the area around the village of the same name near Val Brembana. It is a mild cheese, as is the slightly less popular Fontina which comes from Piedmont. For a tangier taste, try the goat's cheese from Como's High Briaza area. If that is not sufficient to excite your taste buds you need Gorgonzola from the village of the same name near Milan. Gorgonzola is a blue cheese with an indescribable 'bouquet'.

For dessert you will usually be offered ice cream or fruit, as Italy has few sweet specialities. *Panettone* is a Milanese speciality that has spread north and south, a light cake made with sultanas and lemon rind, while *castagnaccio* is a cake made of chestnut flour with pine nuts and sultanas.

Drink

Italy's annual output of over 9,000 million litres of wine makes it the world's largest producer. The wine is categorised according to the state's grading system. DS is Denominazione Semplici – with no quality standard. DOC is Denominazione di Origine Controllata – wine to a defined quality standard and from officially recognised growing areas. DOCG is Denominazione di Origine Controllata Garantita, wine of the highest standard.

Lombardy and Piedmont produce some excellent heavy red wines, including Barolo but Lake Garda produces the most famous wines. Soave is a dry white, Bardolino a light dry red and Valpolicella a full-bodied red. Traditionally these last two wines are the correct accompaniment for a meal of lake trout.

Fresh produce taken from the lake area's citrus belt

Staple ingredients – plump olives, fruity wines and pasta in variety

MALNATE

MAP REF: 110 B3

The countryside east of Varese is arid, unlike the lush green valleys to the north. The SS342 Como road twists through parched landscapes and dusty villages. The first village, Malnate, big enough to be called a town, is perched on a hill and approached by hairpin bends. It is an undistinguished place, but the Villa Rachele-Ogliari is worth visiting. This interesting building houses a transport museum with steam locomotives, stage coaches, horse-drawn trams, old bicycles and a great deal more.

From Malnate a narrow road leads north to the Swiss enclave of Mendrisiotto, passing through a number of pleasant hill villages.

MELIDE

MAP REF: 110 B3

Lake Lugano is crossed by a whole collection of road and rail bridges linking Bissone and Melide, villages that stand on opposite banks of one of the narrowest points on the lake. Melide is a pleasant village, home of the Swiss Miniature (see opposite), and the start point for the *funivia* (cable car) ride to Carona. You can also walk from Melide to the summit of Monte San Salvatore, though this involves a climb of almost 700m and most visitors will prefer to take the cable car from nearby Paradiso. At the top there is a

Statuesque cypresses frame the view in Morcote's Scherrer Park

restaurant and the views take in the peaks of the Bernese Oberland and Monte Rosa and the Valais Alps, as well as Lake Lugano.

THE MENDRISIOTTO

MAP REF: 110 B3

The Swiss enclave that lies south of Lake Lugano, sandwiched between the Italian regions of Como and Varese, is known as the Mendrisiotto after its chief town, Mendrisio. The area is rarely visited but deserves to be more popular for its woodland and gardens and the cool of the Val Múggio, which offers a wonderful contrast to high summer's lakeside heat.

The Val Múggio is a short but delightful valley which evolved an early form of refrigerator. Pits were dug close to glaciers or near slopes that concentrated the winter's snow. These pits were roofed with slates, insulated with straw and fitted with a small, narrow door. In winter the pit/building would fill with ice and snow, and the insulation would (hopefully) keep the ice intact throughout the summer when the ice house would be used to cool milk, butter and other perishables. A few of these *neveres* still remain on the slopes of Monte Gereoso, Sasso Gardena and Monte Bistino, and they make a fascinating find.

The Val Múggio is reached from Balerna, a town that is now virtually continuous with Chiasso. Balerna is an ancient town; there are Roman remains, and the ruins of Pontegana castle are certainly

pre-Lombard. Later the town was an important religious centre.

In the valley itself the first villages are upper and lower Morbio, the lower village dominated by the superb church of Santa Maria dei Miracoli, built in the early 17th century on the site of an old castle. Canéggio, the next village, has narrow alleys of arcaded houses and retains a medieval mill. Several more fine hill villages, many having examples of the valley's typical rural architecture, are passed before Múggio, the highest village, is reached. Múggio is superbly positioned and has a splendid central fountain. The village was the birthplace of Simone Cantoni, the architect who designed Como's Villa dell'Olmo.

Chiasso, close to the mouth of the Val Múggio, is a border town which, despite the frontier, merges with Italy's Ponte Chiasso. The border is easily reached on foot but driving takes a little longer, especially at weekends when motorists from Italy queue to take advantage of Switzerland's cheaper petrol. Despite the existence of 12th-century documents referring to the name, Chiasso has the feel of a modern town, one that has grown up around the huge railway complex. Architecturally there is little that is old; the best buildings – most notably the Liberty-style Palazzo Zist – date from the late 19th or early 20th century.

Mendrisio, the ancient capital of the area, feels much older than Chiasso and has numerous 15th-

Lake steamers, fairytale castles and the peaks of Matterhorn – a glimpse of the Swiss Miniature

and 16th-century buildings. Best of all is the Palazzo Torriani, dating from the 15th century and the church of Madonna delle Grazie, a medieval building that incorporates the rooms of a 12th-century hospital.

Close to the town are several delightful villages. Novazzano stands right on the Italian border and is surround by vineyards and woods. Villa Riva, in the nearby hamlet of Boscherina, is a superb neo-classical building, though it is not open to the public. At Stabio there is a museum to the history of the area and rural life. The village also has a number of interesting houses, and is a good centre for walks on Monte Albano and the nearby hills, walks that wander in and out of Italy. Rancate is home to Ticino's Cantonal Art Museum, housed in the Grosse Palast, the old town hall, comprising over 200 works by Ticino artists.

Finally, for the finest walk in the area go to Meride, a pleasant village of narrow streets, from where a nature trail climbs up Monte San Giorgio. The 7km trail includes 10 stop points, at each of which the local geology, flora and fauna are explored. Leaflets on the trail are available from local tourist offices.

MORCOTE

MAP REF: 110 B3

From the southern side of Lake Lugano, near Porto Cerésio the eye is drawn across the water to Morcote, a village idyllically situated below the cone of Monte Arbostora on a finger of land poking into the lake. Not surprisingly the village is known as the 'Pearl of the Lake'. On closer inspection the illusion of perfection is reinforced; the maze of alleys, the beautiful houses, the park, the harbour and the old church, with its tree-shaded cemetery, are all exquisite. Many believe that Morcote is the most picturesque village in Switzerland. So delightful is the village as a whole that it seems a pity to pick out individual places, but the church of Madonna del Sasso, with its 16th-century frescos and detached campanile, and the lovely Scherrer Park, with its mostly local trees and shrubs, should be on every visitor's itinerary.

Morcote, Switzerland's most picturesque village

THE SWISS MINIATURE

Those who do not have the time to visit the whole of Switzerland should visit the village of Melide where the Swiss Miniature reproduces all of the country's major tourist attractions. Towns, monuments and castles are reproduced at 1:25 scale and mostly in the original building materials of stone and wood. In addition, the Swiss transport system is modelled, with cable cars, cog railways and boats all represented: in total there are over 3km of model railway. At night the models are floodlit.

Although the miniature might be seen as the ideal outing for children it is, in fact, a great day out for visitors of all ages, the more so for the setting in 1ha of parkland beside Lake Lugano.

PONTE TRESA

MAP REF: 110 B4

The bridge of the name is a fine-arched red granite structure crossing the Tresa river which takes the outflow from Lake Lugano into Lake Maggiore. The bridge also crosses from Italy into Switzerland. Swiss Ponte Tresa is a tiny village, little more than a frontier post. Italian Ponte Tresa is bigger and has a very pleasant lakeside walk a little way out of the town, from where the view of this last bay of Lugano is exquisite.

PORLEZZA

MAP REF: 110 B4

In Roman times this was *Portus Retiae*, the gateway to the Retiae, the folk who occupied the country beyond. In medieval times the town was famous for its artists: the della Porta family produced many notable artists, sculptors and architects, including Guglielmo who was the best student of Michelangelo. Another native of the town, Michael Sanmichele, was a military architect employed by the cities of Verona and Venice.

By the time of these artists Porlezza had moved from its original site, the first town having been destroyed by a landslide. Legend has it that San Maurizio, coming to the town, was refused customary hospitality by the morose townsfolk. To teach them better manners he called down a landslide - the same one that also separated Lakes Lugano and Piano - which destroyed all but the church now dedicated to him. The ruins can still be seen on the other side of the bay from the town. Recent excavations have not supported the legend however: Maurizio was a very early saint, but the landslide probably occured in the 17th century, by which time Porlezza had already moved to the shallower side of the bay.

PORTO CERÉSIO

MAP REF: 110 B3

This tiny harbour village is more renowned for the view it offers to Morcote, across the water, than for its own attractions. That is a shame because Porto Cerésio is a lovely little place. The lake front is a delight - with views along two arms of the lake - and the village itself is a huddle of typically Italian shops and houses.

VALSOLDA

MAP REF: 110 B4

Travelling east along the lake from Lugano the visitor enters Italy at Oria, birthplace of the Italian writer Antonio Fogazzaro. Beyond is San Mamete, a pretty village at the entrance of the beautiful, but

The handsome harbour village of Porto Cerésio, a place of exceptionally good views

rarely visited, Valsolda. The valley can be driven a short way, as far as the remote hamlets of Castello, Puria and Dásio, but from there on it is the preserve of the walker in search of peace and natural beauty. A fine, but long, walk goes from Dásio to Cavargna. Castello has an interesting musuem to the art and history of the Valsolda.

MOTOR TOUR

Allow 2 hours for this 45km tour of Val Cavargna.

From Porlezza take the Menággio road to reach Piano Porlezza, beside Lake Piano.

Piano Porlezza
Originally this delightful, tree-fringed lake was part of Lake Lugano, but the huge landslide that destroyed the site of the first village of Porlezza also separated off Lugano from this small stretch of water. Now only a river joins the two.

From the village of Piano Porlezza take the road signposted to Val Cavargna, swiftly arriving in the valley's first village, Carlazzo.

Carlazzo

It is probable that Carlazzo was once fortified to protect the entrance to the Val Cavargna and one of the village houses is still called Il Castello (the Castle). The campanile of the church has a Romanesque base, but was made taller, probably in the 17th century when the church was rebuilt.

Beyond Carlazzo the valley becomes increasingly attractive as the road rises up the craggy, wooded flank of Monte Pidaggia. The tiny church of San Ambrogio (probably 13th century, which would make it the oldest in the valley) is passed before Cusino is reached, a village with a rickety church, and a collection of pleasant houses. On again is San Bartolomeo Val Cavargna, the largest village in the valley, with a church that, despite recent rebuilding, houses some fine medieval artwork.
Ahead now is San Nazzaro Val Cavargna from which the road from Cusino and Monte Pidaggia can be seen in all its splendour. Finally Cavargna is reached.

Cavargna

This picturesque village is located at 1,071m on the lower slopes of the hills that rise to Monte Garzirola. Above the village stands the Holy Wood, so-called because it protects Cavargna from avalanches. The village church is modern and decorated with contemporary artwork, some of it by local artists. Elsewhere, be sure to visit the attractive Museum of the Valley. This comprises four rooms; one an old Val Cavargna village smithy, the others dealing with the sanctuary church of Santa Lucia, which stands on the Swiss-Italian border high above the village, the agriculture of the valley and the local craft of wood turning.

From Cavargna the route leaves Val Cavargna, following Val Rezzo through Búggiolo, a beautiful hamlet set among pine forests and alpine meadows. Below the village, Val Rezzo becomes more rugged, but the road leaves it, bearing east to Molzano and Córrido. In Córrido fork right to return to Porlezza.

MONTE TAMARO

Rifugio Tamaro which stands on Motto Rotondo, at 1,928m. From this second rifugio the summit of Monte Tamaro is easily reached by a rocky path.

The view from the summit of Monte Tamaro (1,961m) is spectacular, taking in much of Swiss Ticino as well as Lake Maggiore and the high Valais Alps around Monte Rosa. If the second stage of the *funivia* has not been completed when you visit the area then you may already be exhausted by your climb and content to make this the literal pinnacle of your walk. If the second stage has been completed then the walk can be extended, as follows.

From Tamaro's summit follow the signs for Bassa di Indemini, the col between Tamaro and the next peak, Monte Gradiccioli. The Bassa is at 1,723m and from it the path continues to the Bassa di Montoia. Beyond this second col, at 1,791m, several paths meet. Take the right-hand path which traverses below Monte Gradiccioli, continues to Monte Pola and from there on to Monte Lema. On the latter part of this long walk, on the ridge between Pola and Lema, the route follows the Swiss-Italian border. However, our route bears left on the path to the summit of Monte Gradiccioli, at 1,935m.

The view from Gradiccioli is little different to that from Tamaro, although there is a better view down towards the Italian Lake Maggiore, but climbing two peaks over 1,900m in one walk is a great achievement.

Because of the geography of the ridge, the outward journey must now be reversed.

Close to the Swiss border, the long lake vistas are part of Porto Cerésio's appeal

VAL CAVARGNA

MOUNTAIN WALK

This superb 6.5km walk visits the high peaks of the Sottoceneri, in the Swiss canton of Ticino. Allow at least 2 hours.

Start in Rivera and take the Monte Tamaro funivia (cable car) to Alpe Foppa, at 1,530m. The funivia is currently in the process of being extended to Motto Rotondo, about 400m higher. If the extension has been completed you carry on up to the top, omitting the first part of this walk. Otherwise take the path which goes southwest along the rocky rib of Motto Rotondo, passing the Rifugio Rotondo at 1,850m where a well-earned drink and snack is available. Now continue up the path to

VALCUVIA

MAP REF: 110 B3

Between Varese and Laveno is the Valcuvia, a beautiful and lush valley that threads its way between wooded hills. At Casalzuigno a road heads up the northern flank of the valley, going around Monte Nudeo to reach Lake Maggiore. The first village the road reaches is Arcumeggia. At first sight this is a typical Italian hill village of houses piled on top of each other and a maze of narrow alleys – but it is distinctively different. In the 1950s the village invited the leading Italian artists of the day to fresco the outside walls of the houses, and this tradition has carried on ever since. Regular art courses are run in the village, under the patronage of Milan's Brera Gallery; the 'artist in residence' stays at the Casa del Pittore, the painter's house and, as well as leading the course, he or she adds another fresco to the village. Over the years the village has therefore become an outdoor gallery of contemporary Italian painting, as well as being an extraordinary and unusual sight.

Parking in Arcumeggia is difficult but, once accomplished, a walk around the village is a constant delight. Some of the works are comic, some serious, some thought provoking, but all are of interest. Choosing favourite works is a matter of personal taste, but Giovanni Brancaccio's *Girl at a Window* and Aligi Sassu's *Cyclists* are both great fun.

Your visit should also include a trip to the village church since many of the visiting artists have contributed painted panels to the Via Crucis (Way of the Cross).

VARESE

MAP REF: 110 B3

The town of Varese is probably pre-Roman in origin, though little that now remains outside of the museum is older than 16th century. Indeed, apart from its very heart, Varese is a modern town which will appeal more to the shopper than to the casual stroller or anyone interested in old buildings. The town was once known as the 'Garden City' because of the beauty of the surrounding hills and countryside, but recent expansion has somewhat limited the view, except towards Monte Campo dei Fiori ('the Mountain of the Field of Flowers'). Several parks also justify the name, including the gardens of the Villa Ponti located in the northern part of the town, known as Biumo. Ponti is actually two villas, one in neo-classical style, the other in what is usually termed 'eclectic', in other words, a mixture of many different styles. Together the villas form a conference centre and the surrounding gardens have good trees and borders.

TOWN WALK

This 2km walk, covering the main sights in Varese, starts from the APT (Tourist) Office, near Piazza Ragazzi del Novantanova.

From the tourist office walk into the main square, with its cluster of modern buildings, and cross Via Volta, the main road, to reach the edge of the old town. Take Via Marconi ahead, then bear left to reach Del Bernascova, the symbol of the town.

1 Del Bernascova is the name given to the superb 77m

Arcumeggia, in the Valcuvia, is a typical hilltown of tumbling houses and narrow alleys

campanile designed by the local architect Giuseppe Bernasconi. The campanile, which is detached from all other buildings, was begun in 1613, but not finally completed until 1774. With its several storeys, numerous balustrades and its final dome – which is more garlic than onion – it is a magnificent work. At the base of the campanile are the baptistery of San Giovanni and the basilica of San Vittore. The baptistery, an Italian National Monument, is the oldest building in Varese, dating from the 12th century. It is an austere but interesting building with internal frescos that date from the 13th and 14th centuries. The basilica is later, being 16th century, and was designed by Bernasconi and Pellegrini, though the façade is more recent. Inside there are 16th-century frescos and some very elaborate wood carving.

Return to Via Volta and turn right. To the right now is Corso G Matteotti, with excellent shops and a real feeling of age – just the place to spend a while exploring. We continue along Via W Marcobi, bearing left into Via Luigi Sacco to reach the Palazzo Estense.

2 The palazzo is another Italian National Monument. It was built in baroque style, and on a huge scale, in the mid-18th century by Francesco II d'Este, Duke of Modena. The palazzo is now the town hall, but visitors are occasionally allowed inside. They are most definitely allowed into the superb garden surrounding the palazzo, which now forms the Varese Public Garden. The garden was designed in the formal style

Aligi Sassu's fresco of cyclists in Arcumeggia

and has wide walkways and a circular pond with a central fountain.

Walk through the gardens, then go up the terraced section to reach the Villa Mirabello.

3 The 17th-century Villa Mirabello is less sumptuous than the Palazzo Estense, but is no less attractive. The villa houses the town museum with collections from the local Bronze and Iron Age cultures, together with more recent history. There is also a collection of moths and butterflies.

From the villa it is possible to walk eastward to return to the APT office, but it is far better to go back through the garden into Via Luigi Sacco and retrace the outward journey.

Varese's sumptuous 18th-century baroque Palazzo Estense

THE SACRO MONTE (SACRED MOUNT)

The long ridge of Monte Campo dei Fiori rises to the northwest of Varese. As early as the 10th century a pilgrimage church had been built on the slopes of the mountain, and later a statue of the Virgin, reputedly owned by the Apostle Luke, was brought to the church. The statue – known as the Black Virgin because it is carved from dark wood – significantly enhanced the church's standing as a centre for pilgrims. In the 16th century San Carlo Borromeo decided that the church deserved a better approach and he devised a plan to build a Via Crucis (Way of the Cross) lined with chapels. Work on the chapels took many years, but today all 14 are complete. They are laid out along a 2km rising path and each is dedicated to an incident in the life of Christ, illustrated in paintings and statuary. All the chapels are of interest, but the seventh, the Flagellation of Christ – with frescos by Francesco Mazzucchelli (known as Il Morazzone) – is regarded the finest. Close to the final church of Santa Maria del Monte, in which the Black Virgin still stands, there is a small village, with two museums. The villa of the sculptor Ludovico Pogliaghi – who designed the central doors of Milan cathedral – is now a museum to his work. The Baroffio Museum houses the art collection of its founder, Baron Baroffio, and some works of art originally from the church of Santa Maria del Monte.

LAGO DI COMO (LAKE COMO)

The French author Stendhal went into raptures at his first sight of the landscape around Lake Maggiore. Later in his travels he also visited Lake Como, after which he wrote: 'What can one say about Lake Maggiore, about the Borromean Islands, about Lake Como, unless it be that one pities those who are not madly in love with them'.

Lake Como is smaller than both Maggiore and Garda, having a surface area of 148 square km, but it is the deepest of the lakes and its maximum depth of 410m- between Argegno and Nesso - also makes Como the deepest lake in Europe. Lake Como also has the longest perimeter of any of the lakes, at over 170km. The reason for this extreme length is the lake's inverted Y shape caused by the division of the glacier that carved out its valley. The diversion was caused by the hard and high triangle of land known as the High Brianza that now separates the Como and Lecco arms of the lake.

The River Adda, which drains the lake, flows out from the Lecco arm, the Como arm having no outflow. This gives a wonderful integrity to the city of Como which is not divided by a river, unlike most other lake cities. The disadvantage can be seen in times of heavy rain when the water backs up in the Como arm, causing the lake to flood the lakeside roads of the city and turning Piazza Cavour into a swimming pool, to the frustration of local shop and café owners.

The two arms of the lake are quite different in character. The

Top: southern Lake Como. Below: traditional craft, crafted lovingly

Lecco arm was cut between high peaks: to the west are the higher ridges of the High Brianza, to the east the huge and impressive rock towers of the Grigna. The steep cliffs mean there are few harbours and access to the lakeshore is difficult; they have also made the lake a shady, sombre place. As a consequence there are few villages and little to detain the visitor.

By contrast, the Como arm was cut between the lower side of the High Brianza and the less steep peaks of the Múggio and Intelvi valleys. The lake here is open and sunny, the harbours numerous, the shore flat or terraced. Here there are villages which, in the 19th century, attracted the tourists of the European Romantic era, including Flaubert, Tennyson, Goethe, Shelley, Browning, Tchaikovsky and Liszt.

Liszt was so entranced that his daughter - who grew up to be Wagner's wife - born in Como in 1837 was named Cosme after the lake. The rich followed the famous, building villas that are still the hallmark of the lake. The Villa d'Este, in Cernobbio, is the greatest of these, but the Villa Balbianello and the great villas of Bellágio and Varenna are almost as good, while Villa Carlotta is one of the highlights of a trip to the area.

The strange geography of the lake has resulted in a variety of different names for each of its three arms. To the Romans the

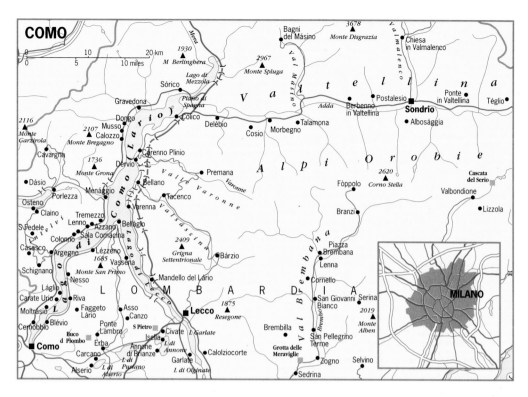

lake was *Lacus Larius*, and this name is still seen in the villages of Gera Lario, to the north, Faggeto Lario, in the Brianza, and Pianello del Lario, home to the lake's fascinating boat museum. The modern name is Como, the lake and city sharing the name, but this does not please the inhabitants of Lecco, who maintain a healthy rivalry with their more famous neighbour. For them the arm of

the lake that ends at their city is Lake Lecco, whatever the maps might say. To add further to the confusion the northern section of the lake, the stem of the inverted Y, is occasionally referred to locally as Lake Cólico.

If we accept these names, then the lakes of Como, Lecco and Cólico meet at Punta Spartivento, the 'Point that Divides the Wind', surely the most romantically

named feature on any of the lakes. In the lee of the Point is Bellágio, known as the 'Pearl of the Lake' and said by some to be the loveliest village in Europe.

Lake Como is well situated for excursions. To the north lies the Valtellina, one of Italy's main skiing centres, while to the south lies Milan, northern Italy's capital.

Tremezzo rises from Como's waters

Spring attracts numerous visitors to the charming villa gardens that are a feature of Lake Como

ARGEGNO

MAP REF: 110 B3

This pretty town of red-tiled houses stands at the mouth of the Intelvi valley in a wooded inlet of the lake. Just to the north is the *funivia* (cable car) station to Pigra, one of Lake Como's finest viewpoints.

BELLÁGIO

MAP REF: 110 C4

Bellágio is known as the 'Pearl of the Lake' and well deserves the title. From the lake itself the town is breathtakingly beautiful and if the tourist traps can be ignored in favour of a stroll through the steeper part of the town, then the beauty is maintained on shore. The town does not sit on the point of the triangle that divides Como's waters – the aptly named Punta Spartivento, the 'Point that Divides the Wind' – but on the westward, the leeward, side.

So beautiful is the site and the village, called the loveliest in Europe, that many villas have been built here, designed to take full advantage of the views. The Villa Melzi d'Eryl, to the south, cannot be visited, but its superb gardens can. Villa Serbelloni, above the village, has a terraced formal garden and is owned by New York's Rockefeller Foundation.

BELLANO

MAP REF: 110 C4

Bellano has some fine old sections and its lake front has monuments to two famous sons of the town, the scientist Boldoni and the writer Tommaso Grossi. Another Boldoni is said to have introduced the silk industry to Como. The church of Santi Nazaro e Celso is strikingly beautiful, with a façade of contrasting colours and a superb rose window.

Close to the town is the best *orrido* in the lake district, a deep, narrow, gorge cut by the Pioverna stream. The gorge can be entered by a series of walkways and ladders; the spray, incessant noise and the beauty of the rocks makes this a thrilling outing.

CERNOBBIO

MAP REF: 110 B3

Though Cernobbio is a pretty town the visitor is inevitably drawn to the Villa d'Este, arguably the finest hotel on the lakes, and one of the most sumptuous private villas ever built. The villa was built in the 16th century by Cardinal Gallio and is now much as he left it, though subsequent owners have altered the grounds – adding the long water-garden ramp and the mock castle behind the house. During the 19th century the villa served as the headquarters of the Austrian commander-in-chief and, later, of Baron Ciani, Cavour's agent, so its position in the history of the struggles of the

Risorgimento is assured. From 1816 to 1817 it was home to Caroline of Brunswick, wife of George IV. Her behaviour scandalised local residents but Londoners were pleased by her absence, having devised the following rhyme:

'Most gracious Queen, we thee implore
To go away and sin no more;
Or if that effort be too great,
To go away at any rate.

BOAT TRIP

There are several different options for boat trips on Lake Como, all of them offering fine views. On the northern reach of the lake the prospect to the peaks of the Berlinghera and to Monte Legnone are superb, while on the Lecco arm of the lake the dolomitic mass of the Grigna to the east and the peaks of the High Brianza to the west make exciting backdrops. Our trip takes the Como arm of the lake. Here the peaks are lower and less rugged and the landscape more genteel, but the villages and villas that front the lake offer their best faces to the traveller, making for a magnificent trip.

Boats leave Como from the Piazza Cavour quay, one of the best departure points on any of the lakes. As the boat clears the breakwater, look to the left for a good view of the Villa dell'Olmo. Ahead now is Tavernola after which the boat docks at Cernobbio, giving a glorious view of the Villa d'Este and its unique floating swimming pool and parkland. Above the village rises Monte Bisbino.

North of Cernobbio Lake Como is narrow and twisting and there are striking differences between the villages on the eastern and western shores. Blévio, opposite Cernobbio, is smaller and less exuberant. The reason, of course, is that Cernobbio receives more sun, so it has more villas and a brighter feel. Blévio gets the evening sun in summer, and enjoys glorious sunsets. It has a few villas including the Villa Ruspini, surrounded by shrubs and flowers.

After Blévio the boat visits Moltrásio then Torno, a very pleasant village with a church dedicated to San Giovani that has a reliquary holding a piece of Holy Nail (from the cross). Close to Torno is the Villa Pliniana, glimpsed from a distance as the boat crosses to Carate-Urio, and then back to Faggeto Lario.

As the boat heads north now

LAGO DI COMO

Bellágio
Cadenabbia
Tremezzo
Lenno
Ospedaletto
Sala Comacina · Villa Carlotta
Colonno · I Comacina
Argegno

Lago di Como

Lézzeno

1685 ▲ M San Primo

Torriggia
· Nesso
1325 · Careno
▲ Carate-
M Bisbino Urio
· Riva
Moltrásio · Torno Faggeto Lário
Cernóbbio
· Blévio
· Tavernola
Villa dell'Olmo

COMO   0 2 4 6 8 km
        0 1 2 3 4 miles

After docking at Argegno the boat moves on to Colonno and Sala Comacina before giving the visitor a superb view of Ospedaletto's campanile, and a close up view of Isola Comacina. The best is yet to come, however, for the boat, after visiting Lézzeno, rounds Punta di Balbianello so giving a view that is not available to visitors who travel by road – that of the Villa Balbianello standing at the very tip of the headland.

Beyond Lenno another treat is in store – the view of Villa Carlotta at Tremezzo. Beyond, lies Cadenabbia before the journey comes to an end with the crossing to Bellágio, the aptly named 'Pearl of the Lake', a breathtakingly beautiful village when viewed from the water.

To return to Como it is best to take the *aliscafo* (hydrofoil); the journey is a lot quicker and considerably more exciting, even if your second sight of the trip's main highlights are somewhat curtailed.

there is the first long view of the lake, with the mountains that define the Val d'Intelvi visible above the next elbow. Torriggia is passed on the way to Nesso, and then the boat clears Punta della Cavagnola on its way to Argegno, allowing the longest view of the trip so far, all the way to the peaks around Monte Legnone above the village of Bellano.

COMO'S VILLAS

The Italian lakes have always attracted travellers in search of beauty and peace, as well as wealthier settlers who built luxurious villas for their own convenience and the envy of others. Sirmione, on Lake Garda, is believed to have been the site of a Roman villa built by the poet Catullus, and Pliny may have had a villa on Lake Como. The Golden Age of villas, however, occurred in the 19th century when Lake Como's romantic beauty and equable climate attracted the likes of Queen Victoria, Stendhal, Flaubert, Tennyson and Liszt.

The roll call of Como's villas includes the famous 16th-century Villa d'Este at Cernobbio, a masterpiece of opulent design, while the 18th-century Villa Carlotta, near Cadenabbia is renowned for its magnificent collection of rhododendrons and azaleas. Varenna's Villa Monastero is among the most beautiful of all the lake's mansions and the Villa Balbianello, near Isola Comacina, has the added attraction of being approached from the lake.

Of all Como's villas the gloomy Pliniana is the most mysterious of all. Pliny was born at Como in AD23 and his writings include a description of a curious well on the eastern shore of the lake – the water in the well rose and fell several times a day for no apparent reason. The locals maintained that the cause was a mixing of the lake waters with those of a river from hell, but it is now more widely believed to be a form of rock syphon.

There is no evidence to suggest that Pliny had a villa at this spot, but his name was given to the mansion built in the 16th century by Count Giovanni Anguissola when he came here in self-imposed exile after murdering the evil Pier Luigi Farnese. Despite its sombre look – and the legend that it is haunted by the Count – it has attracted many visitors: Rossini wrote *Tancredi* here and Napoleon stayed after the Battle of Marengo. Sadly the villa is not open to the public.

The captivation of Lake Como's shores is enhanced and their tranquillity accentuated by the flaming rays of the setting sun

LAKE DWELLERS AND THEIR BOATS

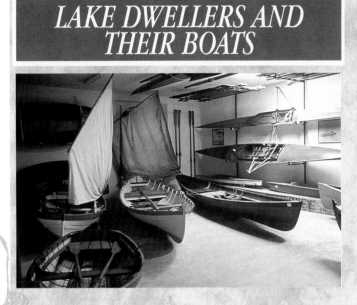

Many years ago it was discovered that Isolino Virginia, the tiny island in Lake Varese, was partly artificial: the natural island had been extended by driving piles into the lake bed to support a timber platform. The village created by the early lake folk was a miniature Venice surrounded by water, and thus safe from casual attack, with an ample supply of fish.

Similar villages have been found on nearby Lake Monate, at La Torbiere, the bog at the southern tip of Lake Iseo, and at Lake Ledro, near the northern tip of Lake Garda. At the latter site the remains of more than 15,000 piles were found in 1929 when the lake level was lowered during work on a hydroelectric scheme. The finds from the Ledro site can be seen in the lakeside village of Molina di Ledro. Those from Isolino Virginia are diplayed in the Varese Museum, though some are housed in the island's own museum and information centre.

It is now believed that the folk who constructed these pile dwellings were at the transition from the neolithic to the Bronze Age, and that they migrated from the Danube region, using the high Alpine passes to travel into Italy. Almost nothing is known of their lifestyle, though it is conjectured that they fished with primitive nets and used an early form of canoe, originally little more than a hollowed-out tree.

Over the centuries the techniques of boat building improved, especially when ideas from the sea-faring folk of the Mediterranean and Adriatic ports arrived in Lombardy. The lifestyle of the lake dwellers also altered. Whereas in the earliest times the lakes had simply been a source of security and food they now became trade arteries, linking the high Alpine passes to the rivers of the Lombardy Plain.

The lakes and rivers became increasingly important in times of war since control over them allowed the rapid transfer of troops and supplies as well as permitting a trade blockade to be maintained. Fleets of war galleys patrolled some of the lakes, often at great cost (see page 104).

By the 13th century several specialised craft had been developed and these remained unchanged until modern times, when the advent of steam and diesel engines changed the whole shape of lake travel. Visitors interested in seeing examples of the various boat types should visit the Boat Museum at Pianello del Lario on Lake Como.

THE GONDOLA

The gondola is linked with Venice to such an extent that many visitors are surprised to discover that this type of boat was also the workhorse of the lakes. Lake gondolas were bigger than their romantic Venetian counterparts, being around 16m long and about 5m wide. Very large versions – up to 25m long – were also built.

Above the water, the gondola was noted for its elegant curved lines. Below the water the boat had a flat bottom, making it suitable only for lake travel. It was therefore used to carry bulk cargo, which was off-loaded on to smaller craft for transport along the region's rivers and canals. The other main difference from today's gondola was the power source. It was too big to be moved by manpower alone so the gondola had a mast, with a large triangular sail woven from hemp and dyed with tannin for protection from sun and rain. For calm days there were also very long oars; most boats had two, but some larger versions had as many as 10. Steering was by means of a stern-mounted rudder.

The original gondolas differed from their modern relatives in being undecorated, though the colour - black from the waterproof coating of pitch - was the same. The most that these older craft would have had by way of decoration was a name and a family or town pennant flying from the masthead.

THE NAV

This was a lake fishing boat. It was small - about 7.5m long - with a round hull and a flat bottom. Interestingly, the bow was both higher and broader than the stern. The boat had two pairs of oars which were used for power and steering, though a sail could be drawn up if it was operating far out on the lake.

THE BATTÉLL

This is the most famous of the lake boats and the one that the visitor is guaranteed to see. The harbour at Isola Pescatori, for example, is usually filled with *battélli*, though on Maggiore, as elsewhere, they are now more frequently called *lucias* after the heroine of Manzoni's book *Il Promessi Sposi (The Betrothed)*. In construction the *lucia* is similar to the *nav* , but it was round bottomed and had no sail. In useage it served not only as a small fishing boat, but also as a passenger ferry operating between the lake villages in the days when roads were poor and dangerous.

THE QUATTRASS

The *quattrass* was developed at the northern end of Lake Como. In essence this was a punt, a flat-bottomed, square-sectioned boat either poled or rowed by two oars from the standing position. It is believed that the modern gondoliers technique of leg

rowing developed from the need to keep one hand free for the fishing nets.

THE CAVALLINE

Sadly the Pianello Museum does not have an example of the *cavalline*. This twin-hulled boat, used on Lake Maggiore, was powered by a horse harnessed to a treadmill between the hulls which powered a paddle-wheel via a series of winches and pulleys. Even more astonishing must have been the horse-driven passenger boat on Lake Garda. In the early 19th century, just before the coming of steam, the *Manubrio* plied the waters driven by eight horses which walked in circles around the deck harnessed to the drive shaft of the engine.

LAKE STEAMERS

Steam reached the lakes in 1827 when the steamship *Archduke Ranieri* offered a passenger service on Lake Garda. After the Austrians were ejected from the area no similar service operated on the lakes for over 50 years until the Lake Navigation Companies came into being, operating scheduled passenger services on steam-driven paddle boats. With the coming of diesel power some of the romance departed from lake travel. Even so, the system has been reinvigorated by speedier *aliscafo* (hydrofoil) services and by the reintroduction of night-time travel - the perfect way to see the floodlit buildings of the lakes.

The latest innovation to reach the lakes, super fast jet hydrofoils

Rowing boat from a more leisurely age, with hoops to support a canvas awning

COMO

MAP REF: 110 B3

Como is an elegant city wonderfully set at the end of the western arm of Lake Como. The Romans ousted the Celts from here around 200BC and the city was rebuilt by Julius Ceasar. Rebuilding was needed again in the 12th century when Como was almost destroyed during the Ten Years' War with Milan. Between these two events the city was an early convert to Christianity and the names of early saints and martyrs are attached to the major churches. Sant'Abbondio stands close to Via Regina, a name that recalls the rule of Queen Theodolinda, and is a masterpiece of the Maestri Comacina (local architects and builders), a magnificent twin-towered building. The basilica of San Carpoforo, in the suburb of Camerlata, is in very early Romanesque style.

On the hill above this same church is the Baradello Tower, all that remains of a 12th-century castle. The view to Como from the 35m tower is superb, though it is doubtful if Napo Torriani would have agreed. When he was defeated in battle by Ottone Visconti in 1227, a cage was attached to the outside of the tower in which Napo and his family were placed. Open to the elements the prisoners died one by one until finally only Napo was left – and he brought his misery to an end by smashing his head against the tower wall.

Como's Piazza Cavour (which floods at times of high rainfall) with the Duomo behind

TOWN WALK

Allow $1^1/_4$ hours for this 4km walk around Como.

Start from Piazza Cavour, with its elegant pavement cafés and glorious views. Walk up Via Plinio to reach the Broletto.

1 The Broletto is the old Court of Justice, built in 1215 with alternate layers of black and white marble and superb arcades. To one side is a campanile that dates from the same period, though its top section was added in 1435. To the other side is the austere façade of the Duomo (Cathedral). The cathedral took several centuries to complete and is an important example of architecture in transition. This western end is Romanesque, but the eastern end, with its domes and semi-domes, is in the much more exuberant Renaissance Gothic style. Be sure to see the 16th-century tapestries illustrating biblical texts.

Continue along Via Vittorio Emanuele II, bearing right into Piazza San Fedele.

2 The square is another joy, with its arcaded shop fronts and the basilica of San Fedele on the eastern side. The basilica is 11th century and has a beautiful apse.

Ahead now is the maze of the old town with its narrow streets and tiny shops. Follow the signs to Porta Vittoria.

3 The tower is 40m high with huge scalloped openings and an impressive doorway; it dates from the 12th century when it built as a gateway in the town walls.

Head back into the old town, going left in Via Rovelli to see the house where Volta was born (Via A Volta No 10) before going through the city wall to Viale Varese. Turn right and walk to the lakeside where the Tempio Voltiano (Volta Temple) stands beyond the city gardens. Continue around the lake to the gardens of Villa dell'Olmo.

4 The villa is named after a cluster of elm trees that have now, sadly, gone. It was built in the late 18th century and is today used for concerts and exhibitions.

Return along the lakeside to Piazza Cavour.

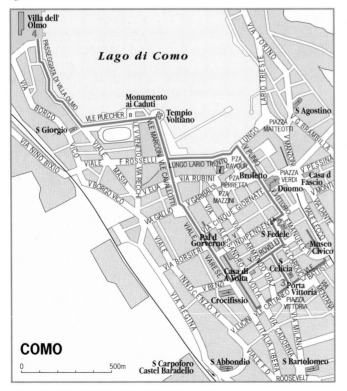

ALESSANDRO VOLTA

Alessandro Volta, the man who gave his name to the volt, the unit of electrical force, was born at No 10, Contrada di Porta Nuova on 28 February 1745. After his death the street was renamed Via A Volta, a nice gesture, though the house itself was renumbered 62, which is baffling. Volta received a conventional schooling, but no direct training in physics. Despite this he was soon experimenting in the subject and in 1765 he published an important paper on electricity and magnetism.

Volta earned his living as a schoolmaster in Como until, somewhat belatedly in 1778, he was made Professor of Physics at Padua University. He maintained his association with Como, marrying in the Church of San Provino in 1794 and eventually retiring to a local house, by which time his fame had spread throughout Europe. He continued his researches for many years in a laboratory at the base of the Torre di Porta Nuova which, ironically, is now used as an electricity substation. Volta died in Como on 5 March 1827, the same day as his great friend and fellow scientist, Laplace, died in Paris.

Today Como's pride in its most famous son can be seen in the statue that stands in Piazza Volta, close to Piazza Cavour, and in the impressive Tempio Voltiano (Volta Temple) on the lakeside where many of Volta's documents and scientific instruments are on display.

GIUSEPPE GARIBALDI

Guiseppe Garibaldi was born in Nice – then part of the Kingdom of Sardinia – on 4 July 1807 and he spent his early years as a merchant seaman. After a meeting in 1833 with Giuseppe Mazzini, another hero of the Risorgimento, Garibaldi took up the cause of Italian unification, inciting an uprising in Genoa in the following year for which he was condemned to death – fortunately the sentence was passed in his absence, Garibaldi having fled to South America. There he fought against the Brazilians, became a commander in the Uruguayan Navy, was shipwrecked once, tortured several times and injured often, once seriously. In the duller moments, of which there were few, he worked as a shop assistant in Montevideo, was married, and fathered three children.

In 1848, learning of an uprising in Italy, he returned with a few fellow exiles to support the cause. Because of his enthusiasm and enormous energy Milan made him a general, but this early uprising failed, his wife died, and Garibaldi moved to New York. He subsequently worked as a candlemaker in China and a merchant seaman in Australia before moving back to Italy (by way of London) in 1855 to settle as a farmer on the island of Caprera off Sardinia.

When war erupted again in 1859 Garibaldi once again joined the cause, becoming a general in Camillo Cavour's Piedmontese army and taking a force to San Fermo, a small village just outside Como. There he defeated the Austrian Marshal Urban, marched into Como, and there proclaimed the city free of Austrian rule and part of the new Italy.

Unfortunately Garibaldi's vision of a united Italy did not accord with Cavour's plan for a greater Sardinia. Garibaldi gathered a few followers, the famous I Mille (The Thousand), and landed in Sicily in 1860, determined to unite it and the southern mainland with northern Italy. After defeating the Neapolitan army Garibaldi won control of Sicily. He then invaded the mainland, capturing Calabria and Naples, before marching on Rome.

With unification almost complete Garibaldi became a member of the new Italian parliament, turning down a request from Abraham Lincoln to lead the Union Army, though ultimately he became a nuisance to the new Italy by constantly seeking new targets for his private army. Finally he retired to his farm on Caprera, dying on 2 June 1882. Today most Italian cities commemorate Garibaldi in some way. In Como, the Palazzo Olginati houses the Giuseppe Garibaldi Museum of the Risorgimento which covers the history of the man and the events of Italian unification.

The gardens of Lake Como's Villa Carlotta (see page 67) are among the most splendid in Europe and a highlight of a visit to the lake

MOUNTAIN WALK

Monte San Primo is the high point of the Brianza. This 8km walk to the summit lasts 3 hours. It begins at the entrance to the Parco Monte San Primo, reached by driving south from Bellágio on the Magreglio road to Guello and taking the road that ascends from there some 8km to the park. From the square by the ski-lifts go back to the road and walk along it until you reach the gate that closes it off to cars. Continue on the gravel road beyond the gate to Alpe delle Ville, at 1,121m. Now go left on a track, signposted to the Rifugio Martina, which crosses the Alpe del Picet, the Alp of Robins. The Rifugio Martina has a restaurant that is open from June until October. Take the track behind the *rifugio*, which rises steeply into and through woodland. Beyond, open alp is crossed to reach the summit of Monte San Primo.

Monte San Primo, at 1,686m, is the highest peak of the Brianza – or of the Triangola Lariano, as the area between the two arms of Lake Como is sometimes called. From the peak the view extends to Switzerland's Monte Generoso, the Grigna, the Cornu di Canzo and across the Lombardy plain to the Apennines. The cross on the summit is inscribed: 'Justice, Freedom, Peace; give your name to these'. The radio mast is for the use of the local forest fire wardens.

Go east along the summit ridge, passing Cima del Costone (1,614m) and then go down to the Bocchetta di Terre Biotte, close to the top station of the ski-lifts. From the Bocchetta take the track signposted Route 39 to climb Monte Ponciv (1,453m). Stay with the track as it turns north to reach Monte Forcella (1,329m) and then follow what is, in winter, a blue run to the Alpe del Borgo, a hostel now used by schoolchildren who stay for courses on the local ecology. From the Alpe a metalled road leads back to the car park at the start point of the walk.

Standing at the summit of Monte San Primo above a sea of cloud

MOTOR TOUR

This 80km tour, lasting 3 hours, takes in the best of the villages and high peaks of the Brianza north of Como.

From Como take the road to Bellágio, which leaves the city at the Brunate end of the bay, passing the funivia *(cable car) station. Follow the narrow road all the way to Bellágio but be cautious and watchful for other traffic especially on the sharp bends - of which there are many. You will pass through several attractive villages, and enjoy splendid lake views to the left, before reaching Bellágio, perhaps breaking the journey for coffee in one of the town's several lakeside cafés.*

Leave Bellágio by taking the steep and bending uphill road that heads for Magréglio. At the village of Guello there is a choice of routes to be taken: turn right here to Cernobbio if you wish to have a closer look at the highest peaks in the Brianza (see the Monte San Primo Walk, left). Otherwise continue ahead on the main road which travels steeply uphill to reach the beautifully sited chapel of Madonna di Ghisallo.

Madonna di Ghisallo
Alongside the chapel is a monument dedicated to the world's cyclists. The hill you have just driven up is renowned in the cycling world and the monument, takes the form of a cyclist raising his arm in a triumphant salute. From here there is a beautiful view

of the Lecco arm of Lake Como, with a backdrop formed of the Grigna peaks.

Continue the drive into Magréglio.

Magréglio
This pretty village stands beside the River Lambro, called the Menaresta (Intermittent) in the local dialect because it occasionally disappears to flow underground.

Beyond Magréglio the road drops down the Vallassina, the lovely valley of the Lambro river, to Asso.

Asso
This light-industrial town, which gave its name to the Vallassina, has a long history – a Roman inscribed stone is set in the 21m tower, all that remains of a 10th-century castle. The excellent church of San Giovani Battista was built in Renaissance style in the 17th century.

From Asso follow the signs to Canzo.

Canzo
This is another light-industrial town which gave its name to the Corni di Canzo, the Horns of Canzo, a series of picturesque peaks standing above the Lecco arm of Lake Como, east of the town.

From Canzo take the main valley road which drops down towards Erba. Beyond Erba bear right along the main road to return to Como.

CÓLICO

MAP REF: 110 C4

Cólico is a town with a chequered history. It stands at the northern end of Como near to the Spluga Pass, and to the Valtellina, which meant that the site was at the crossroads of numerous military expeditions. Just to the north, the Piano di Spagna was given to erratic flooding. Not surprisingly, therefore, Cólico was only occupied sporadically until peace and land drainage meant a more settled existence. Today the town is a pleasant spot, usually used as the starting point for trips to the abbey at Piona.

The abbey is a quiet place, set on a crooked finger of headland that encloses the small bay of Lake Piona, south of Cólico. It was founded by Cluniac monks in 1138 but is now occupied by Cistercians. The abbey buildings are very beautiful, especially the cloisters, and the abbey shop sells an assortment of drinks distilled by the monks. These include the intriguingly named St Bernard's Elixir.

DÉRVIO

MAP REF: 110 C4

The headland at Dérvio makes it the narrowest point on the lake and it was, not surprisingly, fortified from the earliest times, the remains of walls and towers still being visible. Today the town is a centre for the feldspar industry, the stone being brought here from the Valle Varrone, the valley that runs up towards Monte Legnone, for crushing. Dérvio is also a centre for local crafts.

The name of the nearby village of Corenno Plinio is said to derive from its early Greek settlers who came from Corinth, and from Pliny the Elder who loved the site. It too has the remains of ancient fortifications.

ERBA

MAP REF: 110 B3

This modern industrial town is renowned for furniture making and marble working; it is also a centre for the building trade, as the nearby (and overhead!) cement works shows. It has an important exhibition centre that, throughout the year, hosts events that vary from local crafts fairs to dog shows. Within the town the large number of splendid old villas hint at Erba's 18th-century past as a resort centre for the wealthy.

Close to the town, reached by a track from Crevenna, is the Buco

del Piombo – a natural chasm, 100m deep, formed in lead-grey rock (hence the name), in which were found the remains of cave bears and some palaeolithic tools. The chasm was fortified by the Romans and in medieval times.

FAGGETO LARIO

MAP REF: 110 B3

This complex of small villages is named after the bundles of sticks (faggots in English) that were once exported from the wooded valley

Ancient cloister at the Cistercian Abbey of Piona, south of Cólico

of the High Brianza leading back from the lake to the mountain hamlets of Molina, Lemma and Palanzo. Each hamlet is exquisite, especially Pallanzo, where the road ends, with its old castle tower and fine campanile. The nearby lake village of Pognana Lario has several churches, one of which, San Miro, is Romanesque and decorated with frescos on the interior and exterior walls.

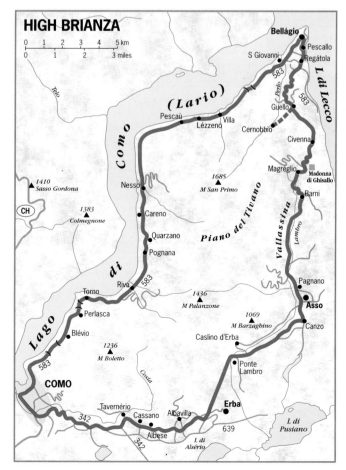

HIGH BRIANZA

COMO AND ITS SILK

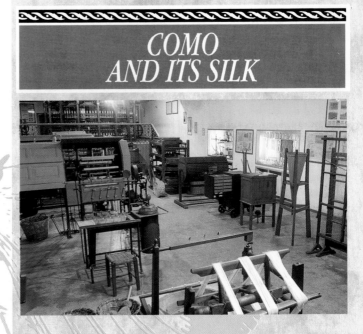

The *Bombyx mari* moth is now extinct in the wild but it was once a native of China. The moths are large – around 5cm long – and pale grey with brown markings. In all *Bombyx mari* would be an unremarkable moth were it not for the cocoon spun by the caterpillar, a huge creature – about 8cm long – that feeds ravenously on the leaves of the white mulberry. When it is ready to pupate the caterpillar spins a cocoon from a single continuous thread of silk.

Top and above: Garlate's Silk Museum, housed in an old silk mill that retains some original machinery

Chinese legend tells of the discovery of silk by Hsi Ling Chi, the young wife of the Emperor Huang Ti, in about 2640BC. That may be an exaggeration, but it is certainly true that silk clothing was worn by Chinese noblemen many hundreds of years before Christ, and that they kept the method of its production a closely guarded secret. Only in the 3rd century BC was silk exported outside of China, first reaching India, then the Persian Empire and, finally, Europe. For centuries the countries of the west endeavoured to discover the secret of this fabulous material, though it was not until the mid-6th century AD that silk production began in Constantinople – after Persian merchants smuggled moth eggs and mulberry leaves out of China in hollow bamboo poles.

Early silk was probably made from cocoons found in the wild, but the Chinese soon realised the haphazard nature of this gathering method. Instead they captured live moths and started a controlled breeding programme. Gradually the wild moth became extinct. Changes brought about by years of selective breeding produced larger numbers of eggs and larger caterpillars (or silkworms) but left the females unable to fly; even the males can barely flutter their way around the breeding cages in search of a mate. Another great sadness of the process is that virtually all the caterpillars are killed after they have spun their cocoons. The cocoon is spun from a single thread so that if the mature insect were allowed to emerge it would break the thread.

The silkworms are killed by heat or steam. Next, the silk threads are wound onto reels. The single thread from each cocoon is between 1,000m and 1,500m long but only 0.025mm thick, so many threads are drawn together to form a silk filament.

From 30 grammes of moth eggs about 35,000 silkworms will emerge to consume about 500kg of mulberry leaves. Natural wastage is quite high and only about 25,000 silkworms will survive to produce cocoons, these yielding about 6kg of reeled silk. Once the thread has been reeled it is 'thrown'. Throwing is a plying process in which many filaments are combined to form a workable yarn. The silk yarn can then be woven on a loom just like any other fabric.

Silk cloth is very strong, yet very light and a superb insulator, being both warm in winter and cool in summer. It is also an excellent dye fabric, taking and holding all colours; a remarkable variety of intricate patterns can be made as a result. Though early Chinese silk fabrics and designs are exquisite, it is now accepted that the silk industry had its Golden Age in Renaissance and post-Renaissance Europe, when production was centred on Lombardy.

In the 17th century Como was the capital of wool production in Lombardy while Milan was the main centre for the production of silk. In the early years of the 18th century, however, a variety of factors combined to change this. The system of internal taxation introduced by the occupying Spanish administration ended silk production in Milan. Production moved to Como where the new silk millers, whose business acumen had been honed by years in the wool trade, employed several new techniques imported from nearby Switzerland and from further afield in northern Europe.

As a result of these innovations Como was able to derive immediate benefit from the enlightened ideas on government, trade and taxation that followed in the wake of the Austrian takeover of northern Italy. Soon Como became the silk centre of the Habsburg Empire, its products dominating the markets from Frankfurt to Leipzig, as well as those of Vienna itself. The Como industry expanded rapidly: a survey in 1733 indicated that 2,500 of the city's population of 14,000 were employed in the silk industry. Allowing for the families of the workers, that implies that Como was virtually a one trade city dedicated to silk.

During the years that followed Como remained the leading centre for silk production and at the forefront of the industry in terms of production techniques. A Como man, Cesare Bonanone, was the first to develop a continuous production method. He imported various machines and tools to Como, modified some of them, and set up a process that employed 600 people – some in small units, others working at home. He had 30 silk looms in factories, another 100 in homes, 14 spinning rooms and two dye works. Soon he was exporting silk to centres outside the Habsburg Empire, such as Turin, in Piedmont, and Lyons, in France.

Como's industry continued to expand until the end of the 18th century, then consolidated in the early years of the 19th. In the middle of the century, however, a mysterious epidemic all but wiped out the local silkworm population. This, together with increasing competition from cotton and raw silk imported from the East, caused the local industry to go into sharp decline. Como's industry survived by going up market and producing luxury silks that were now, more than ever, the preserve of the rich. In 1878 Como silk was the hit of the Paris Exhibition and at the beginning of this century Como still had more than half of Italy's working silk looms. Later, as the cost of manufacturing the basic silk rose, the industry entered yet another new phase, with silk being imported and made up locally into quality finished goods.

That is where Como's industry is today; several local companies are involved in weaving, dyeing and printing the finished products, most of which go for 'export' to the fashion industry of Milan. Few of these local companies have more than 100 employees and the majority have less than 50. Because of the small scale of the Como industry, it has been able to maintain a reputation for quality and for adapting quickly to changes in manufacturing techniques and fashion.

Only a limited range of goods in local silk is available to the visitor in Como – a couple of shops sell scarves and ties. To obtain a better range of products it is necessary to shop around or to ask at the tourist office. The reason is obvious when the 'real thing' is found – though silk is beautiful to look at and to wear, it is not at all cheap to buy.

Anyone interested in finding out more about the local industry should visit the Silk Museum in Garlate, a little way south of Lecco. The museum, housed in an old silk mill which retains some of its machinery, explains the industry from egg to finished garment.

The bold colours and intricate patterns of modern Como silk

GRAVEDONA

MAP REF: 110 C4

Gravedona was the senior member of an early medieval triumvirate known as the Tre Pievi (the Three Parishes), the other member towns being Dongo and Sórico. The alliance maintained a war galley, with a crucifix to make the boat invincible, which patrolled the northern reaches of the lake keeping pirates at bay.

Within the town is western Como's last great villa, Palazzo Gallio, built by Cardinal Tolomeo Gallio on the ruins of an old castle. The villa was known, somewhat cryptically, as the 'Villa of Delights', but it now serves as the town hall and it can be visited on request. The church of Santa Maria del Tiglio is also worth visiting. It dates to the 12th century, but was built over a 5th-century Roman church, part of whose mosaic flooring is still visible.

LECCO

MAP REF: 110 C3

Lecco is Lake Como's second city, a less elegant town than Como, but one with a fine position, tucked under the shapely rock peaks of the Resegone and the Grigna. The town is built on the eastern bank of the Adda, the lake's outflowing river. The southernmost of its two bridges – the one furthest from the lake – was built in 1336 by Azzone Visconti. The bridge has survived, despite the rigours imposed by modern traffic, though it has lost its original drawbridge section.

Within the town there are several sites recording Manzoni's links with the city; part of his famous novel, *I Promessi Sposi* (*The Betrothed*) is set in Lecco. The town museum deals with the development of lake fishing and the town's history, while the Risorgimento Museum, housed in a tower of the old castle, covers the area's involvement in the events of that period.

LENNO

MAP REF: 110 B4

Lenno is the first village of the Tremezzina, or the Azalean Riviera, an area of the western shore of Lake Como famous for the luxuriance of its shrubs and trees – not just azaleas but also oranges, lemons, olives and magnolias. It is now believed that Pliny's Villa Comoedia stood on the shore near Lenno since the Roman poet wrote of fishing from his window.

Nearby, at Azzano, less happy times are remembered, for it was here that Benito Mussolini and his mistress Clara Petacci were shot on the morning of 28 April 1945 .

The huge rock towers of the Grigna form the backdrop to Lecco

The path from Piani d'Erna, on Monte Resegone, leads towards contorted and eroded stacks of Dolomite. Experienced climbers are often seen scaling these giant monoliths, pitting their skill and courage against nature's creation

THE DOLOMITES AND THE VIA FERRATA

In 1789 Deodat de Dolomieu was travelling from his Paris home to Rome when he stopped in Valle Isarco below the Brenner Pass. Being a keen mineralogist his eye was taken by the pale local rock. It was clearly a form of limestone, but not one with which he was familiar. Dr Dolomieu took a sample and found that it was not the normal form of calcium carbonate limestone; instead the Isarco rock was made of a mineral previously unidentified by science, a compound of calcium and magnesium carbonate. This rock is now called Dolomite, in Dr Dolomieu's honour, and the peaks formed from it are known as the Dolomites.

The rock of the Dolomites was laid down in thick sheets during the Triassic Period. In the Tertiary period the land masses of Europe and Africa collided and the Dolomite sheet was raised and contorted. This contortion, together with the corrosive affects of millions of years of frost and snow, wind, rain and sun, have created the spires and towers we see today, forms which are, at the same time, fantastic and beautiful. The main Dolomite peaks are outside the area covered by this book but the Brenta Dolomites are within a day-trip of Lake Garda, and the rock spires of the Grigna vary little from the 'real' Dolomites.

Once, these sheer rock spires were out-of-bounds to ordinary mortals, but some are now climbed by less experienced climbers using *Via Ferrata*, iron ways consisting of steel pegs and ladders. To complete a Via Ferrata requires specialised equipment and should not be taken lightly.

ALESSANDRO MANZONI

Alessandro Manzoni was born on 7 March 1785, the son of a wealthy owner of an estate near Lecco. He did not have a happy childhood. Almost from birth he was rejected by his mother who gave him to a wet nurse, packed him off to boarding school at five and finally left the boy and his father in favour of an even wealthier Milanese. Manzoni married in Paris in 1808 before returning to Italy in 1810 to live in Milan. There he published various works and began the first draft of his masterwork *I Promessi Sposi* which deals with two lovers, Renzo and Lucia, and their lives in an occupied Italy. Though this was published in 1827 Manzoni continued to work on it, producing a 'final' version in 1840.

Manzoni's final years were as unhappy as his childhood. His beloved first wife died in 1833 followed by his second wife and seven out of his nine children. A nervous disorder, which had afflicted him in middle years, grew steadily worse. Despite this his public acclaim grew. Sir Walter Scott hailed *The Bethrothed*, the English version of *I Promessi Sposi*, as the finest book ever written, and the Italians adored him – when he died in 1873 he was given the unusual honour of a state funeral.

Today Manzoni's house in Milan is a shrine to the writer, and Lecco is very proud of its most famous son. There is a statue to him in the town's Piazza Manzoni and a museum of Manzoniana in the 18th-century Villa 'Il Caleotto' where he lived as a boy. Lecco also organises an annual 30km cycle race, the Pedalata Manzoniana which visits the sites mentioned in *I Promessi Sposi*.

MOUNTAIN WALK

Start at the cable car station to the east of Lecco. You can either take the cable car to Piani d'Erna, where the walk begins, or go on up to the summit of Resegone and follow the 5km walk in reverse, in which case it is downhill all the way. Allow 3 hours.

Walk to the right of the Piani d'Erna cable car station, dropping

down through trees to a path. Follow the path left to a road, then go right along the road to reach the gates at its end. Take the mule track to the left, signed Route 1 and marked by red and white paint on trees and rocks along the route. To the left, after 800m, a path marked Route 22 goes off to the left; you may wish to follow this to reach the base of Pizzo d'Erna and to see the Via Ferrata that climbs the dolomite rock face.

Continue along the mule track to reach a large *albergo* (inn/hotel), near to where Route 4 joins Route 1 from the right, and then the alpine hut complex of Costa. Here leave the mule track to climb the steps on the left, between the huts, to reach a steep track that leads to the Rifugio A Stoppani.

Go up the track behind the *rifugio*, passing a spring, the Acqua del Cop, and crossing a stream. Ignore Route 6, right, which goes off towards the Passo del Fo, and bear left to reach Piano Fieno, a small, but obvious, section of flat land among the trees. Now follow the signs for Route 7 which heads due north and gently upwards to reach the wide Bocca d'Erna just below the top station of the cable car at the summit of Resegone. After a pause at the coffee shop, the cable car can be used to return to the start.

·FESTIVALS·

Historical events, often stormy in nature, have left the lakes area with a rich legacy of festivals. Many of these commemorate local battles while others reflect the desire of a community under foreign occupation to maintain its own identity. Often these events are religious in nature, though some reflect the secular heritage of the lakeland towns and villages.

LAKE MAGGIORE

The most famous of Maggiore's events is the International Music Festival held in Stresa. This is held over a four week period during August and September and draws some of the world's finest musicians.

Not to be outdone, Ascona, on the Swiss shore of Lake Maggiore, also holds a festival of classical music. The Ascona festival lasts from the end of August until mid-October, the overlap with the Stresa event allowing some performers to appear at both.

At Laveno, on the opposite side of the lake from Stresa, an extraordinary event takes place at Christmas. On 20 December divers set up a crib beneath the waters of the lake close to the old harbour. The tableau is then floodlit and, on 24 December, a statue of the baby Jesus is lowered into position in the underwater cribs. Because of the clarity of the lake waters the crib is quite clearly visible and makes a haunting picture. Why the crib should be placed underwater is not understood, the event being very ancient. Since it predates floodlighting the Nativity scene must also have suffered from poor visibility in its earliest years, which only adds to the mystery.

An event which takes place in most of the Italian villages of Lake Maggiore, and in some of the valleys north of Varese, is the Riso e Lago, a festival of traditional food. From mid-September until mid-October restaurants in the villages offer a festive menu featuring lake fish and rice, as well as local cheeses and soups and a celebration dessert. A leaflet, from tourist offices, gives details of the venues and their menus, as well as the recipes for each of the main courses.

Other events that are worth

Above: Verdi's *Aida* staged in Verona's Roman amphitheatre. Below: outdoor mass in the ruins of Isola Comacina's church

considering if you are in the area at the right time are the polenta festival at Cuveglio in early July, an event that involves consuming masses of rib-sticking maize-meal pasta; the Va! Cannobina folklore festival at Gurro in mid-July, which includes costumed processions and traditional music and dance; the Quarna Sopra folk festival in late July, at which both local and international groups sing and dance; and the antiques market and firework display in Sesto Calende in mid-July. This market celebrates the Sextum Merecantum, the Roman market which, it is believed, gave its name to the town.

LAKE LUGANO

As befits a city of Lugano's stature it mounts a full programme of events. Of particular note are the Jazz Festival in the first week of July and the Music Festival in the last week of July, which concentrates on classical music.

More traditional are the Maundy Thursday and Good Friday processions in the town of Mendrisio close to the southern shore of the lake. These processions are thought to be the best of their kind in Switzerland, and have been carried on for centuries. On Maundy Thursday the procession re-enacts Christ's journey to Calvary, with all the participants dressed in costume. On Good Friday the procession is more sombre, with various religious groups accompanying a dead Christ and grieving Virgin Mary in a torchlight journey through the town.

LAKE COMO

The most spectacular of all the lake festivals takes place on Lake Como on the weekend following the feast of St John the Baptist, 24 June. The event takes place on and around the island of Isola Comacina and commemorates the destruction of the island's city in 1169 by an army from Como. On the Saturday evening there is a spectacular firework display designed to symbolise the battle. First of all candles burn on the lake itself – floating in glass jars – to depict the encircling of the island by the Como fleet. Next multicoloured rockets light up the sky, a reminder of the ferocity of the battle. Roman candles mounted on tall poles around the island's shore are then lit: as they change colour from white to red they symbolise the island's invasion and the slaughter of its

people. Finally, there is a general firework display symbolic of the final burning of the city.

During the festival no one is allowed on the island itself. That changes on the next day, Sunday, when a religious procession starts on the mainland, continues as a procession of boats and ends with an island procession to the ruined church of San Giovani where an outdoor mass is celebrated. This colourful procession is followed by races between the traditional lake boats.

LAKE GARDA

Lake Garda has no big festivals but many of its towns and villages do have interesting traditional events. Bardolino, famous for its red wine, has a grape festival in September, while nearby Garda has a fish festival in July. This event is called the Sardellata, literally the Sardine Festival, and it includes numerous events on the lake itself. Inland, Cavaion Veronese has an asparagus festival in July. Many villages hold races in traditional lake boats; perhaps the best of these being at Gargnano where the event is combined with an international sailing regatta.

Nearby, on the Tignale, the evenings of 3, 4 and 5 January aremarked by the Canto della Stella – literally starlight singing; processions at several venues on the plateau re-enact the journey of the Three Wise Men to the acompaniment of choral song . A similar festival is held at Desenzano at Christmas. At mid-Lent both Gargnano and Gardone hold 'Hag's Trials', at which the effigy of an old woman is burnt on a bonfire, a festival that recalls the darker side of medieval life.

To the north of the lake, the village of Arco is unusual in celebrating its Austrian past with a procession of folk in full Habsburg costume. At nearby Ponte Caffero/Bagolino the Compagna di Ballori gives an annual demonstration of local dance accompanied by the traditional *sunadut*, a group consisting of violins, a guitar and a *bassetto*, a three-stringed bass 'guitar'. During the festival (held in summer but times vary so consult the local tourist office) the locals wear traditional costume and there is a day – long carnival. Finally, in September, a firework spectacular is held at the castle in Sirmione.

Verona hosts a season of Shakespeare plays in June and July, and the world-famous open-air opera season in July and August; both in the Roman amphitheatre.

At Isola Comacina, the festival that commemorates the island city's destruction in 1169 culminates in a religious procession

LÉZZENO

MAP REF: 110 B3

Lézzeno is the collective name given to 17 hamlets strung out along the southern shore of Lake Como opposite Ossuccio. Each hamlet has good views towards the Azalean Riviera, Isola Comacina and the peaks of the opposite shore and towards the northern section of the lake. Close to the final village, the real Lézzeno, is the Buco dei Carpi, the Carp Hole, a lake cave which attracts shoals of fish. The hole can only be reached by boat and is worth visiting in the evening when the light of the dying sun causes a multi-coloured light show on the water.

Within the village the church of Santi Quirico e Giulitta is worth visiting for the beautifully frescoed interior, much of the work dating from the 16th century.

The view from Bellágio over Punta Spartivento to Monte Grona

MANDELLO DEL LARIO

MAP REF: 110 C3

Mandello, located on the northern shore of the Lecco arm of the lake, is best seen from the opposite shore, when the backdrop of the Grigna peaks can be seen to perfection. Mandello sided with Como in the Ten Years' War with Milan, and was destroyed in 1160 as a result, though the remains of the old walls and castle are still visible at the lakeside. Much later, under the rule of the Sforzas, a battle took place at Mandello between the Sforza navy and Il Medeghino, an infamous Lake Como pirate – despite the odds against him, the pirate escaped to fight another day. Later still, Mandello became prosperous as a result of the silk trade and stone quarrying: Mandello stone was used to build Como's cathedral. Within the town the Church of San Lorenzo is 9th century, and is built on the foundations of a Romano-Christian church.

An old tower in the village of Maggiana, above Mandello, is known as Barbarossa's Tower because of a tradition that he spent some time there in 1158.

MENÁGGIO

MAP REF: 110 B4

Menággio sits at the mouth of the pass between Lake Como and Lugano. As a result it is a bustling town, a good place for window shopping or searching out local art and craft work. From the town there are many fine excursions into the surrounding mountains – southwards to Monte Grona (see walk right) and northwards up the Val Sanagra towards Monte Bregagno.

MOLTRÁSIO

MAP REF: 110 B3

A new road on Como's western shore bypasses the villages of Moltrásio, Carate Urio and Láglio, leaving them quieter than they once were, and friendlier to the visitor in search of a little peace. In Moltrásio, the Villa Passalacqua is a fine 18th-century mansion that is open to public, and the church of Sant'Agata is a beautiful Romanesque building. The village is split by the delightful gorge of the Torrente Vesporina which also has a pleasant tree-shaded upper area.

Carate Urio has a Via Crucis (Way of the Cross), lined by 14 chapels high above the village, while Láglio's town hall houses an exhibition of fossil remains, including those of cave bears, found in the 'Bear's Hole', a cave which lies a stiff 1 $^1/_2$ hour walk away.

MOUNTAIN WALK

This fine walk is waymarked throughout by red paint markers and follows Routes 27 and 28 to Rifugio Menaggio on the slopes of Monte Grona. Allow 2 hours for the 5km walk, but add another 2 hours if you decide to extend the walk to climb to the mountain's summit. To reach the start point, take the Lugano road out of Menággio then turn right for Loveno. Going through that village you will pass the Chiarella mineral water 'factory' – which has a free fountain, though no large containers are allowed. Continue through Bréglia until you reach the end of the road.

From the end of the road follow the mule track that rises through beautiful woodland. Watch now for a well-signposted, but slightly hidden, path to the left which leads to a house with a prominent fountain. The path forks here and you should take the left-hand path. This turns south, through a deep narrow valley, before climbing the far valley side, passing a TV repeater station to reach Rifugio Menaggio.

At the *rifugio* running cold water is available from an animal drinking trough, and more conventional refreshments are served daily in summer and at weekends in spring and autumn. The view to Lake Como is superb from here, virtually the whole northern end of the lake being visible, while Punta Spartivento and Bellagio are prominent to the south. If you walk across the face of the *rifugio* and then southwards, you will reach another vantage point from which Lake Lugano, as well as Lake Como, can be seen.

To return, reverse the outward route. Alternatively you can extend the walk by taking the

MONTE GRONA

La Forcoletta

1736
M Grona   Rif Menaggio

1419

Bréglia

0   1 km

more difficult, but aptly named, Via Panoramico (signed Variante A of Route 28) from the *rifugio*. This goes behind the *rifugio*, through a narrow gully and across the face of Monte Grona, with a view of Lake Lugano ahead and of rock climbers to the right. The path now passes between spectacular rock towers to reach a steep and treacherous grassy path. Be careful – a fall here could be very serious. The difficulty increases as height is gained, the final climb to the summit – at 1,736m – being assisted by a wire rope.

To descend go away from the ascent route to reach La Forcoletta (1,611m). One section of the descent requires help from another *in situ* rope. From there a path, marked by red and yellow paint splashes, leads easily back to the Rifugio Menaggio.

The russet-coloured roof-tiles of Menággio contrast with blue Lake Como

MOUNTAIN WALK

This demanding walk of 11km requires a long half-day, or even a full day when rests are taken into account. In exchange it offers a superb climb to Grignone, the highest Grigna summit from where the view is magnificent. The route is waymarked throughout with splashes of red and yellow paint, and the route numbers are given at each fork in the path. To reach the start point take the road from Varenna through Esino Lario and Cainallo, continuing to Vó di Moncodeno where parking is easy.

Take Route 25 from the car park, a wide track with an expanding view of the Grigna. After about 30 minutes you will reach a fork; follow Route 25, an undulating

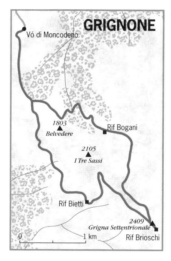

track that leads to another fork. Here go right on Route 24, walking through woodland, to reach a path that hugs the steep rocky face of the Grigna, to the

left. Soon you will reach a natural rock arch – the Porta Prada – within which a crucifix has been set. Beyond the arch take the path that is clearly visible, but occasionally devious where it crosses steep ground, to reach the Rifugio Bietti.

Go behind the hut and follow the steep zig-zag path up to the Grigna ridge. The temperature drops steadily as you climb, and when the ridge is finally reached there is invariably a cooling breeze. Go right and up the ridge path towards the now-visible summit. Close to the summit a chain is provided to assist progress, but beyond you will reach a wide path which passes a chapel and continues to the *rifugio*.

Rifugio Brioschi is open all year and has beds and a telephone as well as food and drink. From the cross at the summit (at 2,409m) the panorama includes the Bernina Alps, Monte Rosa and the Matterhorn to the north together with Milan and the Lombardy Plain to the south.

Return along the ridge and descend past the chains. Instead of reversing the outward route, continue from the bottom of the chains down a path that is obvious at first but becomes more difficult to follow once more level ground is reached. Just keep going downhill: all possible routes are funnelled to the Rifugio Bogani from where a single, and very obvious, path traverses another impressive rock face that falls away from the Grigna. This path rejoins the outward route at the first fork; simply reverse this outward route to return to the Vó di Moncodeno car park.

Porta Prada, sheltering a crucifix, arches over the path to the Grigna ridge

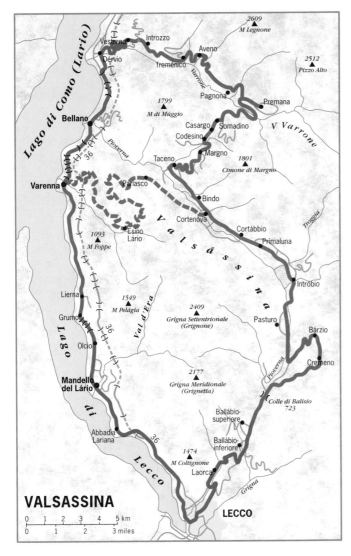

VALSASSINA

```
0   1   2   3   4   5 km
0        1        2      3 miles
```

LECCO

MOTOR TOUR

Mountain hamlets, a famous waterfall and folk art are all included in this 3$\frac{1}{2}$ hour, 105km drive of the Valsássina.

From Lecco take the Bárzio/Ballábio road; this rises from the lake towards the right-hand side of the rock mass of Monte Coltignone, the first peak of the Grigna range. Go through Ballábio and continue to the Colle di Balísio.

The Colle di Balísio
The Balísio Pass lies at the head of the enchanting Valsássina, one of the most beautiful of the region's valleys, green and pastoral, yet bounded on its western edge by the shapely rock masses of the Grigna peaks.

Just beyond the Balísio Pass, turn right on the road signposted to Cremeno.

Cremeno
This pretty village is set among meadows, rocks and woods. The

church houses a fine 16th-century polyptych.

Continue to Bárzio.

Bárzio
Pietro, the father of the novelist Alessandro Manzoni (see page 59) was born in this village which now has all the high-rise trappings of a modern ski resort. From the village a chairlift rises to the Piani di Bobbia, at 1,850m the main local centre for skiing and walking. Within the village, the Medardo Rosso Museum displays the works of this turn-of-the-century Impressionist sculptor.

Continue on the same road until you rejoin the main valley road, then turn right going down the valley. To the left is a turning for Pasturo, the location of Agnes's house in Manzoni's novel The Bethrothed. Continue to the village of Intróbio.

Intróbio
The waterfall on the Troggia river above Intróbio is so beautiful that Leonardo da Vinci came here to view it when he was working in

Milan. It is interesting to speculate whether the great man, who was working on his *Last Supper* at the time, visited the Intróbio churches, all of which have early frescos.

Continue to Primaluna.

Primaluna
This was once the 'capital' of the Valsássina and the valley road was protected by a castle built by the della Torre family, though little now remains. The church of Santi Pietro e Paolo has some fine wood carving. Within the village is the Museum of the Valley, dealing with its history and folklore.

Continue down the valley, with magnificent views towards the Grigna and the lower peaks of Monte Legnone, to reach Cortenova. From here there is a choice of routes. The road to the left goes through Parlasco before winding a tortuous, but lovely, route over the pass near Sasso di San Defendente and into Esino Lário, a town of many villas that is sometimes known as the 'Pearl of the Grigna'. From Esino you can drive down into Varenna and follow the lakeside road back to Lecco.
The alternative is to continue down the main valley road to Taceno, a delightful spot, and turn right on the road that leads to the Val Varonne, another beautiful valley with, at its head, the village of Premana.

Premana
The village is famous for its craftworkers, who specialise in wrought iron, and for the costumes worn by the women. The costumes, and the local dialect, are quite distinctive and show Venetian influence.

From Premana a road drops down to reach Lake Como at Dérvio and from here the lakeside road south, through Bellano and Varenna, rapidly brings you back to Lecco.

NESSO
MAP 1234

Picturesque Nesso is the only village along the peaceful eastern shore of the Como arm of the lake around Punta della Cavagnala. The village still has a section of its old wall; the castle and the rest of the wall were destroyed during a battle between Il Medeghino, the Musso-based pirate, and Francesco I Sforza in 1531. Where the Torrente Nesso reaches the lake there is a small gorge which can be viewed from the bridge close to the shore.

OLIVETO LARIO
MAP REF: 110 C3

A narrow road from Bellágio follows the western shore of the Lecco arm of the lake. This shore has few settlements but offers wonderful views of the Grigna across the water. Oliveto is the only village of substance and its name refers to the olive groves that provide a gentle contrast to the rock towers of Grigna. In late medieval times Oliveto's remoteness allowed it to function as an independent state. In the village there is a delightful little harbour and a rock topped with the chapel of the Madonna del Moletto, the Virgin of the Jetty, containing good, but poorly preserved, frescos.

PIANELLO DEL LARIO
MAP REF: 110 C4

Pianello is a tiny, but picturesque, village whose major attraction is the fascinating museum of lake boats (see page 50).

Two villages lie to the north. Musso stands beneath the Sasso di Musso, its sides quarried out for the marble used to build part of Como's cathedral and the whole of Milan's Arch of Peace. This natural fortress was once topped by a castle defended by Il Medeghino, a ruthless pirate. The pirate was born Gian Giacomo Medici in Milan, but came here as a youth after killing another boy in a fight. From Musso Il Medeghino terrorised the northern lake. Resisting all attempts to subdue him he eventually sold the castle to the Duke of Milan, living out the remainder of his years as a free, and rich, man. He even ended up with a tomb in Milan's cathedral.

Nearby Dongo, one of the three villages of the medieval Tre Pieve alliance, is famous as the spot where Mussolini's flight to freedom was halted in 1945. Many of his party were executed at Dongo on the day after their capture, while Mussolini and Clara Petacci were driven south to meet their fate at Azzano.

SALA COMACINA
MAP REF: 110 B4

The lake shore between Sala Comacina and Punta di Balbianello is often called the Zocca dell'Oli, the Olive Hollow, because of the abundance of olive groves.

Opposite Sala is Lake Como's only island, Isola Comacina, measuring a mere 800m by 400m.

Isola Comacina once supported a thriving community, one of the richest on the lake. The island village was called Crisopoli, the City of Gold – and not Christopoli, the City of Christ, as is sometimes quoted – and was the envy of many other lake towns, most especially Como. During the Ten Years' War between Como and Milan, the island sided with Milan. Como did not forget and when the village rose again, after its initial defeat, Como's army devastated the island killing all the inhabitants and levelling their houses. Today it remains largely uninhabited, apart from an excellent restaurant and a few studios occupied by artists on scholarships from Milan.

Opposite the island is Ospedaletto with a church whose campanile is the most photographed of any on Lake Como. The slender Romanesque tower is topped by a very pretty Gothic bell turret. In nearby Ossuccio the church has a 3rd century Romano-Christian altar, while above the village a 17th-

Ospedaletto's Romanesque tower topped by a Gothic bell turret

century Via Crucis, with 14 chapels, climbs to a sanctuary. Higher still, and reached by a stiff walk, is the basilica of San Benedetto in Val Perlana, the finest Romanesque church on the lake.

From any of these lake villages boats will take visitors to the Villa Balbianello which stands at the point of the headland of Balbianello. The romantic little quay, with its statue of St Francis offering a welcoming hand to the guest, is one of Como's most photographed scenes. The statue dates from the time when the villa was a convalescent home for Franciscan monks. The present building is an 18th-century extension of that home, built under the direction of Cardinal Angelo Durini, a sombre man who slept between black sheets in a black bedroom with a coffin beside his bed to remind him of his fate each morning when he awoke. The bedroom forms a curious contrast to the riotous colour of the villa's beautifully tended gardens.

THE SMALLER LAKES

MAP REF: 110 B3, C3, C3

Three small lakes – Alserio, Pusiano and Annone – lie between the Lecco and Como arms of Lake Como, while to the south of Lecco there are two more – Garlate and Olginate.

The first lake reached from Como is also the smallest, Lake Alserio. Carcano, one of the two villages close to the lake was heavily fortified in the early medieval period, its castle playing a role in the Battle of Tassera when Barbarossa fought the Milanese. Barbarossa held the castle and his troops were winning the battle until villagers from nearby Erba joined the attack,forcing him into the open. His army fled and the Milanese destroyed the castle. Alserio, the village that shares the lake's name, was once a fishing port, with a lucrative license to supply the Dukes of Milan. Lake Pusiano is larger than Alserio and has a small island named after the cypress trees which grow on it. The villages that surround the lake have fine villas, a memory of the more idyllic time before the cement works arrived.

Lake Annone, near Lecco, is almost split in two by a thin peninsula where the village of Isella has one of the region's most romantically sited campsites. A bridge linking the tip of the land spit and the mainland was destroyed by the Spanish in the 17th century though the piers can still be seen. The bridge joined Isella to Annone di Brianza, a village with a beautiful, spear-like campanile. On the lake's northern shore is Civate from where a 2-hour walk leads to the church of San Pietro al Monte and the Oratory of San Benedetto high up on Monte Rai. The little complex dates from the 8th century and is one of the most important sites – both architecturally and historically – in Lombardy.

Lake Garlate lies immediately south of Lecco. The village of Garlate, near the lake's southern tip, has a fascinating museum to the local silk industry (see page 56). South again is the tiny Lake Olginate the final lake of the area.

SÓRICO

MAP REF: 110 C4

The most northerly village on Lake Como is Sórico, located opposite the Piano di Spagna, an area of marshland between the inflowing rivers Mera and Adda. The marshland is named after the Spanish governor of Milan who built a castle on a hillock above the marsh, marking the limit of Spanish territory in northern Italy. The castle must have been a miserable posting for the occupying soldiers – the marsh was so unhealthy that the original fishing settlement was abandoned in the Middle Ages in favour of today's village, sited further away from the sinister, disease-ridden bog. Both the marsh and Lake Mezzola, to the north, are now important sites for breeding and migrating birds. Sórico's church is dedicated to San Mirus and pilgrims come here to pray for relief from pain.

TREMEZZO

MAP REF: 110 B4

Most visitors come here to see the Villa Carlotta (see opposite), missing the remainder of the picturesque village and the delightful lakeside walk which continues through an avenue of trees – celebrated by Longfellow as 'a leafy colonnade' – into

The fresco-filled, 11th-century church of San Giovanni, Varenna

The manicured gardens of the Villa Carlotta, laid out from 1850 onwards

Cadenabbia.

Cadenabbia has a car ferry port linking Como's western shore with Bellágio and Varenna. Most of its fine villas have now been turned into hotels. Verdi stayed in one while working on the score of *La Traviata*. Close to Cadenabbia is Griante, the Grianta of Stendhal's novel *The Charterhouse of Parma*. Stendhal describes the village as having a sublime view of the lake – and so it has. The Villa La Collina is now the headquarters of the Konrad Adenauer Foundation, named after the former German Chancellor who frequently stayed here during his years in office, and after his retirement. The villa stands on a superb hilltop site surrounded by elegant gardens.

VARENNA

MAP REF: 110 C4

Varenna is built around a final spike of rock that falls from the Grigna. The position had strategic importance, commanding both the Como and Lecco arms of the lake, and the gaunt remains of an old castle – said to have been the last home of Theodolinda, the 7th-century queen of the Lombard's – testify to this. When Isola Comacina was destroyed by Como those islanders who managed to escape the slaughter came here and boosted the town's prosperity by opening the black marble quarries for which the town became famous. A later native of Varenna, G B Pirelli, went on to found the huge industrial firm that is now famous both for its tyres

and for its calendars which have now become highly prized collector's items.

Today Varenna is a beautiful place with a mass of piled-up houses intersected by narrow alleys. Of considerable interest is the Ornithological and Natural History Museum, which has a display of local mammals and of all the bird species found in the locality. The 11th-century church of San Giovanni and the 13th-century church of San Giorgio both have fine frescos.

Of greatest interest, however, are the two villas at the southern end of the town. Villa Cipressi, in Via 4 Novembre, with its excellent terraced gardens falling down to the shore, is beautiful enough but it cannot really compete with the nearby Villa Monastero. This villa dates to the early 13th century and was built for Cistercian nuns who had been evicted from Isola Comacina. Three centuries later rumours about the nuns' behaviour – the locals referred to the villa as the House of Lovers – persuaded San Carlo Borromeo to close the convent. Today it is used as a science centre and the view from the arcaded terraces is excellent.

Close to Varenna is Fiumelatte, a village named after a stream that emerges from a cave above the houses and meets the lake after 250m, making it the second shortest stream in Italy. The name means Milk River, because in spring, when the Grigna snows are melting and the river is in full spate, its waters appear to be a milky white.

THE VILLA CARLOTTA

The Villa Carlotta is the most famous of all Lake Como's villas and the highlight of a visit to the lake. Many who come assume, understandably, that the 'C' above the entrance stands for Carlotta, whereas it actually refers to the Clerici, the family who built the villa in the early 18th century. The Clerici were not, however, responsible for what we see today. Most of the works of art were executed while the villa was owned by Count Sommariva at the beginning of the 19th century and the gardens were laid out from 1850 by a later owner, Princess Carlotta of Prussia, who gave her name to the villa.

Inside, every ceiling is a masterpiece of the plasterer's art, and there are several priceless works of art. Of these the best are the sculptures of Antonio Canova. His *Mary Magdalene* is a brilliant evocation of anguish, while *Cupid and Venus* is a wonderful portrayal of tenderness.

The gardens contain over 500 tree and shrub species including some 150 different rhododendrons and azaleas, many of them planted in the Azalea Avenue. When in bloom this makes one of the finest sights in Europe. In addition there are many beautiful camellias and wisterias, a fern valley, a magnificent rock garden and an all-pervading scent from the blossoms of the numerous citrus trees.

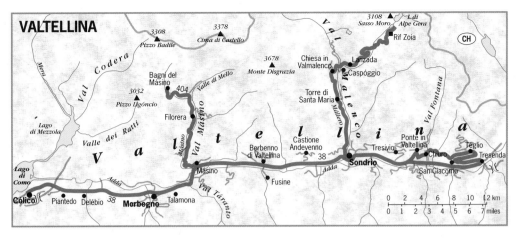

VALTELLINA

MOTOR TOUR

The River Adda flows down from
the high Alps to meet the Po near
Cremona – thus says the classic
geography of the river, but the
Adda has two unusual features.
The first is that, at its northern
end, the river flows east to west,
unlike the other local rivers which
flow north to south. The second
unusual feature is that, for part of
its length, the river in fact
becomes Lake Como. The east-
west section of the Adda's flow is
known as the Valtellina, a valley
with a long history. Several of the
high Alpine passes, running north
to south, end in the Valtellina.
Control of the valley therefore
ensured control of the passes.

*Our 170km tour, lasting
4 hours, starts from the northern
end of Lake Como. From Cólico
follow the road northwards,
ignoring the turning to
Chiavenna, and continue to
Morbegno on the Sondrio road.*

Morbegno

This pleasant town has a delightful
bridge, the Ponte di Garda, built in
the 18th century with a semi-
circular arch. The town also has a
fine natural history museum.
Nearby, the Val Tártano is one of
the most beautiful of the local
valleys.

*Continue along the main valley
road to reach Sondrio.*

Sondrio

This is the undisputed capital of
the Valtellina, its strategic
position, halfway along the valley,
resulting in a long and violent
history. The Middle Ages saw
bitter feuding for control of the
town and, in 1620, the Spanish
Governor of Milan ordered the
slaughter of all of the town's
Protestants. Even the peace that
followed Napoleon's Italian
campaign was shattered a few

years later when the Torrente
Mállero, which bisects the town,
flooded disastrously. Today the
stream is enclosed in a solid
concrete channel. Masegre Castle,
the last of many to be built on the
site, stands on one bank.

Piazza Campello lies at the heart
of the town surrounded by the
Palazzo Communale (the Town
Hall), a fine 16th-century building
with an unusually textured façade,
and the 18th-century church of
Santi Gerasio e Protasio.

To the north of the square is the
oldest section of the town, though
continuous rebuilding means that
little is now older than the 18th
century. A glorious exception is
the Palazzo Lavizzori in Via
Pallavicino, a 16th-century
mansion with a marble doorway.
Eastwards from Piazza Campello is
the Palazzo Quadrio which houses
the Museo Valtellinese, a museum
to the history and art of the valley,
including Roman and Etruscan
finds. A second museum, at Via
Ragazzi del 99, deals with the

area's natural history and geology.

A little way from the town the
church of Madonna della Sassella,
an interesting 15th-century
building with some good artwork,
stands among the vineyards that
produce grapes for Sassella, the
area's famous red wine.

*Continue eastwards along the
valley, but turn off to visit the
village of Ponte in Valtellina.*

Ponte in Valtellina

Set off the main valley road, and
close to the mouth of Val Fontana,
Ponte is one of the artistic
highspots of a trip to the
Valtellina. The church of San
Maurizio was built in the 14th
century and is famous for its fresco
by Bernardino Luini. There is also
a very rare 16th-century bronze
ciborium or tabernacle. A small
museum beside the church
displays further items relating to

**Vineyards spill down to Sondrio,
capital of the Valtellina**

its history and art. Another museum, in Via Ginnasio, deals with the history and folklore of the area. Elsewhere, a monument commemorates Giuseppe Piazzi (1746-1826), who was born in Ponte and discovered the first asteroid.

Head back towards the main valley road but, before reaching it, turn left to Chiuro and continue along an exacting road to Téglio.

Téglio

The Valtellina is named after Téglio, which was the most important town in the valley in the Middle Ages. Téglio also claims to be the home of *pizzocheri*, a pasta made from black flour and served hot with butter. Every autumn the town celebrates the Sagra dei Pizzocheri, a festival at which the dish is served in all the local restaurants.

Within the town, seek out the Palazzo Besta which is the finest palazzo in the Valtellina – its superb courtyard is surrounded by two storeys of arcades and frescoed walls. The town museum, the Antiquarium Tellinum, has an interesting collection on the rock engravings, perhaps dating to the Bronze Ages, found in the **nearby** valleys. Two churches are also worth visiting: the Romanesque San Pietro has an 11th-century campanile, while the 15th-century Santa Eufemia has some interesting artwork.

From Téglio return to the main valley road and head west, back towards Sondrio and Lake Como. At Sondrio, turn right for a visit to the Val Malenco which ends beneath the massive bulk of Pizzo Bernina, the highest peak of the Bernina Alps at 4,050m.

Madesimo, one of Lombardy's best-known and most popular ski resorts

Head for Chiesa, the Val Malenco's chief town.

Chiesa in Valmalenco

The town has a good collection of the minerals for which the Valmalenco is famous. Over 150 types have been found here, making it the premier site in the Alps for mineralogists and crystal hunters. The quarries that can be seen in the valley work a particular form of green serpentine known as Malenco marble.

From the village of Chiesa in Valmalenco a twisting and occasionally difficult road heads off to the Rifugio Zoia from where a superb walk of about 1 hour visits the lonely, but beautiful, lakes of Campomoro and Alpe di Gera nestling beneath the peak of Sasso Moro (3,108 m).

Return to the main Valtellina road, heading westwards, but turn off to the right at Masino to visit the Val Másino.

The Val Másino

This valley heads north to end close to the Pizzo Badile, one of the major peaks of the Bernina Alps at 3,308m. The north face of Badile is ranked, alongside the north faces of the Eiger and the Matterhorn, as one of the six most challenging climbs in the Alps. To the east of the valley is Monte Disgrazia, a giant peak of 3,678m said to be the home of the Gigiat, a huge goat or Alpine Yeti which remains as elusive as its Himalayan counterpart.

From the Val Másino it is a short drive back, along the main Valtellina road, to Lake Como.

SKI RESORTS AND MOUNTAIN EROSION

The high peaks of the Valtellina are home to some of the best-known ski resorts in Italy. Livigno and Bormio - venues for a recent World Skiing Championship - lie to the northeast of the valley, Madesimo to the northwest and Aprica in the valley itself. These resorts contribute substantially to the local economy. As skiing is also a healthy pastime, enjoyed by millions of visitors in lovely surroundings, the situation would appear to be ideal. In reality these ski resorts have had a detrimental effect on the local environment and serious doubts are now being expressed about the wisdom of unabated development.

One concern is the amount of rubbish and sewage from the resorts which places a very large burden on local services. Even more serious is the effect on the local ecology, resulting in the destruction of precious high alpine meadows and trees and damage to the local hydrography. Flash floods and landslides have become more frequent because the felling of forests and the stripping of top soil has destroyed the area's ability to absorb water and release it slowly. Landslides killed 17 people and made more than 500 others homeless in 1983. In 1987 floods and landslides killed another 20 people, cutting Bormio off from the lower valley. Such ominous events are causing valley dwellers to hope that those in charge of future developments will learn from the harsh lessons of the past.

MILANO (MILAN)

Milan (map ref: 110 B3) began as a Celtic settlement in the middle of the Lombardy Plain, hence it was called *Mediolanum*. In 222BC the Romans occupied the town after a crucial battle against the Celts. The town grew to be one of the largest in the Roman Empire.

It was here, in AD313, that Constantine the Great signed the Edict that gave freedom of religion to the Christians, and here that San Ambrogio (St Ambrose) lived in the late 4th century, becoming the town's first bishop. Subsequently the city headed the Lombard League, which defeated Barbarossa in 1176, and gained independence as a City State before coming under the sway of the della Torre family, then the Visconti and finally the Sforzas.

In the years of the Risorgimento the city fought valiantly if, at times, with some subtlety. When Giuseppe Verdi's operas were being performed at La Scala, the whole city was daubed with VIVA VERDI, because VERDI was an acronym for Vittorio Emanuele Re D'Italia. Mussolini was elected parliamentary member for Milan in 1921, though the city had lost all enthusiasm for Fascism by the time the city was battered by air-raids in 1943. Today Milan is Italy's economic capital, a world centre for the fashion industry, a cultural city with priceless works of art and home to two of Europe's most distinguished football teams – in short, one of the great modern cities of Europe.

TOWN WALK I

This 40-minute walk will introduce you to the many highlights of the city centre.

Start in the Piazza del Duomo and walk between the north side of the Duomo (cathedral) and the front of the Galleria, passing La Rinascente, a well-known shopping centre. Turn right along the back of the cathedral. To the left is the Palazzo dell'Orologio, named after its clock, flanked by statues of Day and Night. At the end of the palazzo turn left into Piazza Fontana.

1 The piazza is named after the fountain designed by Piermarini and erected in 1782. Turn round now for a fine view of the cathedral. To the left is the entrance to the Palazzo Arcivescovile, the 12th-century Archbishop's Palace. It is a rather dull and sombre building, but must have been livelier (and noisier) when the archbishop's mules were kept on the ground floor, with the horses of the clergy on the floor above.

Walk alongside the Palazzo Arcivescovile to reach the Palazzo Reale, to the left.

2 The Royal Palace was given to the city by the King in 1920. Mozart's first opera was performed here, when he was only 14. Today the palace houses a gallery of contemporary art and the Museo del Duomo.

Cross the Piazza del Duomo to the entrance to the Galleria.

3 The Piazza del Duomo has recently acquired two Metro entrances but these have not changed the character of the magnificent square, one of the finest in Europe. It is dominated by the west front of the cathedral, although some time should be given to the impressive equestrian statue of Vittorio Emanuele II, a bronze sculpted by Ercole Rosa in 1896.

The Galleria that bears the King's name was built in the 1870's and was modern for its time, with a glass and ironwork cupola and fine mosaics.

Go through the Galleria, noticing, to the right, Savini, Milan's most famous restaurant. At the far end of the Galleria is the Piazza della Scala, with the famous opera house, the Teatro alla Scala, standing to the left. Cross in front of the 16th-century Palazzo Marino, on the right of the square, and turn right along its northern flank. At the end a right turn leads to Piazza San Fedele where a statue of the novelist Alessandro Manzoni faces his favourite church. Bearing left pass Casa degli Omenoni to reach, to the left, Piazza Belgioioso.

4 Casa degli Omenoni, the House of the Giants, is named after Leone Leoni's sculptures on the façade. To the right of the piazza is the 18th-century palace of the Belgioioso d'Este family, while at the end is Alessandro Manzoni's House, now a museum devoted to the writer.

Go through the piazza to reach the Museo Poldi-Pezzoli on the right-hand side.

5 The museum houses one of the finest art collections in the world, including Antonio Pollaiolo's famous *Profile of a Young Woman*.

From the museum go down Via A Manzoni back into the Piazza della Scala.

6 La Scala was built in 1778 by Piermarini and the opera season runs from early December until May. The theatre holds around 2,000 people and is lit by the famous Lampadrio di Boemia chandelier which has a bulb for each day of the year. The Museo Teatrale, in the same building, covers the history of the theatre. The statue in the square is of Leonardo da Vinci and four of his favourite pupils.

Walk past the front of La Scala, keeping right into Via Santa Margherita to reach Via Mercanti. Cross over into Piazza dei Mercanti, the old market square.

7 Entering this quiet square you pass the arcaded Palazzo della Ragione, the old magistrature, built in 1233. The relief on the rear wall, in the square, dates to the same year – and shows Oldrado da Tresseno, one-time city governor. The iron rings on the arcade columns – for tethering horses – are decorated with a snake, the Visconti family emblem. Opposite stands the 17th-century Palatine School with the 14th-century Loggia degli Osii to the left and the Palazzo dei Notari, the Palace of the Lawyers, to the right – an inscription here notes that in any dispute only the lawyers grow fat.

Via Mercanti leads back to the Duomo.

IL DUOMO (THE CATHEDRAL)

Milan's Duomo (Cathedral), begun in 1387, took 400 years to complete and is the third biggest in the world. The cathedral, built of dazzling pinkish-white marble from Candoglia, is 157m long and the western front is 68m wide. The tip of the Madonnina, the gilded statue on top of the highest spire, is 108m above the ground. Over 3,000 statues adorn the interior and exterior.

Inside a red light shines high up in the nave to mark the position of a True Nail from the Cross of Christ which is brought to the floor once each year so that it may be seen by the faithful. Close to the entrance is a bronze strip set in the floor. A hole high in the roof allows the sun to strike the line twice a year, at noon on 21 June and 21 December. At one time the Milanese used these events to reset clocks and calendars, but building subsidence means that the sundial is no longer accurate. The Duomo's crypt holds the body of San Carlo Borromeo. The body lies in a silver and crystal casket, a gift of Philip IV of Spain, dressed in bejewelled vestments. The head is covered by a silver mask modelled from the saint's death mask. The highlight of the cathedral is the roof. Stone stairways, and the flat slabs of the roof itself, give safe access to well-protected viewpoints where you can see the gilded statue of the Madonnina. In deference to the Madonnina no building in Milan was allowed to be higher. Of late this unwritten agreement has been breached, but only for buildings well away from the cathedral. The result is a wonderful view of Milan .

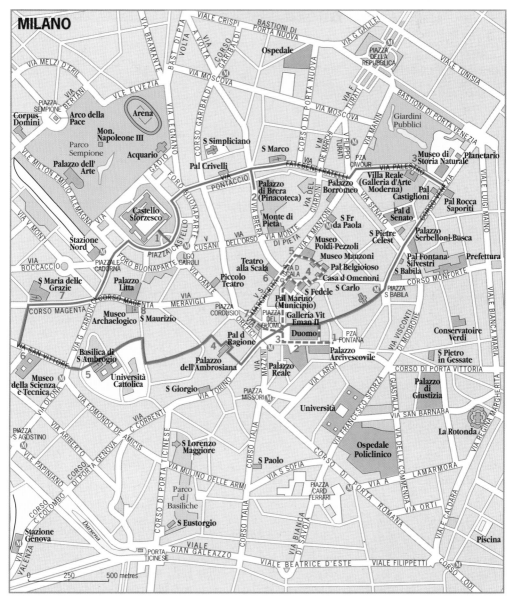

TOWN WALK II

The second of our walks takes in the artistic highlights of the city, including Leonardo da Vinci's renowned *Last Supper* fresco. Allow at least 2 hours for the 7km walk and much longer if you plan to visit each museum in detail. (See Walk I for map)

Start at the Castello Sforzesco (whose military history is explained on page 102).

1 The Castle Museum, housed in the domestic apartments of the Sforza Castle, includes one of the finest collections of antique medieval instruments in Europe and a beautifully displayed collection of arms and armour. The fresco of intertwining oak branches in the Sala delle Asse, the Room of Beams, was painted by Leonardo da Vinci, but the original work has suffered from comprehensive restoration. The excellent paintings collection includes work by Mantegna and Tintoretto, but pride of place goes to Michelangelo's *Pietà Rondanini* depicting the Virgin supporting the dead Christ. This was Michelangelo's last work and it is usually said that he died before its completion. This is not true: the artist stopped work because he decided that man could not capture God in paint or stone. Even unfinished the Pietà is a work of power and genius.

From the castle's Clock Tower entrance, turn left, following Piazza Castello to reach Via Lanza. Turn right up this street, continuing along Via Pontaccio. The Palazzo Crivelli to the left here is 17th century and has a fine wrought-iron balcony. Go right at Via Brera to the Palazzo di Brera, Milan's art gallery.

2 The beautiful, arcaded courtyard of the Palazzo di Brera is dominated by Antonio Canova's bronze statue of Napoleon. The gallery, reached up the elegant stairway, has works by Raphael, Titian, Luini and Tintoretto – to name just a few – but the real masterpiece is Andrea Mantegna's *Dead Christ*, a phenomenal achievement of colour and perspective.

Return to Via Pontaccio, turning right into Via Fatebenefratelli. Walk to Piazza Cavour, passing the church of San Marco, to the left, which contains a magnificent rose window. Go left

Antonio Canova's bronze statue of Napoleon outside the Palazzo di Brera

across Piazza Cavour to reach Via Palestro which leads to the Villa Reale.

3 Villa Reale (the Royal Villa) is a superb neo-classical building that presents its best face to the park at the rear. It houses Milan's Modern Art Gallery with works by Renoir, Cézanne, Monet, Gauguin and Picasso, as well as many leading Italian artists such as Marino Marini, whose statue in the courtyard greets the visitor.
Across Via Palestro is the city's Public Garden, a delightful place with a miniature railway.

Continue along Via Palestro to Corso Venezia and turn right. The neo-classical Palazzo Rocca Saporiti, to the left, is topped by Roman deities, while Palazzo Castiglioni, to the right, is riotously art nouveau in style. Further on, to the left, is the 15th-century Palazzo Fontana-Silvestri, Milan's oldest 'private' house. Bear right in Piazza Santa Babila for Corso Vittorio Emanuele II. Via Monte Napoleone, off to the right here, is Milan's most exclusive shopping street. The Corso also has fine shops and an outdoor sculpture display. Cross Piazza del Duomo, bearing left to exit along Via Torino. Turn right into Via Asole to reach Piazza Pio X1 and the Ambrosiana Gallery.

4 The 17th-century Palazzo dell'Ambrosiana houses some very fine paintings including works by Botticelli, Luini and Caravaggio. Here too is Leonardo da Vinci's *Portrait of a Musician*.

Go along Via Moneta and turn left into Via Bocchetto. At the road junction go across into Via Podone and follow it to Via Sant'Orsola. Go right at Via Cappuccio, then left into Via Santa Valeria, following it to the Basilica di Sant'Ambrogio.

5 The remarkable basilica was founded by St Ambrose, Bishop of Milan, in AD379 though much of the fabric now dates from the 8th to the 12th century. The Volvinio altar, made in AD835, is one of the world's finest examples of the goldsmith's art. The crypt holds the mummified bodies of Sant'Ambrogio (St Ambrose), San Gervaso and San Portaso.

Go through the basilica, exiting by a Roman column with two curious holes at the base; legend says they were made by the horns of the devil when St Ambrose threw him out of the church. Cross into Via San Vittore to reach the Museum of Science and Technology, to the left.

6 The museum has a superb collection, including a complete full-rigged ship and full-size jet

Works by Marino Marini in the gardens of Via Palestro's Modern Art Gallery

LEONARDO DA VINCI'S LAST SUPPER

Leonardo da Vinci's *Last Supper*, in the refectory of Milan's Dominican convent, is one of the greatest works of Renaissance art. Preliminary drawings (now in England's Windsor Castle) show that, from the outset, Leonardo decided to capture the dramatic moment when Christ told his disciples that one of them would betray him. Judas, the third figure to the left of Christ (as viewed) is shown clutching a bag of money, while the other disciples start back in alarm.

For the work Leonardo decided to use an unusual technique: normally the fresco artist painted on wet plaster which absorbs the pigment giving a permanent image, but this requires very fast painting and leaves no margin for error. Leonardo chose to paint on dry plaster – a technique known as tempera. The advantage was that he could develop his work over time – in practice he spent two years on the fresco completing it in 1497 – but the technique had a serious drawback. Inadequate adhesion meant that the paint soon began to flake. Restoration work was necessary by the 16th century and has continued ever since.

To protect the fresco, the light level is kept low and visitors are kept at a distance. This means that the view is barely adequate and it is best to study Leonardo's marvellous depiction of hands, robes, and expressions with the help of the illustrated guides on sale.

fighters. Especially good is the exhibition dealing with Leonardo da Vinci's inventions.

Continue along Via San Vittore, then go right into Via B Zenale to reach the church of Santa Marie delle Grazie.

7 Leonardo da Vinci's renowned *Last Supper* fresco (1497) is in the refectory of the adjoining convent. The church - especially the apse - is also a masterpiece, a soaring structure of red brick and cream terracotta. Be sure to see the apse from the delicate Cloister of the Frogs, the smaller of the convent's two cloisters.

From the church go along Corso Magenta, crossing Via G Carducci, to reach the Museo Archaelogico (Monastero Maggiore) on the right.

8 The Monastero Maggiore has wonderful frescos by Bernardino Luini and the monastery itself houses Milan's Archaeological Museum.

Backtrack up Corso Magenta and turn right into Via Carducci to return to Castello Sforzesco.

Frescos by Bernardino Luini in the monastery church of San Maurizio

BÈRGAMO, BRÈSCIA AND LAGO D'ISÈO (LAKE ISEO)

Between Lake Como and Lake Iseo, a distance of 60km, there are several valleys but no lakes. This is because the east/west ridge of the Orobie Alps, separating the two lakes, blocked any significant glacial flow from the high Alps and limited the size of local glaciers. Only where the east/west ridge was broken by the Val Camonica, which cuts between the Orobie Alps to the west and the Adamello range to the east, could a large glacier break through. In the Val Camonica that glacier created Lake Iseo.

Despite the absence of lakes there is much else to see between Como and Iseo. Of particular interest is Bèrgamo. Italy is justly famous for its Renaissance cities and tourists flock to Venice, Florence and to Verona, Mantua and Padua in the Lombardy Plain. Fewer people are aware that Bèrgamo's Città Alta, the high city set on top of the hill behind the modern city, is an entrancing time capsule. The old city retains its medieval walls and is entered through the original gates; cars are excluded and, as a result, we are offered a glimpse of how the Italy of the City States must have appeared. There are beautiful Renaissance buildings set around cobbled streets, churches that are jewels of the architect's art, profusely decorated to make them miniature art galleries. There are narrow, enclosed streets from which the visitor emerges to catch sudden glimpses of far-off hills or nearby towers – in short Bèrgamo is a delight.

North of Bèrgamo two fine valleys work their way back towards the high Orobie ridge. The Val Seriana has a long history and has resisted the march of time sufficiently well to offer another glimpse of the medieval architectural and artistic heritage of Italy. Only in its lower reaches, close to Bèrgamo, has the valley's agricultural economy been replaced by industry. Higher up the valley is very beautiful, the high peaks offering a superb background for walks. One such walk takes in the Cascata del Serio, one of Europe's highest waterfalls.

The second valley is the Val Brembana, a little less serene but more unspoilt because its geography meant that it was inaccessible to motor vehicles

Above: old and modern Bèrgamo juxtaposed. Below: elegant archways in Piazza Vecchia in the Città Alta (Upper City)

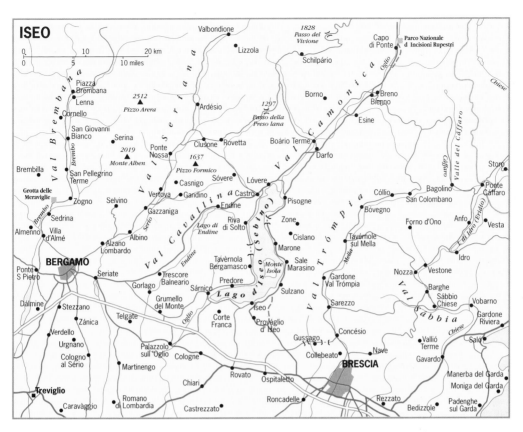

ISEO

0 10 20 km
0 5 10 miles

Valbondione · Lizzola · 1828 Passo del Vivione · Capo di Ponte · Parco Nazionale d Incisioni Rupestri

Piazza Brembana · Lenna · Cornello · 2512 Pizzo Arera · Ardésio · Schilpário · Borno · Breno · Bienno · Esine

San Giovanni Bianco · Serina · Clusone · Rovetta · Boário Terme · 1297 Passo della Preso lana · Darfo

Brembilla · 2019 Monte Alben · Ponte Nossa · 1637 Pizzo Formico · Sóvere · Lóvere · Stóro

San Pellegrino Terme · Casnigo · Endine · a Castro · Pisogne · Cóllio · Bagolino · Ponte Cáffaro

Grotta delle Meraviglie · Zogno · Vertova · Gandino · San Colombano · Anfo · Vesta

Sedrina · Selvino · Gazzaniga · Riva di Solto · Zone · Bóvegno · Forno d'Ono · Idro

Almenno · Villa d'Almé · Albino · Lago di Endine · Marone · Tavérnole sul Mella · Vesta

BERGAMO · Alzano Lombardo · Tavèrnola Bergamasca · Monte Isola · Sale Marasino · Gardone Val Trómpia · Nozza · Vestone · Idro

Ponte S Pietro · Seriate · Predore · Sulzano · Sarezzo · Barghe · Sábbio Chiese · Vobarno

Dálmine · Stezzano · Gorlago · Trescore Balneario · Sárnico · Iseo · Concésio · Vallió Terme · Gardone Riviera

Zánica · Telgate · Grumello del Monte · Corte Franca · Prováglio d'Iseo · Gussago · Nave · Gavardo · Saló

Verdello · Urgnano · Palazzolo sull 'Oglio · Cologne · Collebeato · BRESCIA

Cologno al Sério · Martinengo · Rovato · Ospitaletto · Rezzato · Manerba del Garda · Moniga del Garda

Treviglio · Chiari · Roncadelle · Bedizzole · Padenghe sul Garda

Caravàggio · Romano di Lombardia · Castrezzato

until relatively recent times. Oddly, in view of this isolation, the valley village of Cornello del Tasso gave birth to Europe's first postal system.

Lake Iseo is the fifth largest of the lakes, measuring 24km long and 5km wide at its broadest point. At that same point the lake is almost filled by Monte Isola, the largest island in any of the lakes and, indeed, the largest island of any European lake. Iseo is a tourist lake, its villages well known for their sailing facilities and their beaches. Monte Isola differs in that the old fishing villages have not yet been completely absorbed by tourism. That, and the fact that the island is free of cars, makes it a good place for a quiet stay. Lake Iseo fills the lower part of the Val Camonica. Higher up, the valley is more ruggedly beautiful, confined by the ridges of the high peaks. Near Capo di Ponte there is one of Europe's finest ensembles of prehistoric art, the rocks of the valley floor having been engraved with domestic and hunting scenes. So important is the site that it has United Nations protection.

To the southeast of Lake Iseo is Brèscia, Lombardy's second city. Brèscia has some of the finest Roman remains in the lakes area and a number of interesting buildings and museums. The complex on Cidneo, the hill beside the city, is particularly good. North of the city lie the Val Trómpia, famous in history as the centre of the Venetian arms

industry, and the Val Sabbia which contains little Lake Ledro, one of the smallest of the lakes, but also one of the prettiest.

Monolithic medieval towers, built for the purpose of defence, spring up from the narrow alleys of Bèrgamo's Città Alta

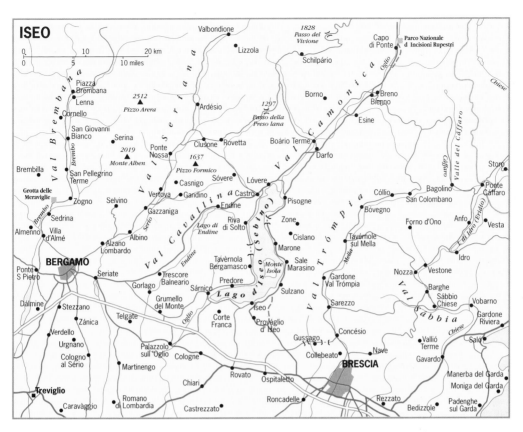

BÈRGAMO
MAP REF: 110 C3

Bèrgamo consists of two distinct parts, the upper medieval city and the lower, more modern, one. The upper city commands a natural fortress that was settled by both the Celts and the Romans. In early medieval times it was a City State and a member of the Lombard League, but it was taken over by Milan in 1264 and remained Milanese for 150 years until it was taken by the Venetians to become part of the Serenissima, the Venetian Republic. During the Risorgimento, Bergamo sent 180 men, the largest contingent, to join Garibaldi's force of I Mille (The Thousand), earning itself the title Città dei Mille.

The main sights of the lower city are grouped around the central Piazza Matteotti and the Sentierone. On the southern side of the piazza is the Donizetti Theatre and a statue of the composer. Just to the east is the church of San Bartolomeo with its large altarpiece by Lorenzo Lotto, who was born in the upper city. To the west, the church of Sant' Alessandro in Colonna stands beside a column said to mark the spot where St Alexander was martyred in AD297.

The composer Donizetti sits entranced by his muse in this magnificent memorial to Bèrgamo's most famous son

TOWN WALK

This 1 hour walk covers the main attractions of the compact and traffic-free città alta (upper city) of Bèrgamo, reached by rack railway from the station in Viale Vittorio Emanuele II, in the lower city. The rack railway is a fascinating way of reaching the upper city: you climb aboard and within a couple of minutes you have travelled 500 years back in time, burrowing through the well-preserved city walls built in the 16th century by the Venetians.

From the top station go left to follow Via Donizetti, turning right then left to reach the Piazza Vecchia, at the heart of the upper city.

1 Both Frank Lloyd Wright and Le Corbusier believed that the Piazza Vecchia was as good as any Renaissance square in Italy. At the centre is the Contarini Fountain, erected by the Venetian mayor Alvese Contarini in 1780, complete with Venetian lions. Another lion adorns the façade of the Palazzo della Ragione, though this is a replica of the original which was smashed when the

townsfolk rebelled against their Venetian rulers. In front of the palazzo is a statue of the poet Torquato Tasso, while to the side is the 12th-century Torre del Comune which can be climbed for a remarkable view. On the far side of the square is the 17th-century town hall, which now serves as the town library.

From the Piazza Vecchia travel through the arcades of the Palazzo della Ragione to reach the Piazza del Duomo.

2 The Duomo (Cathedral) is a simple building, much altered in the baroque era, its white façade almost hidden by flanking buildings. Alongside is the most remarkable church of Santa Maria Maggiore, built in the 12th century when the citizens, exhausted by war, plague and famine, were in need of spiritual assistance. The

elegant church is entered through an elaborate red and white marble porch added to the main structure in 1350. In the sumptuous interior you will find Donizetti's tomb, some magnificent 16th-century Florentine and Flemish tapestries and much more.

Equally ornate is the elaborate Colleoni Chapel, a masterpiece of Renaissance art, built up against the side of the church. Bartolomeo Colleoni was a *condottiere* (mercenary) who twice captained the forces of Milan against those of Venice, and twice captained Venice against Milan. In the course of his many adventures he not only managed to retain his head, he also amassed a small fortune which he used to fund the chapel and the tombs inside for himself and his daughter. He also paid for a statue of himself, on horseback, which he asked to have set up in front of San Marco in Venice. The

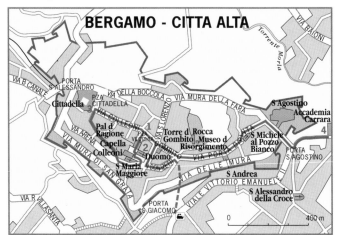

wily Venetians agreed, but erected the statue in a minor square in front of the School of San Marco, rather than in the city's prestigious main square.

On the fourth side of Piazza del Duomo is a delightful 14th-century polygonal baptistery that once stood within Santa Maria Maggiore.

With your back to the Colleoni chapel take the furthest exit, right, from the Piazza del Duomo. This passageway leads directly to Via Arena past the Donizetti Institute with its small museum. Take the next right turn then turn left into Via San Salvatore which leads to the Cittadella.

3 The 13th-century Cittadella houses the Museums of Natural History and Archaeology, each of which contains interesting collections. In the same piazza is the 13th-century Torre dei Adalberto, also known as the Tower of Hunger.

Directly behind the Cittadella is the Porta Sant'Alessandro city gate which leads to Number 14 Borgo Canale, the Donizetti Birthplace Museum.

From Piazza Cittadella take the superb Via Colleoni back to Piazza Vecchia, continuing straight along Via Gombito to reach the Torre del Gombito and the Piazza Mercato dei Fieno with its medieval tower houses. To the left here is the Rocca *housing the Museum of the Risorgimento.*

Continue back to the top station of the rack railway and turn left in Via Porta Dipinta to reach the Porta Sant'Agostino city gate beyond which there are good views of the town walls. Go through the gate and turn left into Via della Noca to reach the gallery of the Accademia Carrara.

4 The Academy was founded in the 18th century by Count Giacomo Carrara to display his many magnificent paintings, including works by Raphael, Titian, Botticelli, Rubens, Bellini, Velasquez and Mantegna, among others. The collection of work by artists of the Venetian school is especially good.

Retrace your steps to the railway station by means of Via della Noca and Via Porta Dipinta, or descend to the lower town along Via San Tommaso and Via Masone.

GAETANO DONIZETTI

Gaetano Donizetti was born in Borgo Canale, in Bèrgamo's upper city, on 29 November 1797, the fifth of six children of a very poor family with no musical tradition. Nine years later, in 1806, Johannes Simon Mayr, the music master at Santa Maria Maggiore, opened a charitable school for the training of choirboys with Donizetti as one of its first pupils. Mayr immediately recognised Donizetti's gift for music and, in 1815, arranged for him to study at Bologna. When Donizetti returned to Bèrgamo two years later he began to write in earnest. An opera performed with success in Rome in 1822 led to a commission from the Naples Opera House, and in the next eight years Donizetti produced no less than 23 operas, culminating in *Anna Bolena* (1830) which was a huge success in Milan. From then until 1842, when Verdi wrote *Nabucco*, Donizetti was the foremost Italian composer. In that period he produced his most enduring works – *Lucia di Lammermoor*, *Don Pasquale* and *L'Elisir d'Amore*.

The emergence of Verdi coincided with a decline in Donizetti's health, probably re-emergence of syphilis. Increasingly erratic in his behaviour, Donizetti returned to Bèrgamo where he died on 8 April 1848. He was buried in the lower city's Valtesse cemetery but, in 1875, his remains were transferred to the church of Santa Maria Maggiore. In 1951 they were moved again and no longer lie close to Vela's 1855 monument in the church.

Bèrgamo's Duomo is one of many fine buildings in the Città Alta

THE RISE AND FALL OF CITY STATES

From the 11th century onwards the cities of Italy underwent a dramatic change, brought about by local factors and external events. The chief local factor was a doubling of the population. External events, notably the Crusades, created the need for fleets of ships, and for active ports on the Mediterranean and Adriatic shores. Genoa, Pisa and Venice rapidly rose to become the premier European ports, with fleets that soon dominated the trade routes from the Near East, Africa and Spain, while the cities of the Lombardy Plain – Milan, Bèrgamo and Verona – grew prosperous on overland trade. In addition, the growth of travel on the continent, particularly in pilgrimage traffic to Rome, helped the rise of Florence and Siena. The rapid growth of commercial trading in the cities led to the rise of a merchant class and to the development of a banking system. The latter was at its most finely tuned in Milan, so much so that even today the centre of London's banking world is in Lombard Street, a tribute to its northern Italian origins.

Top: Verona's Piazza dei Signori, centre of Medieval civic life, with a statue of Dante. Above: *Portrait of a Musician* (attributed to Leonardo da Vinci) in Milan's Palazzo dell'Ambrosiana, a typical Renaissance work of art

The development of trade not only created a prosperous merchant class, but also a wealthy and powerful feudal aristocracy, men who amassed fortunes by taxing the countryside, and grew richer still by controlling the cities and the city markets. They, as much as the merchants, were anxious for the borders of trade to be extended and for its volume to be increased. As the cities increased in wealth and power the central Italian state began to collapse. Italy's geography, a long narrow country in which overland communications were poor, had allowed its early break-up into separate states, the Normans having invaded Sicily and the southern provinces, while Rome's Papal State held the centre and the north. In the face of the rise of the cities of the north, Rome was powerless to prevent further

fragmentation. Soon the Papacy held only an area in the centre, while the north was controlled by the new cities: the age of the City States had begun.

The Lombard League
The most interesting aspect of the City States of the late 12th century was their rule by a *commune*, a council whose members were, nominally, elected by the townsfolk. In practice power fell into the hands of a small number of ruling families. Each City State controlled the country around it, offering the peasant farmers protection against lawlessness in exchange for the food and wine they produced. Inevitably there were conflicts between adjacent cities for territorial control, since more land meant greater wealth. Milan, for example, fought Como in the Ten Years' War.

Even so, the City States recognised the need for, and the strength of, unity when an outside force threatened. Such a threat erupted in the wake of the Milan-Como war when the German Holy Roman Emperor, Frederick I, known as Barbarossa because of his red beard, marched into Lombardy and set Milan ablaze. Alarmed at the prospect of Barbarossa expanding southward, the leading cities – Venice, Verona, Vicenza, Milan and several others – combined to form the Lombard League. Barbarossa marched against the League in 1176, but was heavily defeated at Legnano and forced to sign the Treaty of Constance which gave the cities control of northern Italy. Fifty years later, when there was a renewed German threat, a second League was formed.

The Signori

In the 13th and 14th centuries many of the City States lost their democracies to leading families, the *signori*, who seized power and maintained it for many years or lost it later in a power struggle with another noble family. In both Milan and Verona the *comune* lost control to the della Torre and della Scala families respectively. The della Scala family was responsible for building the formidable array of Scaligeri castles on Lake Garda.

It is difficult to pin down the precise reasons for the decline in City State democracy, especially as some cities retained their independence right into the modern era, but most experts now agree that intercommunal warfare left many cities exhausted and ripe for the intervention of a strong leader who would restore confidence and prosperity. In addition, the Black Death ravaged through Europe at this time, reducing the number of folk working on the land. Food shortages, difficult trading conditions and the collapse of the banking system made the whole system vulnerable to change. Some cities avoided the collapse into signorial rule, including Venice and Genoa, the chief sea-trading ports. Even in these cities, however, deomocracy was replaced by an oligarchy, with power vested in a relatively small number of families. The Doge of Venice was never the supreme ruler, rather more the city mayor. Throughout the medieval period Venice rose in influence, its Republic, the somewhat grandly termed Serenissima, eventually becoming the longest surviving of all the City States and extending to

include the whole of Lake Garda, plus the cities of Verona, Bèrgamo and Brèscia.

Milan is the archetypal *signori*-dominated city. After the della Torre family seized power, around 1260, there was a continuous power struggle between themselves and the Visconti which ended when Ottone Visconti became ruler of Milan in 1277. The Visconti family enjoyed supremacy for two centuries. In the main Visconti rule was beneficial to the Milanese but the neighbouring states were always concerned about their ambitions, never more so than when Gian Galeazzo Visconti moved southward to challenge Florence – he died, however, before a full scale war broke out. When the last of the Visconti died without a male heir, Milan was almost immediately taken over by Francesco Sforza, a *condotterie* (mercenary) who had led the city's defence against Venice and married the daughter of the last Visconti. The Sforzas then ruled Milan until the invasion by France in the 16th century effectively ended the reign of the City States, the states being too small to compete with the major European superpowers.

The Renaissance

Before the final eclipse of the City States they gave Europe what many consider to be the finest element in its cultural heritage, the Renaissance. The *signori* and the merchant guilds vied with each other to commission palazzi and churches, richly decorated with the finest works of art, and the fruits of this era are what draw visitors to Italy today.

Michelangelo's unfinished last work, the *Rondanini Pietà* in Milan's Castello Sforzesco

·BRÈSCIA·

Lombardy's second city (map ref: 111 D3) has nothing like the presence of Milan, or the grace and elegance of nearby Bèrgamo, but it is a pleasant enough place with much of interest. The city's name is Celtic – from *brix*, meaning hill – which the Romans merely transcribed into *Brixia*. Later it was the capital of Lombardy and Ermengarda, daughter of the local ruler, King Desiderius, left from here to marry Charlemagne – returning, to the convent of San Salvatore, when he repudiated her.

In the 11th century Brèscia joined the Lombard League against Barbarossa, before falling prey to the duke's of Milan and Verona. It became Venetian in the 15th century and fought valiantly for 10 days against the Austrians in 1849, supplying one of the great leaders of the independence rebellion, Tito Speri. Another great son of the town was Arnold of Brèscia, a 12th-century Benedictine monk who travelled to Rome to preach against the materialism and ungodliness of the Church. The pope listened, then had him hanged.

good works of art and a treasury whose precious reliquary contains a piece of the True Cross and a Holy Thorn.

To the left of the Rotonda is the 'new' cathedral, built in baroque style in the 16th century, although the dome, one of the better features of the building, was not completed until 1825. Inside the cathedral is austere to the point of bleakness despite the beautiful white marble.

Behind the cathedral, at No 3 Via Mazzini, is the Biblioteca

Queriniana, a library founded by Cardinal Querini in the 18th century and housing some beautiful old religious books and a 6th-century Gospel binding.

The final public building in the square is the Broletto, the 13th-century town hall. This has a fine courtyard, and incorporates the 11th-century Torre del Popolo, Brèscia's oldest building.

From the piazza go beneath the Clock Tower, taking the passageway into the Piazza della Loggia, the city's best square.

2 There are, in fact, two loggias, or covered arcades: ahead is a magnificent 16th-century building in fine Renaissance style designed, in part, by Palladio. To the left is the Monte di Pietà loggia of 1484 with an extension dating to 1591.

An archway by the post office and the Monte di Pietà loggia leads south into the Piazza della Vittoria.

3 This 'Victory Square' was built of grey marble in 1932: some call it a fine example of the Fascist style, others describe it as dire and deathly, and yearn for it to be demolished.

Cross the piazza to its far end and turn left to join Via Giornate. Turn right, passing the Grand Theatre, and turn left in Corso Zanardelli, the main shopping street. At the end of this street turn right into Via San Martino della Battiglio. After 200m turn left into Via Moretto and follow this to Piazza Moretto and the Pinacoteca Tosio Martinengo.

4 The art gallery is housed in a plain 16th-century building and

TOWN WALK

This 1 hour walk around the city centre starts in the Piazza Paolo VI.

Before the walk starts in earnest take a gentle stroll around the piazza.

1 The 16th-century clock tower – is similar to that in the Piazza San Marco in Venice and was built when the Venetians controlled Brèscia. Opposite is the Rotonda or Duomo Vecchio (Old Cathedral). This curiously shaped building dates to the early 12th century. Inside there are some

Left: Brèscia's Castello. Above: the Rotonda or Old Cathedral

comprises two collections bequeathed in 1908. The paintings cover the period from the 14th to the 18th century and include works by local artists such as Foppa, Lorenzo Lotto and Giovanni Battista Moroni – one of the finest of 16th-century portrait painters.

The gallery also houses some outstanding antiquities – notably the magnificent Cross of Desiderius, an 8th-century wooden crucifix overlaid with silver and set with around 200 gemstones. The cross is said to have been given to the convent of Santa Giulia by King Desiderius. This, and several other items, will be transferred back to the Museum of Christian Antiquities when restoration work on the Convent of Santa Giulia (see below) has been completed.

From the gallery recross Piazza Moretto and turn right along Via Crispi and Via Gallo to reach Via dei Musei.

5 Straight ahead is the Capitoline Temple of AD73 and the Roman Museum (see Roman Remains, right). Turning right you will pass the 16th-century convent of Santa Giúlia. Once restoration is completed this will house the Museum of christian Antiquities and the Civic Museum. The convent complex includes two further churches. San Salvatore is Byzantine in style and was rebuilt in the 9th century – it was to this convent that Ermengarda retired after her rejection by Charlemagne. The church of Santa Maria in Solario is 12th century Romanesque.

Just before Santa Giulia take the Via Piamarta road to reach the superb church of San Pietro in Oliveto.

6 The church is 12th century, with 16th-century cloisters. True to its name, it stands among olive trees. Alongside is the Cydnean Hill with an array of buildings on its plateau: Roman remains, the ruins of the 5th-century church of San Stefano, a 5th-century Byzantine arch, the delightful 13th-century Mirabella Tower and the 15th-century castle. This played a key role in the independence struggle with Austria and fittingly houses the Risorgimento Museum, together with the Luigi Marzoli Museum of Arms, a superb collection of medieval arms and armour. Elsewhere on the Cydnean Hill there is a small zoo and an observatory, the whole set in excellent parkland.

Exit from the castle into Via Contini which leads down into a small square close to the Piazza del Duomo.

Street musicians serenade visitors to Brèscia; a form of entertainment little changed over the centuries

THE ROMAN REMAINS

Italy's lake district has surprisingly few Roman remains – with the honourable exception of Verona – because so many buildings of the era were subsequently quarried for their fine masonry. The Capitoline Temple in Brèscia, commissioned by the Emperor Vespasian, survived because it was buried under a landslide and only rediscovered in 1823.

Beyond is the Roman Museum which holds finds from the site. Of these, the finest piece is the *Winged Victory*, a wonderfully fluid bronze statue, which may have stood on the temple pediment. .

Of the few other Roman remains in the lakes area, the best are also close to Brèscia, on the southern tip of Lake Garda. At Desenzano del Garda a villa has been excavated, revealing some interesting mosaics, while at Sirmione the remains of the baths have been discovered. These are known as the Grotte di Catullo (the Caves of Catullus) because it is known that the 1st-century BC poet had a villa at Sirmione. Here, too, there is a site museum displaying the best of the excavated finds.

CAPO DI PONTE
MAP REF: 111 D4

Capo di Ponte, halfway up the Val Camonica, is a good centre for visiting the valley's prehistoric rock engravings (see opposite), as well as being an interesting town. The nearby church of San Siro, on a hill above the river, is fascinating and dates mostly from the 11th century but with older sections and excellent frescos. Another nearby church, San Salvatore, was once the abbey church of a Cluniac monastery.

South of Capo di Ponte is Breno, the Val Camonica's major town, which has the ruins of an early castle, dating in part from the 9th century, and a museum to Camonican history. The parish church has frescos by the 14th-century painter Pietro da Cemmo.

Further down the valley, Esine is a pretty village with several churches, each with good frescos, including more works by da Cemmo. Cividate Camuno, the next village south, was the Roman capital of the valley. A few remains from the Roman period are visible, though the better pieces are to be found in the town museum, which deals with the history of the Val Camonica as a whole. The tower that dominates the town is 12th century, evidence of Cividate's long history as a strategically important valley site. The Cividate churches also have frescos by the 14th-century artist, da Cemmo.

Clusone boatman

Rovetta, another pretty village close to Clusone.

CLUSONE
MAP REF: 111 D3

This extremely picturesque village has an exuberant town hall, in Piazza dell'Orologio, a square that is named after the town hall's 16th-century astronomical clock, the work of Pietro Fonzago, a local man. Close by, the Oratario del Disciplini, a small chapel beside the church, is frescoed with a masterpiece of 15th-century art. The work, slightly damaged but sufficiently intact to make its point clearly, is a Dance of Death, with Death, represented as a skeleton wielding sword and musket, gathering in the nobility and the clergy. The point of such eerie works was to impress a superstitious peasantry as they left the church, but also to boost them with the thought that death claimed the rich and powerful as well as the poor. There are other frescos in the oratory, and a fine Fantoni *Deposition*.

A museum devoted to the work of the Fantoni family of 16th-century artists is to be found in

CORNELLO DEL TASSO
MAP REF: 110 C3

Visitŏrs to the Val Brembana usually head up the valley from San Pellegrino Terme towards Fòppolo and may, as a result, miss little Cornello altogether. It is now down to a mere handful of inhabitants and has little enough to detain the visitor. Yet tradition has it that this village has had a huge impact on the world in which we live.

In the 13th century the local Tasso family started a business transporting goods by mule across the high pass into the Valtellina and from there down to Bèrgamo and the Lombardy Plain. In time the family began to carry messages as well as packages and then, realising this was good business, they began to offer similar services to the great cities of Venice and Rome. In the 16th century the family expanded their business further still, into Germany and France, creating Europe's first postal service.

Local people further claim that a

German arm of the family gave themselves a more Teutonic name, Taxis, and started a service of private vehicles for hire, while another arm expanded into Russia and eventually set up the Tass news agency.

FÒPPOLO
MAP REF: 110 C4

The ski resort of Fòppolo is reached by the Val Brembana road which first reaches Piazza Brembana, a pleasant village in a most beautiful position, with stunning views in all directions. Two streams meet at Piazza to form the Brembo river and two valley roads follow the streams back into the mountains. The western fork rises to the San Marco Pass before descending into the Valtellina, while the eastern fork ends at Fòppolo, the most developed ski resort on the southern flank of the Orobie Alps.

The village is set among spectacular scenery and in summer the chairlifts can be used to reach some remarkable viewpoints. The best of these is the summit of Corno Stella, reached after a 3km walk from the chairlift top station. The view from the peak is well worth the effort.

Picturesque Clusone features two exceptional rarities: a 16th-century astronomical clock and *Dance of Death* fresco

THE ROCK CARVINGS OF THE VAL CAMONICA

When the Romans occupied the Val Camonica around 16BC they found a tribe called the Camuni in residence and named the valley after them. The Camuni used the rocks of the valley to record tribal information in the form of paintings or engravings. Few of the paintings have survived the rigours of 2,000 summers and winters, though there are some good examples at Cemmo, near Capo di Ponte, which still show a good colour range. Of the rock engravings many more examples remain.

When archaeologists began to take an interest in the engravings it was soon discovered that they were not all carved at one point in time, some of them predating the Iron Age. Later discoveries near Boario Terme showed that the oldest engravings date back to the earliest neolithic period, certainly 6,000 years ago and perhaps as many as 8,000. Intriguingly these works suggest that the earliest Camuni had already domesticated the dog and the cow and had evolved the rudiments of agriculture. Later engravings include the geometric patterns that imply a developing artistic sense, and the leisure time to devote to it.

In all around 158,000 engravings have now been found, about 75 per cent of them near Capo di Ponte. They represent one of the largest and finest collections of prehistoric art in Europe, so good in fact that in 1979 UNESCO declared the area a World Heritage Site.

The engravings are now contained within the Parco Nazionale delle Incisioni Rupestri, the National Rock Engravings Park, centred on Capo di Ponte where there is also a study centre. Five colour-coded routes can be followed in the park, designed to show the visitor the better works.

All five routes visit the Naquane Rock on which there are no less than 900 engravings. The engravings were made by hitting some form of chisel, possibly an antler, with a hammer to create a stippled effect. The subject matter includes hunting scenes, ploughing with oxen and religious symbols and the engravings have great vibrancy.

LAGO D'IDRO (LAKE IDRO)
MAP REF: 111 D3

Lake Idro is the highest lake in
Lombardy, located at 368m above
sea level. Strangely, the lake is also
exactly 368m deep. To complete
the statistics the lake is 11km long
and 2km wide. It is also a beautiful
lake, surrounded by steep
mountain cliffs that appear to rise
sheer out of the water. As a result,
the road on the western shore is
tunnelled at one point, while on
the eastern shore it ends at the
village of Vesta, from where a
short walk reaches the fine
viewpoint of Prato della Fame.

Legend has it that the lake is
home to the Idro, a monster with a
snake-like body, dog's paws and
seven heads. The monster gave its
name both to the lake and to the
village of Idro, where a painting of
this chimera can be seen in the
church on the coat of arms of the
Pialorsi family, above the organ.
Idro is a resort village with a fine
beach, while nearby Anfo, a
prettier village, is renowned as a
sailing centre. The Rocca d'Anfo,
just oustide the village, is topped
by a castle built, originally, by the
Venetians in the 15th century, but
modified in later years.

The Gaudiesque landscape of
erosion pillars at Zone

GANDINO
MAP REF: 110 C3

In medieval times Gandino grew
prosperous on the manufacturing
of bergamask, a heavy, but
inexpensive cloth. Many of the
houses, and the artwork in the
church, reflect this ancient wealth,
and the Renaissance air this gave
the village almost certainly helped
develop the talents of the sculptor
Bartolomeo Bon and the painter
Giovanni Battista Castello.

The basilica that these two
would have visited in their youth
is topped with a very Byzantine-
looking spire and has a baroque
interior which includes a fine
16th-century bronze balustrade.
There are also some good pieces
by Andrea Fantoni, the 17th-
century baroque sculptor.

The basilica's museum houses a
collection of rare and important
vestments and documents, while
the village's history museum
includes items on the medieval
textile industry. From Gandino a
chairlift rises to the plateau below
Pizzo Formico, a good place for
taking a walk.

In the Val Seriana, close to
Gandino, there are numerous silk
and cotton mills and the lower
part of the valley has an industrial
character. There are, however,
three interesting villages. Vertova
has a 17th-century church
surrounded by porticos that makes
it look like a mother hen with her
chickens. Casnigo also has an
elegantly arcaded 14th-century
church. Ponte Nossa, the last of
the three, is the starting point for
an exciting drive westward on a
road that twists around Monte
Alben to reach the Val Brembana.

GARDONE VAL TRÓMPIA
MAP REF: 111 D3

Immediately north of Brèscia is the
Val Trómpia, a wide, agricultural
valley at first, but one which
becomes more mountainous at its
northern end.

The valley's first town is
Concésio, the birthplace of Pope
Paul VI, but the biggest is Gardone
Val Trómpia. At the time of the
Venetian Republic Gardone served
as the state's armoury and was
both wealthy and heavily
defended. Today the tradition lives
on and Gardone is dotted with gun
and rifle-making factories – the
best known of the locally made
firearms is the Beretta.

Venetian influence can be seen
in the church of Santa Maria degli
Angeli, a fine cloistered church
which is decorated with art of the
Venetian school. There are also
frecos by Paolino da Brescia, the
Brescian artist.

Beyond Gardone, the Val
Trómpia – named by the Romans
after the Celtic tribe of Triumplini
– is a paradise of chestnut woods
and orchards. Tavernole sul Mella
was once the valley's capital, and
from it a devious road reaches
Lake Idro. North again, at Bóvegno
the village houses have a distinctly
Tyrolean look. Here, the church of
San Giorgio has some good wood
carvings, while Pineta Park offers
good walking. At Collio there is a
cable car to Monte Pezzeda, a
good walking area, though a walk
around the village, with its white
houses, geraniums and backdrop
of blue pine trees, is equally
worthwhile. The final village is San
Colombano, a winter sports
centre.

MAP REF: 111 D3

Between Brèscia and the southern tip of Lake Iseo is the wine-growing area known as the Franciacorta, the Free Court. The name was given not because the area was independent but because it was so poor that it was exempt from taxes. Within the area Colombaro is worth visiting to see the magnificant cedar of Lebanon (reputedly Italy's oldest) in the grounds of the Villa Ragnoli. Nearby, Prováglio d'Iseo has an 11th-century Cluniac abbey decorated with 15th-century frescos. Above the village the pretty church of Madonna del Carno offers a superb view of Lake Iseo.

Iseo is a pleasant resort village that shares its name with the lake. The tourist centre of Sassabanek is equipped with several enticing swimming pools. Within the village there are the remains of an Oldofredi castle, now part of the community centre, and a fine church, also built by the Oldofredi family. The tomb of one family member is built into the façade. Close to the village is a marshy area known as La Torbiere, famous for its pink and white water-lilies, bog plants and emerald-green moss. The remains of early pile dwellings have been found in the marsh which is now a plant and wildlife reserve.

Lake Iseo, popular for its resorts and famous for its water-lilies

EROSION PILLARS

Visitors to Lake Iseo who turn off the eastern shore road at Marone to visit the pretty little village of Zone are in for a surprise. The surprise consists of what look like gigantic termite nests that are reached as you round a hairpin bend just before the village of Cislano. Park your car just beyond the bend and walk back to the viewpoint near the road for a look at one of Nature's more eccentric features.

When glaciers come towards the end of their journey, the erosion processes become more uneven and the eroded debris they carry is deposited. The asymmetry of both the erosion process and the debris burden can now lead to the creation of some very weird shapes, of which erosion pillars are the most eye-catching.

The Zone erosion pillars vary in form, some being thin upright sheets of earthy conglomerate with crenellated tops, others being almost pure pyramids or cones. The tallest are tens of metres high and look extremely fragile. The most unusual feature, however, is the occasional boulder perched on top of the pillars, or on top of a point of one of the sheets. Such boulders are 'glacial erratics' brought down by the glacier to be deposited miles from their point of origin – to the confusion of early geologists. Most of these erratics were deposited at ground level, but the build-up of glacial debris means that one was sometimes left right at the top of a debris cone. The boulders add a surreal touch to the scene.

The Zone pillars are not unique, though they are Europe's best examples. Other pillars in the lakes area can be seen near Postalesio in the Valtellina.

LÓVERE

MAP REF: 111 D3

Lóvere stands at Lake Iseo's northern end and is, after Iseo, the lake's principal tourist resort, and one with much more character than the southern town. Lóvere is a delightful place, built on a series of terraces so that it seems to tumble downhill. Because of its strategic position, at the junction of the Val Camonica and the Val Cavallina and at the head of the lake, the site has been occupied for a long time – certainly for more than 2,000 years as proved by the discovery of 4th-century BC remains. Later fortifications have furnished the town with three old towers, two from the 13th century and one from the 14th.

The beautiful church of Santa Maria in Valvendra, in the northern part of the town, has fine 15th-century frescos and good 16th-century carved stalls. Other works of art can be found in the Palazzo Tadini at the lake side. This long and beautifully arcaded palazzo was built in the 18th century and now houses the Galleria dell'Accademia Tadini, a small collection of paintings, sculptures and ceramics. The paintings are of principal interest and include a *Madonna* by Jacopo Bellini and works by Magnasco and Civerchio. In the garden there is a memorial to the palazzo's builder, Faustino Tadini, by Antonio Canova.

From Lóvere the walker can make for Altipiano di Lóvere where there are several fine villas and equally good views. The driver should make for Lake Endine, a secretive little lake tucked into the folds of the Val Cavallina which has maintained its untrammelled Italian character.

PISOGNE

MAP REF: 111 D3

North of Marone the road that follows the eastern shore of Lake Iseo excavates a way through the steep cliffs of the Corna dei Trentapassi. The tunnel is not continuous, a short section of daylight separating the two sections. As you drive this short section, the view to the lake includes a quick glimpse of the *bögn* of Zorzino, a sheer limestone cliff that plunges into the lake.

Beyond the end of the second tunnel lies Pisogne. Within the town the church of Santa Maria della Neve is well worth visiting to see the 16th-century frescos of Girolamo Romanino; these have been called the 'Poor Man's Sistine

The historic town of Lóvere is one of Lake Iseo's principal tourist resorts, with much to engross even the most wearied of travellers

Chapel', which seems to be very unfair criticism disguised as faint praise.

PONTE CÁFFARO

MAP REF: 111 D3

Ponte Cáffaro is the northernmost village on Lake Idro and also the last in Lombardy, the Cáffaro stream forming the border between Lombardy and Trentino. Until 1918 the stream was the border between Italy and Austria, that position explaining the presence of the (now ruinous) castle. From the castle there is an interesting view of the *quadri* (squares), on the Pian d'Oneda. The Pian was reclaimed by Benedictine monks in the 10th century and has always been prized for its fertility. After numerous ownership disputes it was decided to divide the plain into squares by digging drainage ditches. The villagers were then allocated a square by the drawing of lots.

Close to Ponte is Bagolino, a village of narrow medieval streets beside the Cáffaro. The church of San Rocco is one of the most important in the Val Sabbia because of its 15th-century frescos by da Cemmo. Also of interest are the village craftshops, handmade carpets being a local speciality.

THE VAL SABBIA

MAP REF: 111 D3

The Val Sabbia starts at Gavardo, a pleasant town split into two halves by the river Chiese which appears likely to wash away the foundations of several town

houses. The town museum deals with the history of the Val Sabbia and the mountains on its western edge. From Gavardo a road leads off to Vallio Terme, a small spa which sells bottled water and specialises in the treatment of kidney and liver complaints.

The next village is Vobarno where there is a fine 16th-century bridge and the remains of a castle of similar vintage, both built by the Venetians. Sabbio Chiese also had a medieval castle, built on top of the Rocca, a natural fortress. When peace came the castle was transformed into a church or, rather, two churches one on top of the other. Just up the valley is Barghe, a village of no special merit, but one that is wonderfully picturesque when seen with the river in the foreground and the cliffs of the valley edge beyond.

Further on again, Nozza is the old capital of the Val Sabbia while from Vestone a road leads off to Forno d'Ono arguably the most beautiful mountain village in the lakes area.

MOTOR TOUR

Allow 4 hours for this 150km tour of the countryside northeast of Bèrgamo and around Lake Iseo.

If you are starting your tour from the old city of Bèrgamo, follow the signs for Clusone and Edolo. If you are in the newer, lower city, take the peripheral ring road eastward, ignoring the turn to Lóvere and exiting at the next roundabout. In both cases you will soon reach Alzano

Lombardo, the first town at the mouth of the Val Seriana.

Alzano Lombardo

The basilica of San Martino has Antonio Fantoni's pulpit, covered in reliefs and claimed to be the best rococo work in Italy.

Continue along the valley road, through Nembro, to reach Albino.

Albino

This industrial centre is worth a stop for the superb *Crucifixion* in the church of San Giuliano, the work of Giovanni Battista Moroni who was born in the hamlet of Bondo Petello just above Albino. From Albino a *funivia* (cable car) rises to the hill village of Selvino, a centre for walking and skiing.

Further up the valley, a right turn leads to Gandino (see page 84) If you visit the village you can return to the main valley road by going through Cazzano Sant'Andrea and Casnigo. Continue along the valley road through Ponte Nossa to reach Ponte Selva and the turning for

Clusone (see page 82). Go through Clusone, exiting to the right for Lóvere.

This new road follows the delightful valley of the Borlezza river all the way to Lóvere (see opposite). Turn left in Lóvere on the road for Boário Terme – Italy's third largest spa – and the Val Camonica. Turn right off this road to reach Pisogne.

The tunnelled road, with its elusive glimpses of the bögns *(limestone cliffs) near Castro and Riva di Solto, is now followed to Marone (where you can turn off to see the erosion pillars of Zone – see page 85) and on to Sale Marasino.*

Sale Marasino

Arguably this is the prettiest village on Lake Iseo. Close to the lake is the Villa Martinengo whose delightful gardens include the remains of a 1st-century AD Roman villa.

The bulk of Monte Isola dominates all lake views now and will continue to do so as you drive through Sulzano to Pilzone

and on to Iseo (see page 85).

Turn off the main road here, going through Iseo and around the southern edge of the lake through Clusane. Before Sárnico is reached, go left to Capriolo and on to Palazzolo sull'Oglio. This road follows the River Oglio, Lake Iseo's outflow, and crosses the A4 autostrada. In Palazzolo take the SS573 for Bèrgamo/Milan taking the Bèrgamo exit at a round-about some 6km from the town. Continue to Malpaga.

Malpaga

The castle at Malpaga was the 'country house' of Bartolomeo Colleoni, the *condottiere* (mercenary) who built the splendid chapel in Bèrgamo's upper city. The castle (open by appointments only) stands amidst a collection of delightful farmhouses and dates from the 13th century.

Beyond Malpaga the road rejoins the Sério valley, now broad and flat. When the main road, the SS42, is reached, turn left to return to Bèrgamo.

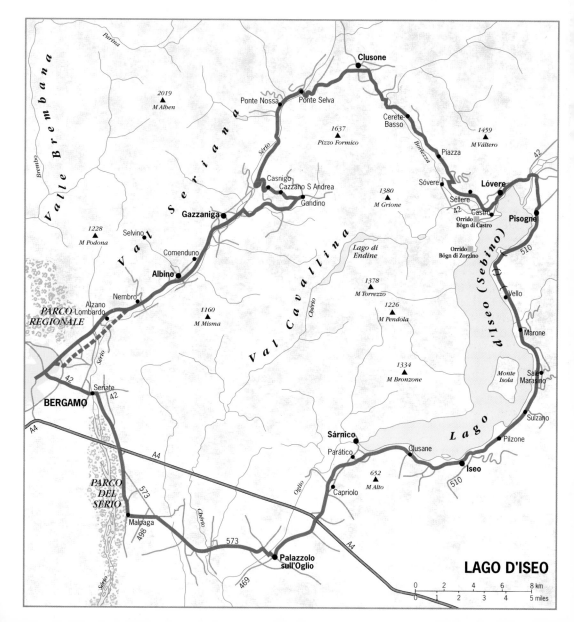

LAGO D'ISEO

The measured architecture of San Pellegrino, the spa town whose bottled waters are drunk all over Italy

SAN PELLEGRINO TERME

MAP REF: 110 C3

At the beginning of this century San Pellegrino was Italy's most fashionable spa, the prosperity of those times being apparent in the architecture of its major buildings, especially the glorious art nouveau structures - the Grand Hotel, the Palazzo della Fonte and the old Casino.

The warm mineral water spring at San Pellegrino has been known since the 13th century at least, but it was not until the 19th century that wealthy Italians developed the social niceties of spa culture. Today San Pellegrino still has a reputation for the curative properties of its water, which is said to be especially good for kidney disorders.

From San Pellegrino a *funivia* (cable car) rises to Vetta from where there are fine views of the town and the valley. Close to the town is the Grotto del Sogno while the village of Serina has delightful frescod and arcaded houses and a huge church with works by Palma il Vecchio who was born in the village.

SEDRINA

MAP REF: 110 C3

Sedrina lies in the Val Brembana, north of Bèrgamo. The valley begins at Villa d'Almè a flourishing little township. Over the river Brembo from here is Almenno San Bartolomeo where the 12th-century circular church of San Tome was constructed on the site of a Roman temple. The church is a marvellous example of the Lombardic Romanesque style and is built, essentially, of three cylinders one above the other. At night floodlighting adds its own magic to the church's splendour .

Sedrina itself is noted for the bridges that link the steep sides of the Brembo valley. Close to the village there are numerous limestone caves, including Buca del Castello, one of Italy's deepest, which make this an important speleology centre. The Grotta delle Meraviglie is open to the public and has a collection of stalagmites and stalactites. Beyond Sedrina is Zogno, the valley's chief town and an industrial centre, but with an interesting museum to the history of the Val Brembana.

RIVA DI SOLTO

MAP REF: 111 D3

From Lóvere a minor road edges its way down the western shore of Lake Iseo passing first through Castro, an old village once heavily fortified with a maze of steep, narrow streets.

Between Castro and Risa di Solto are the *bögns* of Castro and Zorzino - huge, near vertical sheets of limestone that plunge into the lake. From the road at the base of the cliffs the sheer scale of them is difficult to grasp and many visitors will find the view from the lake more satisfying. Beyond the Bögn of Zorzino, which forms a small bay, is Riva di Solto, a very picturesque village from which the view across the lake to the mountains of the Adamello is the best of any on the shore. Further south is Tavernola Bergamasco, another pretty village dotted with the ruins of old fortifications.

VALBONDIONE

MAP REF: 111 D4

Valbondione is the most northerly village of the Val Seriana, a scattered village set in a rugged mountain hollow. A track leads from the village to the lonely farmhouses of Grumetti and then on to the Rifugio Curo, being beautifully sited beside a small lake. The walk is long and climbs continuously, but it passes the Cascata del Serio, the highest waterfall in Europe at 315m. Unfortunately the fall is dry for most of the time because the river has been directed underground to drive a hydro-electric power station. The fall is only visible on certain summer weekends when the plant is being overhauled, and at that time there is likely to be a crowd.

BOAT TRIP

Allow half a day for this round trip of Lake Iseo and a full day if you plan to spend time ashore at Monte Isola. The ferry routes differ so be sure that your boat will call at Sulzano and Marone.

Start at Sárnico, the terminus for the lake steamers. Several companies in Sárnico specialise in making speedboats and international race meetings are hosted by the village. The ferry first visits Clusane, close to the La Torbiere marsh, a village that boasts a 15th-century castle and a special recipe for lake tench - tinca al farno con polenta. The

boat now crosses the lake to reach Predore, a village noted for its vineyards and its numerous historical finds, chiefly from the Roman era. After recrossing to Iseo the boat then moves on to Monte Isola.

Monte Isola

Monte Isola is the largest island on any of the lakes. Cars are banned and it offers a wonderful respite from the world. Monte Isola escaped the chiselling effects of the Ice Age glacier and its single peak thrusts 600m above the level of the lake. Trees cover most of the mountain except to the east where steep cliffs plunge towards the water. The pilgrimage church of Madonna della Ceriola stands on the flat-topped summit. It is a long walk to the church and many visitors will settle for a more leisurely stroll along the tracks that link the island's four villages.

In spring the island is yellow with broom and in autumn it is purple with heather. In summer the ubiquitous flowers form a multi-coloured carpet flowing beneath the stands of chestnut trees and through the vineyards and olive groves. A few village folk make nets for tennis courts and others still fish for a living; their drying nets and small fishing boats, together with the narrow, cobbled streets and the lack of cars, all contribute to a timeless scene. The 15th-century Oldofredi castle in Sensole and the tower of the same vintage in Siviano both add to the illusion.

Beyond the island the boat heads east to Sulzano.

Sulzano

Sulzano is one of the most important sailing centres on the lake, and a starting point for crossings to Monte Isola, whose

The wooded island of Monte Isola, with its single, distinctive peak

steep, wooded slopes make an impressive backdrop to village views. From the village a cobbled street leads to a road up into the mountains. This leads to the 15th-century church of Santa Maria del Giogo, standing around 700m above the lake, with excellent views.

The boat now calls at Sale Marasino and Marone.

Marone

At Marone you will find the ruins of a Roman villa and a museum devoted to the photography of Lorenzo Antonio Predali who worked in the early part of this century. His fascinating pictures illustrate the old way of life of the lakes area.

From here the boat crosses to Riva di Solto, affording views of the whole length of the lake – apart from the elbow around to Sárnico – together with the beautiful hills on either shore. As Riva is approached the view is enhanced by the Adamello mountains to the east and the mouth of the Val Camonica. North of Riva the boat sails close to the bögns of Castro and Zorzino. The view from the boat is the very best one for establishing the sheer scale of these huge and near vertical limestone cliffs. Ahead now the steamer will dock at Castro, Lóvere and Pisogne as it rounds the northern tip of the lake in preparation for the return journey to Sárnico.

LAGO DI GARDA (LAKE GARDA)

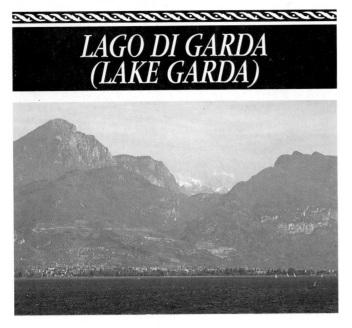

Garda is the largest of the lakes, its water surface covering an area of 370 square km. It is shorter than Lake Maggiore, at 52km, but more than makes up for this by being wider, particularly at its southern end where it broadens to 17km. The reason for this is that Garda extends much further beyond its confining ridges than do any of the other lakes. The glacier that formed the lake broadened out as it reached the Lombardy Plain and laid down a thick layer of moraine behind which the fan-shaped lake was formed. This broad, southern area of the lake is, as a result, relatively shallow in comparison to the huge depth (over 340m) of the deeply gouged northern section.

There are fine beaches at the southern end of the lake where most of Garda's resorts are concentrated. The lake is so popular that almost all the villages on its shore line are now given over to tourism. Only at the northern end of the western shore – specifically the high plateaux of Tignale and Tremòsine and the little fishing village of Campione – can the 'old' Garda still be found. Vestiges remain elsewhere, as a trip around the lake will show. Sirmione, Lazise, Torri del Benaco and Malcésine all have castles dating from the times of the City States, while at Peschiera the heavy fortifications of the Austrian occupation can still be seen.

Oddly, these fortifications were not used by the Austrians when, in 1859, the French and Piedmontese armies marched on Lombardy during the Second War of Italian Independence. Instead, the Austrians moved out of their strongholds to confront the armies of the Risorgimento. The decisive battle was fought at Solferino, just south of Sirmione, a battle whose horrendous aftermath led directly to the formation of the International Red Cross in Geneva (see page 94).

Sirmione itself is an extraordinary place. Here a long and remarkably narrow finger of land pokes up into the lake. At its head is a circle of land that was much prized by the Romans because it is fed with continuous hot water from a spring deep below the lake. Later, the strategic importance of the peninsula was identified by Verona's Scaligeri family who defended it with one of Europe's most beautiful castles – standing in the lake, joined to the land by a drawbridge and supplied, originally, through a defended harbour.

Above and below: dramatic snow-capped peaks rise sheer from the northern end of Lake Garda

Consistent wind speed and direction make Lake Garda perfect for sail-based sports such as windsurfing

At Malcésine there is another Scaligeri castle, this one dominating the lake shore at one of the lake's most beautiful villages. Above the castle and village rises the long ridge of Monte Baldo, known as 'the Botanical Garden of Italy' for the rarity of some of its plant species which are protected by two nature reserves.

Across the lake from Malcésine are the plateaux of Tignale and Tremòsine. To the south is Il Vittoriale, one of the most curious places on any of the lakes, a fascinating collection of buildings designed by Italy's poet-adventurer Gabriele d'Annunzio.

Further south again is Saló, a beautiful town, especially at the lake shore, that is justly famous as the birthplace of the lute maker who produced the world's first violin, and sadly notorious as the capital of the Saló Republic, the last act of Italy's tragic involvement in World War II.

A little way east of Lake Garda is Verona, the city of *Romeo and Juliet*, and before that a Roman city whose archaeological remains are second only to those of Rome in terms of their number and importance. Verona's Roman theatre, its superb Renaissance gardens and its beautiful Romanesque church of San Zeno Maggiore make this city a must for every visitor to the region.

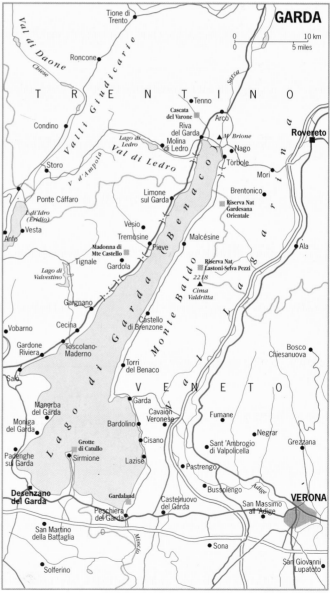

MOUNTAIN WALK

Monte Baldo rises to the east of Lake Garda and its long ridge, being relatively flat, makes it ideal for walking.

You should allow $2^1/_2$ hours for this 6.5km stroll which takes in superb views and rare mountain flora. You may also be privileged to catch sight of an asp viper basking in a sunny spot. If you do keep well away, as this is Europe's most poisonous snake.

From Malcèsine take the cable car to the Monte Baldo ridge, which stands at 1,745m above sea level. The journey takes about 15 minutes and saves several hours of arduous climbing.

At the top station there is a hotel and restaurant, but the main attraction is the tremendous panorama across the lake towards the high peaks of the Adamello alps and the Brenta Dolomites.

Close to the top station are the ski-lifts of Garda's foremost winter sports centre. Go south along the ridge between these, the path dropping down through rhododendron bushes to reach Bocca Tratto Spin, a col located at 1,720m. Beyond this the path climbs continuously, passing the top of a chairlift and heading for

Monte Baldo above Malcèsine

the first of the ridge's peaks which you will reach after about one hour.

Cima delle Pozzette, at 2,132m above sea level, is the northern peak of the Monte Baldo ridge. Looking back there are good viewpoints over the southern peaks and down to Lake Garda.

For most visitors Cima delle Pozzette will be a sufficient goal. There is no alternative but to return along the outward path, but that is no problem as the view is quite different and equally enthralling. Looking north you will see Monte Altissimo (2,079m) at the extreme end of the Baldo chain, as well as the rocky terrace of Corna Piana and the Brentonico valley.

The strong walker can continue south for another half an hour to climb Cima del Longino (2,180m) and Cima di Val Finestra (2,091m) and Cima Valdritta, the highest Monte Baldo peak at 2,218m. The final climb to the top of Cima Valdritta is along a short, tricky path and the same path must be used for the even more difficult descent. The compensation is, of course, panoramic views and a great sense of achievement as you survey the mountain landscape. Return from the high peak by reversing the route.

The ice sheets of the last Ice Age did not reach the top of the Monte Baldo ridge – which explains the survival of the Baldo speedwell (see box) – the high points on the ridge having been sculpted by the elements over the last several million years.

MONTE BALDO

Malcèsine

Valle di Colone

1720
Bocca Tratto
Spin

Selva Pezzi

Val Bona

Baldo

L di Angual

2132
C d Pozzette

Monte

2180
C d Longino

2091
C d Val Finestra

2218
C Valdritta

0   1 km

THE MONTE BALDO NATURE PARKS

The long high ridge of Monte Baldo dominates the eastern shore of Lake Garda. The top of the ridge is a harsh place, planed smooth by wind, rain and snow in winter and bleached by the summer sun. Yet the sheltered western flank of the ridge, overlooking the lake, is a paradise for plants. Such is their variety and profusion that the area is known as the 'Botanical Garden of Italy' and two nature parks have been created. The Lastoni Selva Pezzi Park stretches from Malcèsine to Castello from the ridge to a point about halfway down the slope while the Gardesana Orientale Park is much nearer to the lake and lies a little north of Malcèsine.

A noticable aspect of these parks is the way the tree cover changes as you climb the slope. Close to the lake olive groves are interspersed with holm oak and Mediterranean pine. These trees give way to chestnut then beech and black (Austrian or Corsican) pine. Next comes larch, and some firs, though even these give up the fight at the ridge where only a few hardy alpine flowers are found.

On the lower slopes the flowers include peppermint and camomile. Further up are hellebores, orchids, and gentian. Monte Baldo also has some species unique to the hill – an anemone (*Anemone baldensis*) a bedstraw (*Galuim baldensis*) and a speedwell (*Veronica bonorota*) which is a unique survivor of the pre-glacial period.

BARDOLINO

MAP REF: 111 E3

Above this village rise the terraced vineyards that produce the famous red wines of Bardolino. As with many other Garda villages, Bardolino was fortified by the Scaligeri family of Verona, though only a few ruins and the old harbour remain from that period. The village has no less than five churches, including the tiny 9th-century Carolingian church of San Zeno. The 12th-century church of San Severo has fine contemporary frescos and a superb campanile. Just south of Bardolino, at Cisano, there is a fine museum devoted to the olive oil industry, housed in an old oil mill.

BRENZONE

MAP REF: 111 E3

The villages that lie betweeen Torri del Benaco and Malcésine are collectively known as the Brenzone, a name said to derive from Bruncione who was one of the 12 privileged paladins, or knights errant, in Charlemagne's court. Of these villages the best is Castelletto, an ancient place grouped around the delightful Piazza dell'Olivio with its tall trees. The houses here have creeper-encrusted walls and balconies, external stairways and arched entrances, all of which helps to make the village the prettiest on the lake's eastern shore.

DESENZANO DEL GARDA

MAP REF: 111 D3

Desenzano is the largest town on the southern section of the lake and being close to the A4 *autostrada*. It is also one of the busiest. The old harbour, with its Tuesday covered market, is very picturesque, the new harbour being bigger and more businesslike, as befits the headquarters of the lake steamer company. The town has a long history, the Romans having fortified the area of Capo la Teira, in the higher part of the town, a thousand years before the castle whose ruins we see was built. Perhaps one of the town's Roman citizens built the 2nd-century AD villa which has been excavated by the lake shore. The villa should be visited for the mosiacs of hunting and village life scenes.

Elsewhere, you can visit the house in which Sant'Angela Merici, the founder of the Ursuline order, was reputedly born in 1470. Also worth visiting is the church of Santa Maria Magdalena, which has a superb *Last Supper* by Tiepolo and other fine works, including one by Paolo Veronese.

GARDA

MAP REF: 111 E3

Garda's Palazzo dei Capitani is a visible reminder of the Venetian Republic's influence on Lake Garda since it was once occupied by the Venetian Captains of the Lake. The building is imposing rather than beautiful, though the ground floor arcading does soften the lines. Another fine building is the Villa Albertini, a romantic, castle-like mansion where Carlos Alberto signed the treaty whereby Lombardy was united with Piedmont, an act which many see as the starting point for the Risorgimento. Those interested in local history should also visit the town museum where there are several examples of the ancient rock engravings found at Punta San Vigilio, close to the town.

Monte Garda, towering above the town, is a natural fortress with the remains of a castle on its summit. In the 10th century this was the most important fortification on the southeastern shore of the lake. In AD950 Berenger II, King of Piedmont, imprisoned Queen Adelheid in the castle. Adelheid controlled much of what is now Lombardy and the Veneto. Berenger wished to marry her and increase his kingdom. He was a man of such unpleasantness that Adelheid declined. Some men might have given up or tried harder to please. Berenger was

• GARDA

93

A Venetian flavour, a warm sun and good hospitality lull the patrons of this Garda restaurant

more direct: he locked her up until a visiting priest helped her to escape to the kingdom of Otto I in Germany. Adelheid and Otto soon wed and marched on Italy. their army soon defeated Berenger and Otto was subsequently crowned Holy Roman Emperor in AD962.

Two hundred years after this event the Rocca proved its worth as a defensive position by surviving a year-long siege by Barborossa. Later a castle was built on the summit by the Scaligeri family of Verona. Its ruins are all that now remain for the visitor to see – that and a wonderful view of the lake.

Shady trees line the varied waterfront promenade in Garda

94

SOLFERINO AND THE RED CROSS

The first skirmishes in the long struggle for Italian independence began in July 1848 when Lombardic troops, assisted by an army from the neighbouring Kingdom of Piedmont, faced the forces of the occupying Austrian army at Custoza. On that occasion, and again at Novara in March 1849, the Austrians were victorious and an uneasy peace descended on northern Italy.

Following the defeat, King Carlo Alberto of Piedmont abdicated in favour of his son, Vittorio Emanuele II. In the next ten years the Piedmontese, under the skilful diplomacy of their Prime Minister, Camillo Cavour, forged an alliance with the French and the British by sending troops to fight against the Russians in the Crimea.

Later, in 1858, Cavour signed an agreement with Napoleon III in which Jerome Napoleon, the Emperor's cousin, was betrothed to Princess Clothilde, Vittorio Emanuele's daughter. It was also agreed that France and Piedmont would seek to precipitate a war with Austria.

The Austrians, at first resolutely declined to enter hostilities, ignoring various provocative acts. Finally, just when Napoleon decided to abandon the scheme, Austria handed Piedmont a disarmament ultimatum, and the Second Italian War of Indepedence began. The French army of well over 100,000 men started to arrive in Genoa in the middle of May 1859. On 20 May the French and the Piedmontese won an early skirmish at Montebello. The first major battle took place at

Above: a contemporary artist's memorial to the Red Cross in Solferino. Below: serene enough today – Solferino town and the battlefield

Magenta, to the west of Milan, on 4 June. The result was inconclusive but the Austrians started a general retreat eastwards, evacuating Milan. Had the French pursued them the whole war might have soon ended. Instead, Napoleon and Vittorio Emanuele became embroiled in argument about why the Piedmontese had not joined in the battle, leaving the French to do all the fighting and resulting in the death of 2,000 French soldiers. Even so, the Austrians retreated to the river Mincio, the outflow of Lake Garda, forming the border between Lombardy and Venetia. Franz Josef, the Austrian Emperor, was appalled by this capitulation and the loss of Lombardy; he arrived in Italy to take personal charge of the army and the scene was set for one of the bloodiest battles of the 19th century.

Solferino

The battle of Solferino was actually two battles fought on the same day, 24 June 1859. To the north of Solferino, at San Martino, the Piedmontese army fought the Austrians under Field Marshal von Benedek, while around the village of Solferino itself the French fought the remaining Austrians led by Emperor Franz Josef. The battle, when it came, was very close run. To the north von Benedek stopped the Piedmontese and was on the point of pursuing them when he was ordered to fall back by Franz Josef, who had seen his own army turned by the French. As the Austrians retreated a violent storm broke, rapidly turning the battlefield into a quagmire. Napoleon and his men were weary from the heat and the battle so the Austrians were allowed to retreat, while the victors spent the night on the battlefield, among the dead and the dying, who numbered more than 40,000.

The Red Cross

War in 19th-century Europe was not the total war of today, and civilian life was scarcely affected. That is why Henri Dunant, a businessman from Geneva, who was holidaying near Lake Garda, was able to watch the battle on the 24 June and to visit the field on the following day. What he saw appalled him. There were virtually no medical supplies or medical teams to tend the wounded. Dunant went home and published a pamphlet in 1862 entitled *A Souvenir of Solferino*. He graphically described the battle scene and its aftermath, including

an amputation he had witnessed in which the patient's gangrenous leg was sawn off without anaesthetic. He concluded with a question: 'Would it not be possible to create societies in every European country whose aim would be to assure that prompt and devoted care is given to those wounded in battle?'

Dunant's words had an immediate effect: a conference was convened in Geneva on 26 October 1863. Sixteen countries attended, of whom 12 signed the first Geneva Convention on warfare – which effectively set up an International Committee to protect war wounded and prisoners. The Committee took a version of the Swiss flag as its symbol – a red cross. Today the International Red Cross, and its associated societies such as the Red Crescent, is established in over 100 countries and the Geneva Convention specifies the 'rules' of warfare.

The Battlefield Today

At Solferino, a pleasant village just to the south of Lake Garda, the visitor will find an ossuary chapel containing the bones of around 7,000 French and Austrians who died in the battle, along with a museum to both the battle and the Risorgimento. Here, too, there is a monument to the Red Cross erected in 1959, the centenary of the battle. It is built with stone from every member nation.

At San Martino, where the Piedmontese fought, there is a huge round memorial tower, 64m high; dedicated to Vittorio Emanuele. The view from the top extends over most of the battlefield. Here too there is a museum to the battle and an ossuary chapel.

Castiglione delle Stiviere, to the west of Solferino, is where Henri Dunant stayed on the day of the battle; today it has a museum to the Red Cross movement.

The Ossuary Chapel at Solferino, dedicated to the memory of Jean Henri Dunant and the Red Cross, lined with bones from the battlefield

95

Plaque in Solferino's Ossuary Chapel paying tribute to Dunant and the work of the Red Cross throughout the world

Gargnano's harbour

GARDONE RIVIERA

MAP REF: 111 D3

Gardone deserves its appendage – 'Riviera' because it has an unusually mild winter climate, of benefit to both man and plants. Dr Ludovic Rohden, a 19th-century German expert on climatology, published a paper on the health benefits, which encouraged the Austrian Emperor to build the Villa Albi here for his own use. The building of the villa had a dramatic effect on Gardone's prosperity, though the Emperor never actually came to stay.

About a decade after the Emperor's enthusiasm had been raised Professor Arthur Hruska arrived in Gardone to found a botanical study centre. The result was the Hruska Botanic Gardens, one of the great gardens of Europe, especially renowned for its rockeries. The professors's beautiful work can be visited, but Villa Albi is not open to the public.

GARGNANO

MAP REF: 111 E3

In the 13th century Gargnano was a major religious centre; the Franciscan monastery here can still be seen – though it was substantially modernised earlier this century. The capitals in the monastery cloister are carved with citrus fruits: legend has it that the Franciscans introduced citrus

cultivation to the region. Today the whole town seems surrounded by groves of orange and lemon trees and you can buy fresh local fruit, in season, at the lakeside.

The town hall, a fine 16th-century building, and some of the neighbouring houses still show signs of cannonball damage – Gargnano was bombarded by the Austrian navy in 1886. Elsewhere there are fine villas – such as the striking Villa Feltrenelli – and narrow picturesque alleys. The combination of elegant villas and simpler town houses, with their stone arcading and window boxes, makes Gargnano a delightful place.

LAZISE

MAP REF: 111 E3

Lazise was the main Venetian port on Lake Garda during the 16th century and the harbour still has a cluster of buildings dating from that time. The Venetian defensive walls can still be seen, forming three sides of a square, with the lake making the fourth. To forestall an attack from the lake a chain could be drawn across the harbour entrance – an effective defence against the wooden ships of the day. Within the town there are the excellent remains of a Scaligeri castle – modified by the Venetians – though sadly not open to the public. Elsewhere, the fine

Renaissance church of Santa Maria della Pergolina is worth a visit.

Inland from Lazise, at Pastrengo, is the Garda Safari Park. This consists of three seperate areas: a drive-through safari park, a zoo with a fine reptile collection and a park with full-scale (replica) dinosaurs.

LIMONE SUL GARDA

MAP REF: 111 E3

The last town on the western Lombardy shore of Lake Garda is named after the lemon trees that once made it prosperous, and which still grow in profusion, along with oranges and mandarins. The Gardesana Occidentale, the new road on the western shore, has taken much of the passing traffic away from Limone, leaving it a peaceful backwater. Here you can stroll through the delightful old quarter – with its balconied and flower-bedecked houses – and drink coffee in the old harbour, under the shade of a palm tree, while gazing at the lake or at the dazzling white cliffs above the town.

On a hill near these cliffs is the solitary church of San Pietro, set in an olive grove. An inscription on the exterior wall tells of a plague in 1630, a poor olive harvest in 1822 and a very cold winter in 1857 – the last straw which caused the village served by the church to be abandoned.

D'ANNUNZIO AND THE VITTORIALE

Gabriele d'Annunzio, poet and Italian patriot, was born on 12 March 1863. He began publishing poetry and short stories in his twenties and a decade later he achieved international recognition, especially for his plays. His works were sensuous and ahead of their time.

D'Annunzio was over 50 years old when World War I broke out. Despite that he returned to Italy from Paris to lecture on the need for Italian intervention, and to offer his own services. When Italy entered the war; d'Annunzio was enlisted as a lieutenant, losing an eye when a plane in which he was travelling crash-landed in 1916. His war exploits mirrored his writing – flamboyant, yet brave – and he was richly decorated .

At the end of World War I the former territories of the Austro-Hungarian empire were divided up and part of Italian-speaking Istria was given to the future Yugoslavia. D'Annunzio felt the loss was unfair to Italy and he occupied the city of Fiume (now Rijeka) with a group of volunteers. After the Fiume incident, d'Annuzio settled in Gardone and built his Villa Il Vittoriale degli Italiani which he donated to the State before his death in 1938.

Il Vittoriale is a curious collection of buildings in the art nouveau style, some opulent and some garish. The open-air theatre and the Dalmatian Square are both elegant, while the Prioria is over elaborate. It is difficult to imagine how anyone could find sleep in d'Annunzio's bedroom, yet his study is fascinating – the door was deliberately built low so that visitors had to bow as they entered. The study is dimly lit, as with most of the rooms, because d'Annunzio disliked daylight and had many of the windows painted black.

Elsewhere there is the aeroplane the poet used to fly over Vienna in 1918, a warship of the Italian navy and the car d'Annuzio used in his abortive occupation of Fiume. He is buried in a mausolem in the gardens. Like the man himself, this memorial is larger than life and of questionable taste.

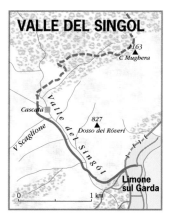

VALLE DEL SINGÓL

COUNTRY WALK

This fine 5km walk from Limone heads inland from the lake to reach the remote and beautiful Valle del Singól. Allow 2 hours.

The Gardesana Occidentale (the SS45 road along the western shore of Lake Garda) cuts through the western edge of Limone, passing close to the church. Find the church and cross the main road to follow Via Caldogno to its end. From there you will find a track bordered on the left by a stream, the Torrente San Giovanni. This leads to a bridge over the stream from where a wide mule track goes up the Valle del Singól.

The Valle del Singól is very beautiful, with several small waterfalls and views to rugged peaks. It has been suggested that the mule track was originally created to carry goods from Lake Garda to Lake Ledro. This may be so, but it seems rather unlikely, since the road that follows the Ponale valley further north would have been an easier route between the two lakes. It is more likely that this track was used to supply the soldiers who were manning the trenches on the Italian-Austrian border during World War I.

You will reach the first set of waterfalls after 2km. To extend the walk further you can continue past the rough track to the left (which goes up the Val Scaglione) and cross a small wooden bridge to reach the ruins of a circular building. The stream is then crossed again and a series of bends beyond leads to the Madonnina (little Madonna) del Mürel set on the rocks to the left.

To return, the outward route must be retraced. Alternatively, hardened walkers can persever ahead to join the extended walk from Tremòsine (see page 105).

Full-size replica dinosaurs in the Garda Safari Park near Lazise

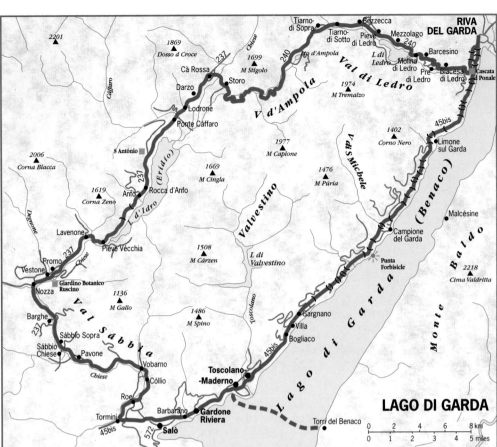

MOTOR TOUR

This 130km drive follows the western shore of Lake Garda and returns north by way of Val Sabbia and Lake Ledro. Allow 3¹/₂ hours.

From Riva del Garda follow the Gardesana Occidentale (SS45) to Campione del Garda.

Campione del Garda

There is a stunning view from here across the lake to Malcésine's castle, the tent-shaped mass of Monte Baldo rising behind. The village itself, a group of houses beneath the cliffs, is the only one on Lake Garda to retain anything like its original feel.

Follow ss45 to Gargnano and the turn off to Lake Valvestino.

Lake Valvestino

The lake is a reservoir set between Val Toscolano and Valvestino, the latter a magnificent valley of rugged hills. From Magasa, the valley's final village, a long, but excellent, walk climbs Monte Caplone, for a stupendous views.

From Gargnano continue to Bogliaco.

Bogliaco

The neat village is set below tumbling vineyard terraces. The old harbour is a fine spot, while the 18th-century Villa Bettoni stands alongside delightful gardens, to which it is linked by a bridge, and houses works by Veronese, Dürer and Holbein. The villa is open on request.

Continue south to the twin towns of Toscolano-Maderno.

Toscolano-Maderno

Etruscan Toscolano was once separated from Roman Maderno by a circular headland but 20th-century development has seen the two join up. Toscolano has one of the prettiest old harbours on the lake. In the main square is Sant'Andrea, a 12th-century Romanesque church with intricate carving around the doorway.

The road now continues past d'Annunzio's Villa Il Vittoriale (see page 97) and the Hruska Botanic Gardens (page 96) at Gardone Riviera, and on towards Salò. At the edge of the town bear right on the road to the Val Sàbbia (signposted to Brèscia) reaching the valley at Tormini. Turn right here and follow the valley past the villages of Vobarno, Sàbbio Chiese, Barghe and Nozza to reach Vestone.

Vestone

The pretty village is set where the Torrente Degnone joins the Val Sàbbia's river Chiese. Close to the river are the Giardino Botanico Ruscino, a botanical park specialising in plants from Val Sábbia.

Continue along the western shore of Lake Idro, taking the ss237 Tione/Madonna di Campiglio road from Ponte Cáffaro. At Cà Rossa turn right on to the ss240 for Lake Ledro and Riva. The new road follows the beautiful Val d'Ampola which carves a dark, narrow way upwards through high peaks (Monte Càdria, to the north, is 2,254m high) past many delightful waterfalls. At Tiarno you reach the head of the valley and the local watershed. The route now follows an infeed stream down to Lake Ledro.

Lake Ledro

The tiny lake is only 3km long and is famous for its ancient lake dwellings (see page 50). Pieve di Ledro, the village at its head is a quiet, pretty resort.

From Pieve you can follow either of the shore roads; the northern route is quieter, the southern prettier. Both roads lead to Molina di Ledro, from where a very steep road drops down the Ponale valley to reach the ss45 near the Cascata del Ponale waterfall. At the main road, go left to return to Riva.

LAGO DI GARDA

CYCLE TOUR

The natural bay formed by the hook of Punta San Vigilio and the finger of Sirmione offers the best cycle ride on Garda. Allow 3 hours for this 26.6km trip (33km with the inland detour).

Leave Sirmione down the peninsula's only road, turning left at Colombare along the main road. The road bypasses Peschiera del Garda, so turn left into the town, crossing the Mincio bridge and continuing past the ancient Austrian fortifications and the Gardaland theme park. When Lazise is reached turn right for Calmasino and Cavaion Veronese. The road climbs now and offers tremendous views of the lake.

Cavaion
The pretty village is set on the flank of a densely wooded hill

Shapely cypress trees echo the towers and fishtail battlements of Malcésine's striking castle

with outcrops of steep white cliffs. The vineyards near the town grow grapes for Bardolino wine.

From Cavaion do not take the road down to Bardolino, but continue north through Affi and Albare Stazione to reach Costermana. Turn left here for Garda.

Costermano
Just outside the village is a huge German war cemetery. In 1955 the Italian government gave the land to Germany in perpetuity and the remains of 22,000 soldiers were transferred from burial grounds throughout northern Italy.

Drop down into Garda and make for the lake steamer quay where any boat (except the aliscafo *– hydrofoil) will return you to Sirmione.*

MALCÉSINE
MAP REF: 111 E3
Malcésine is the highlight of a visit to Lake Garda's eastern shore, a beautiful town set below Monte Baldo, and with one of the lake area's most striking castles. The 14th-century castle, built by the Scaligeri family, is almost intact, its low walls and squat towers grouped around the tall central tower adorned with fishtail battlements. In the courtyard is a bust of Goethe. The great poet came to the town in September 1786. At that time the border between Italy and Austria lay just north of the town and Goethe, who was sketching the buildings and jotting down a few notes, was arrested by an over-zealous official as an Austrian spy. It took Goethe some time to prove his innocence, but he saw the funny side of the

incident and wrote a humorous piece about it in his *Italian Tour*. The Pariani Museum in the castle deals with Goethe's visit and a plaque in the town commemorates the place of arrest – surely a unique memorial. The castle also houses the Museum of the Lake with many fine exhibits, including one on the overland transportation of Venetian war galleys to Torbole (see page 104).

Elsewhere, the 15th-century Palazzo dei Capitani, now the town hall, is a superb building with its pillars and arcades.

MONIGA DEL GARDA
MAP REF: 111 D3
On the southwestern shore of Lake Garda, between Desenzano and Saló, is the Valtenesi, a giant fist of undulating land created by the uneven distribution of morainic deposits from the glacier that carved out the lake. Here there are several interesting villages.

Moniga stands apart from its pretty little harbour. The village, with its castle remains, is still reached through a massive medieval gateway. To the south, Padenghe sul Garda is set on a hill, much of the picturesque village enclosed within the walls of its Venetian fortification. Manerba del Garda, north of Moniga, has developed as a tourist resort because of its sheltered bay. There is a fascinating museum of Valtenesi life in the village.

PESCHIERA DEL GARDA
MAP REF: 111 E2
Peschiera, a fishing village as its name suggests (*pesce* means fish), is located on the so-called Olive Tree Riviera. Pope Leo the Great came here in the mid-5th century and persuaded Attila the Hun not to attack Rome. In the 19th century Peschiera was fortified by the Austrians and huge defensive works remain where the river Mincio flows into the lakes.

Today, Peschiera is unhurried and peaceful, its Renaissance churches and buildings a delight, its gardens a pleasure. Try to be in the main square on the hour when the town hall clock is struck by the beaks of two bronze eagles.

Just outside Peschiera is Gardaland, northern Italy's answer to Disneyland. Here there is a fairground, a circus, a maze, a replica of the ancient Egyptian Valley of the Kings – and gardens where parents can relax while their children burn off their energy.

RIVA DEL GARDA

MAP REF: 111 E3

Riva stands at the northern tip of
Lake Garda, a prosperous and
sophisticated place, very popular
with windsurfers as the lake's
northerly winds are very
dependable. The heart of the town
is Piazza Tre Novembre with its
medieval houses and the Torre
Apponale, a clock tower built in
the 12th century, but rebuilt in the
15th century as part of the town's
defences. Close by is the Rocca, a
moated Scaligeri castle – complete
with drawbridge – which houses a
museum to the area, including
finds from the Lake Ledro pile
villages. Also worth visiting is the
church of the Inviolata in Via
Roma, the road to Arco. This
interesting building has a
beautifully decorated octagonal
sanctuary.

Close to the town, about 4km
along the Tenno road, is the
Cascata del Varone, a 90m
waterfall that drops into a cold,
narrow gorge.

SALÓ

MAP REF: 111 D3

Saló was the home of Gaspare
Bertolotti (Gaspare da Saló) a lute
maker credited with inventing the

violin in the late 16th century.
Gasparo's statue stands in a room
on the first floor of the 16th-
century Palazzo Municipale, the
town hall. The town around the
palazzo is one of Lake Garda's
most beautiful, especially at the
lakeside itself where the views of
the narrow cove and the
luxuriously long promenade are
exquisite.

Away from the water is the
Duomo (Cathedral), a Gothic
building with a soaring interior of
sombre stone relieved by a fine
collection of artwork. Especially
good is the polyptych by Paolo
Veneziano. Alongside the
cathedral is the Palazzo Fantoni
which houses the Biblioteca
Atenco, a collection of old and
rare books. A quite different, but
equally rare, collection can be
found in the Whiskythek in
Lungolago which claims to have
every brand of whisky in the
world on its shelves.

SIRMIONE

MAP REF: 111 E3

From the southern shore of Lake
Garda a peninsula, 3km in length,
pokes out into the water. In places
the peninsula is only a little over
100m wide, but it broadens out at
the tip to create a blob of land

**Riva del Garda's moated Scaligeri
castle houses a regional museum**

where Sirmione sits, protected by
its lovely castle (see page 102).
Visitors must park outside the
town, whose narrow traffic-free
streets merely add to the fairytale
quality. Those with the time
should walk to the very tip of the
peninsula, passing, on the way,
the Grotte di Catullo, the ruins of a
Roman bathhouse.

The thermal springs – the water
emerges at 70°C – that once fed
the baths now supply a spa
specialising in the treatment of
muscular and nervous problems.
Elsewhere within the town the
15th-century church of Santa Maria
Maggiore has a columned porch
and an unusual 13th-century altar
of polished marble, behind which
is a superb wooden screen.

The church of San Pietro in
Mavino is much older, perhaps 8th
century, and was built on the site
of a Roman temple. It has 13th-
century frescos which feature
early examples of graffiti. Outside
the church is the Bell of the Fallen,
completed in 1955 as a memorial
to all those who have died in war.
The bell is rung periodically – the
stone tablet gives dates – and also
serves as a fog warning for lake
fishermen.

Riva del Garda's clock tower

THE SALÓ REPUBLIC

When Mussolini forced Italy into World War II the armed forces were unprepared. Perhaps sensing, too, that the popular mood was not in favour of war, Mussolini hesitated until June 1940 – after Germany had occupied Belgium, the Netherlands and much of France – before committing Italy to the fray. His armies fought poorly in Albania, Greece and Libya. Worse still, in 1942-3, almost half of the 100,000 soldiers sent to the Russian front were killed.

At home the shock of this news led to the emergence of an anti-Facist movement and further eroded public support. When the Allies landed in Sicily in July 1943 Mussolini was forced to give up power. King, Vittorio Emanuele III appointed Marshal Pietro Bodoglio to head a new government which signed an armistice on 8 September. Germany poured troops into Italy to stop the Allied advance, 'kidnapped' Mussolini and made him head of the Italian Socialist (or Saló) Republic, controlling the north of Italy which was still in Axis hands. Mussolini 'ruled' his Republic – in practice he was a puppet dictator – from the town of Saló and from the Villa Feltrenelli in Gargnano.

On 13 October 1943 the new Italian government declared war on Germany. In the spring of 1945, partisans operating behind German lines took control of Milan and many of the northern towns, making Mussolini's position untenable. The Germans attempted to smuggle him out of the country in a convoy of lorries which drove up the western shore of Lake Como en route for the Valtellina and Austria. The convoy was stopped at Dongo on 27 April 1945 and all the Fascist leaders, except Mussolini, were shot. Mussolini and his mistress were driven south on 28 April, but Italy did not want the embarrassment of seeing Il Duce tried as a war criminal, so the Committee of National Liberation ordered his immediate execution at Azzano. The bodies of Mussolini and his mistress were then taken to Milan where they were hung ignominiously upside down, outside a petrol station in Piazza Loretto. The Saló Republic was no more.

BOAT TRIP

The towns ringing southern Lake Garda look magical from the water – allow 3 hours for this trip.

Board the ferry at Sirmione, from where the boat travels south to Peschiera del Garda. Stay on the right-hand side of the boat for this leg for the best views of the Sirmione peninsula and the castle. There are further good views of Peschiera's fortifications as the boat enters the town's enclosed harbour.

From Peschiera the boat heads north to call at Lazise, with its castle, then Bardolino and Garda. Stay on the right-hand side of the boat for a fine view of Garda's Rocca and of Punta San Vigilio.

The Punta SanVigilio is one of the most beautiful places on the lake. Huge cypress trees rise up behind the *chiesetta*, the little church, which is part of the nearby 16th-century Villa Guarienti. The tiny campanile is a gem and the statue in its niche can only be seen from the lake. The villa was used by Winston Churchill when he wanted peace to complete his memoirs. He also painted here, gazing out across the aptly name Serene Bay which stretches to Garda.

On the long crossing to the western shore you will see the huge expanse of Lake Garda to the right, the ridge of Monte Baldo behind the boat and the hills above Gardone Rivieria straight ahead. From Gardone the boat heads to Salò and Porto Portese.

Porto Portese is a little fishing village at the edge of the Valtenesi. In the 15th century Bartolomeo Zoni, the renowned Renaissance printer, set up a press here that produced all the state documents for the Venetian Republic.

The view ahead to Monte Baldo is magnificent as the boat travels between the mainland and Isola di Garda, then across the bay to San Felice.

Isola di Garda is the only true island in Lake Garda. St Francis of Assisi visited the island's 12th-century monastery. Today the island and its villa are privately owned by the Princes of Borghese. San Felice del Benaco is an important Valtenesi town. The 14th-century church of Madonna del Carmine is richly frescoed.

The boat now passes the headland of the Rocca di Manerba – known locally as Dante's profile. You can decide whether the great poet would have been flattered or not by the comparison.

The ferry boat docks at Porto Dusano before returning to Sirmione. If you are on an evening boat you may be fortunate enough to catch sight of the sun setting behind the peaks north of Brèscia, turning the the surface of the lake orange and pink. If not, it is worth visiting Sirmione's shore just to witness this magical sight.

LAGO DI GARDA

Gardone Riviera
Salò
Porto Portese · Isola di Garda
San Felice del Benaco · Garda
Rocca di Manerba · Pta S Vigilio · Villa Guarienti
Porto Dusano
Bardolino
Lago di Garda
Sirmione · Lazise
Peschiera del Garda

0 2 4 6 8 km
0 1 2 3 4 miles

·CASTLES·

In medieval Europe the castle was the ultimate symbol of power. Safe within its walls a feudal overlord could control his territory with the help of a retained group of knights. The poorly armed peasantry had no answer to such tactics. The castle was also a mighty weapon in the event of war. Invading armies were forced to take every castle they passed; failure to do so meant that the castle's occupants could cut the invader's supply line. For that reason medieval wars involved many a long siege of castles built at strategic points, such as at the mouth of a valley or at a river crossing.

Above: the castle at Angera. Below: Milan's Castello Sforzesco, now a palatial art gallery and museum

In the lake's area we see castles everywhere, though most of the region's abundant castles are now ruinous, quarried for building materials as soon as they were abandoned. A few, however, remain almost complete as a reminder of the region's sometimes troubled history.

THE CASTELLO SFORZESCO, MILAN
MAP REF: 110 B3

The first castle on this site was built in the mid-14th century by Galeazzo Visconti. Later, the Milanese, seeing the castle as a symbol of repression, pulled much of it down, so that Francesco Sforza, who came to power in the late 15th century had to start almost from scratch.

Sforza's castle was designed by Il Filarete, the Florentine military architect and one of the greatest castle builders of his day. In subsequent years the castle was badly damaged, first by the explosion of a gunpowder store and then in the Five Day Uprising against the Spanish. Extensive renovation took place at the end of the 19th century so we now see the castle much as it would have looked when built.

The castle is a massive and impressive building, entered, at its city side, through the Filarete Tower, also called the Clock Tower, a perfect replica of the one lost in the gunpowder-store explosion. The tower is 70m high and decorated with a bas-relief of Umberto I on horseback. Around

the tower the outer castle walls enclose a large square, with huge round towers at the two front angles, once surrounded by a water-filled moat. Any attacker who managed to penetrate to this inner courtyard was then faced by a second inner fortress surrounded by a deep dry moat.

The inner castle was itself subdivided and, in extreme circumstances, the castle's defenders could withdraw to the innermost tower, the Rocchetta, from where they could bombard attackers trapped below.

THE BORROMEO CASTLE, ANGERA

MAP REF: 110 B3

The Rocca (Castle) at Angera occupies a naturally defended position which was successively exploited by the Lombards, the Franks, the Torriani, the Visconti and, finally, the Borromeo family. The Borromei, who gained possession in 1450, have held the Rocca ever since, surviving, one way or another, Spanish and Austrian rule and the upheaval of the Risorgimento.

A steep road leads up to the castle's gateway, which, it is believed, was once a Roman watchtower. Any attacker would be forced to reach this gate by running along the length of an embattled wall, all the while under fire from above. In doing so, the attackers would also present their unprotected right-hand sides to the defenders.

Inside the main gate there is a courtyard surrounded by defended walls, the final redoubt being a high tower that commands views over almost all of the castle. After Angera had ceased to play a military role it became a mansion. Its frescoed walls add a splendid touch of colour to the rooms.

THE SCALIGERI CASTLE, SIRMIONE

MAP REF: 111 E3

Sirmione was long recognised as being of strategic importance. The Romans fortified the peninsula, as did the Lombards, though what we now see dates from the 15th century, the work of Verona's Scaligeri family. The main castle consists of a small square block with corner towers defending a taller keep. This is completely surrounded by a long lake-filled moat which is itself enclosed within another wall. The moat was large enough to accommodate a small defensive fleet, with access through an offset gap in the walls.

There was no water gate, but there is a tower at the gap, and the embattled walls had a walkway so that soldiers could fire on attacking craft. On the peninsula side there was a drawbridge and portcullised gateway. Thus, whether attackers approached by land or boat they faced a formidable array of obstacles.

THE SCALIGERI CASTLE, VERONA

MAP REF: 111 E2

Verona's Castelvecchio is a fascinating early castle, built in the mid-14th century; despite later remodelling it retains many aspects of its original design. At first it seems a straightforward rectangular castle with the fish-tail battlements typical of Scaligeri family castles. In reality, the design is more subtle.

The castle is built on the river bank so that one long side, containing the domestic buildings, is protected by a natural moat. As with Milan's Castello Sforzesco, there is an inner curtain wall allowing an inner fortress to be maintained if attackers broke through the outer wall. If the attack penetrated further the defenders could retreat to the Mastio, a taller, more heavily defended tower, from which, as a final insurance, a heavily fortified bridge led across the water to an escape route on the far bank.

The formidable but picturesque defences of Sirmione's 13th-century castle, a stronghold of Verona's Scaligeri family

TIGNALE

MAP REF: 111 E3

Two high plateaux sit above Lake Garda's northwestern shore breaking up the pattern of steep, inhospitable hills. Tignale is the southernmost of the two plateaux, reached by a narrow road that leaves the Gardesana Occidentale shore road north of Gargnano. Six separate hamlets are spread out across Tignale's sloping plateau, which rises by 200m from east to west. Tignale is a place for quiet walks, with excellent panoramic views of the lake. Each of the villages is a delight, though the real highlight is the church of Madonna di Montecastello. As the name implies, the church occupies

Beach marauders and windsurfers making the most of the plentiful supply of summer sunshine and the offshore breezes at Tòrbole on Lake Garda

104

the site of a former Scaligeri castle, standing on a high tree-clad rock close to Gárdola. Inside there are several fine paintings, including a magnificent fresco of the *Coronation of Virgin* attributed to Giotto.

TÒRBOLE

MAP REF: 111 E3

Goethe sailed from Tòrbole on the journey that was to end in his arrest as an 'Austrian spy' at Malcésine. A plaque marks the house where Goethe slept and started work on the drama *Iphigenia*. Another heroic journey began in Tòrbole – that of the extraordinary Venetian fleet which was hauled by oxen and carts across the hills for launch on Lake Garda (see opposite).

The village is a fine one, set beside the inflowing river Sarca, the lake's main source of new waters. The church of Sant'Andrea

should be visited, if only to see the painting of *The Martyrdom of St Matthew* completed by the 18th-century artist Giambettino Cignaroli. It is a superb rendering of cruelty and anguish.

From Tòrbole a road rises to the tiny hamlet of Nago set on a hill above the lake. The hill offers expansive views of Tòrbole and the lake, but is of more interest for the Marmitte dei Giganti, the Giant's Pots, smooth holes bored out from the rock bed by the erosive action of swirling meltwater and pebbles at the end of the last Ice Age.

More fine views are to be had from Monte Brione, the rocky wedge that separates Tòrbole from Riva del Garda. A road climbs all the way up to the summit from where the Sarca valley and the valley of Lake Loppia can be seen.

TORRI DEL BENACO

MAP REF: 111 E3

Torri is the eastern terminus of the Garda car ferry and is, as a result, a busy, bustling sort of place. The old harbour has maintained its original character, however, and is one of the prettiest on the lake. The village name betrays its Roman origins – it was *Castrum Turrium* – though the most prominent feature, the Scaligeri castle, dates from the late 14th century. The castle now houses a fascinating museum which deals with lake fishing, the local olive oil industry, local quarrying and ancient rock engravings. The local quarries are famous for their red and white marble.

The 15th-century Church of Santa Trinita has frescos once attributed to Giotto, but now believed to be the work of his pupils.

TREMÒSINE

MAP REF: 111 E3

Tremòsine is the northernmost of the two high plateaux that rise above Garda's northwestern shore. No less than 17 villages are spread across this beautiful and fertile high plain, dotted with olive groves on the lower slopes and fir trees above.

Walkers come to the area to enjoy the fine views from the 'Balcony of Lake Garda'. The best views are to be had from Pieve, a clifftop village from which virtually the whole of Lake Garda can be seen. Several of the village cafés have terraces that overhang the cliffs, and the view downwards from their parapets is awesome.

TÒRBOLE WAR GALLEYS

In 1424 war broke out between Milan and the Venetian Republic, a war that was to drag on for almost 30 years. The Milanese quickly gained the upper hand, invading the Po Valley and reaching the outskirts of Verona. They also besieged Brèscia; the city offered stout resistance, but clearly could not hold out forever. The Venetians, who still held eastern Lake Garda, decided upon an outflanking manoeuvre, attacking Brèscia from the north by way of the Ledro valley and the Val Sábbia. To do this they needed to hold northern Lake Garda and that meant having a fleet on the lake. But how to get it there?

In February 1439 the fleet left Venice on the backs of oxen. This strange procession made its way to the river Adige near Verona. There the ships were launched and rowed upstream to Roverto. From there they were hauled over land to Lago di Loppio, floated across the lake, and then hauled over the San Giovanni Pass to Tòrbole.

The journey, which involved thousands of men and oxen, lasted three months. By the time they reached Tòrbole the ships needed extensive repairs. In the meantime the Milanese had assembled their own fleet. At a battle off Maderno, on 29 September 1439, the Venetian fleet, still barely serviceable, was almost totally destroyed.

Undeterred, the Venetians tried again. This time they transported materials and tools rather than ships. The ships were built and launched at Tòrbole. This time the fleet was successful - the Milanese were defeated on 5 May 1440, and Brèscia finally liberated.

COUNTRY WALK

This fine walk of 5km explores one of the untouched high plateaux above Lake Garda's western shore; allow 2 hours. The walk starts at Vesio, reached by a winding road from Limone sul Garda.

From the centre of Vesio take Via Orsino eastwards, ignoring the turn to the left for the Valle di Bondo and continuing on towards Fornaci. About 200m after the turning a track (Route

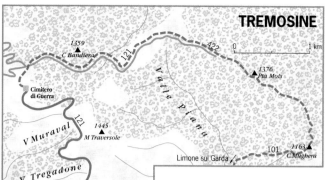

106) is marked on the left: follow this towards the mountains that back the Tremòsine plateau. By a series of hairpin bends this track gains height before making a loop around the peak of Dalvra Alta. Beyond, the track climbs again to reach the Bocca dei Sospiri, a mere bump at 1,026m above sea level, but the highest point on our route.

Continue along Route 106 from

here through magnificent country, going up the western side of Monte Traversole then bearing northwest (as Route 121) to reach a small World War I cemetery. Beyond, the route passes old trenches from the same conflict.

This is a strangely remote place to find reminders of war, but this area formed the front line in the conflict between Italy and Austria. Despite the beauty of their surroundings, the troops endured great hardship, burnt raw in summer, frozen in winter, and always suffering lack of supplies.

Now follow Route 103 to join Route 421 to Fortini. From there take Route 422 to reach Route 101 down the Valle del Singól. Follow this to reach the walk given on page 97, which can be followed into Limone. Buses return to Vesio from here.

That longer walk takes a full 6 hours. Our route from Bocca dei Sospiri follows Route 109 southeast. the twisting track drops down between streams to reach Fornaci. Take the path by the road from the house Fornaci bearing right where it forks and following it back into Vesio.

Rooms and terraces with a view looking across to the Tremòsine plateau

·VERONA·

Built into a sharp bend of the river Adige, Verona (map ref: 111 E2) is a very old city whose Roman remains are second only to those of Rome itself. In the 13th-century, after fierce family feuding, the city fell into the hands of the della Scala (or Scaligeri) family. The most famous of the Scaligeri was Francesco della Scala who called himself Cangrande – the Great Dog – and ruled from 1311 to 1329. When Dante was exiled from Florence he found refuge in Verona and dedicated his *Paradiso*, the third and final volume of the *Divine Comedy* to Cangrande. Ultimately, Verona was absorbed into the Venetian Republic.

Our town walk visits many of the city's finest sights, but the Roman remains north of the river require a separate journey.

Ponte di Pietra takes the visitor across the Adige; the bridge was blown up in 1945 and subsequently reconstructed. The two arches of the left bank are Roman. The contrast of the white stone and the red brick from a 16th-century rebuild makes the bridge very picturesque. Beyond the bridge is the Teatro Romano (Roman Theatre), a semi-circle of marble terraced seating. At the rear of the theatre is the city's Archaeological Museum. The theatre is still used for theatrical performances, notably those of Verona's annual Shakespeare Festival. On the hill behind the theatre is the Castel San Pietro, an Austrian castle on the foundations of an earlier fortress.

South from the theatre, but on the same side of the river, are the 16th-century Giusti Gardens, considered to be one of the finest examples of Renaissance garden design in Italy. The numerous flower beds, fountains and statues are shaded by superb cypress trees and there is an entrancing view of Verona from the tower on the upper terrace.

At the opposite end of the city altogether, beyond the western bend in the Adige you will find the church of San Zeno Maggiore, one of the city's most important monuments. San Zeno is set between a slender 11th-century campanile and a delightful fish-tailed 13th-century tower. This is one of the most beautiful Romanesque churches in northern Italy, its façade completed by a glorious rose window. The doorway is decorated with 12th-century bronze reliefs, while above the high altar there is a marvellous triptych by Mantegna.

TOWN WALK

Allow $1^1/_2$ hours for this 5km walk which covers the main sights in central Verona.

Start in the Piazza del Duomo.

1 Verona's Duomo (Cathedral) is a fusion of Romanesque and Gothic, the simple form of the early church having been transformed by more creative ideas when the façade was heightened in the 14th century. The entrance porch has delightful carvings, perhaps by the same 12th-century craftsmen who carved the porch of San Zeno Maggiore. The nave is high and wide with a beautiful vaulted ceiling. There are numerous works of art, but pride of place goes to Titian's *Assumption*, completed about 1540. Alongside the cathedral is a Romanesque cloister containing fragments of 6th-century mosaic, all that remains of the first church on the site.

From the Piazza del Duomo take Via del Duomo south towards the city centre to reach Sant'Anastasia on the left.

2 Sant'Anastasia is the biggest church in Verona. It was begun in 1290 but the Dominican Friars in charge of the work stopped for breath 30 years later. Work started again in 1423 but stopped 60 years later. This halting progress left the west front incomplete, though the double doorway is a masterpiece nevertheless. Inside look for the two holy water stoups held aloft by *gobbi* (hunchbacks) – oddly charming little figures. There are several fine paintings in the church: the fresco by Altichieri in the Cavelli Chapel (the first on the right) is late 14th century, while Pisanello's later fresco of *St George at Trebizond* has been moved into the Sacristy following restoration.

Above: the palace-lined banks of the Adige. Below: the amphitheatre

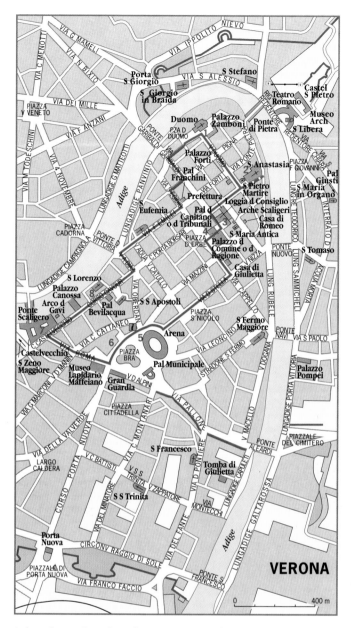

VERONA

0   400 m

Walk past the Torre dei Lamberti, through a passage that leads out into the Piazza delle Erbe.

4 The square is named after an old herb market. Today there is a general market here whose stalls are shaded by wide-brimmed umbrellas. The square has a curiously irregular shape, with fine buildings on all sides. At the northern end – to the right as you enter – the Venetian lion stands on top of a column.

Turn left in the Piazza delle Erbe, exiting along Via Cappello, passing the Casa di Giulietta (Juliet's House) on the left, to reach Via della Stella. Turn right and follow Via della Stella to the Roman Arena in Piazza Brà.

5 The Arena was built in the 1st century AD. It is elliptical, 152m across the long axis and 123m across the short. In its original form the amphitheatre had a three-tier perimeter wall, only a short section – known as the *ala*, the wing – remaining after a severe earthquake in 1183. Inside, stone seating terraces stretch all the way down to the elliptical floor. It is, arguably, the most impressive Roman amphitheatre in existence and still seats some 25,000 people at a time during the opera season.

Cross Piazza Brà by walking along the Listone, the elegant pavement on the northwestern (right-hand) side.

6 The Listone, with its cafés and restaurants, is the social heart of Verona. At the Via Roma end is the Museo Lapidario Maffeiano housing Europe's finest collection of inscribed stones, including ancient Greek, Etruscan and Roman examples.

Continue to the end of Via Roma to reach Corso Castelvecchio, and the impressive castle itself.

7 This important 14th-century castle (see page 103) now houses a museum containing many fine pieces, including works by Mantegna, Veronese, Tintoretto and Tiepolo.

From the castle take Corso Cavour, passing the Arco dei Gavi on the left, an impressive 1st-century AD Roman arch. Further up on the left is the church of San Lorenzo.

8 San Lorenzo is a magnificent Romanesque church. It was rebuilt

A short detour along the right-hand side of the church – with a fine view of the campanile – brings the visitor to Via Sottoriva, a beautiful porticoed street and an almost complete survival from the medieval period.

With your back to Sant'Anastasia cross the square and Via Duomo to reach Corso Sant'Anastasia. Take the second turn on the left, Via Fogge, to reach the Piazza dei Signori.

3 The beautiful square is enclosed by an outstanding range of public buildings. Turning left through a covered passage, you will reach the Scaligeri tombs outside the church of Santa Maria Antica. The tombs are surrounded by a 14th-century iron fence which incorporates a repeated ladder motif – emblem of the della Scalla family and a reference to the literal meaning of their name. Many of the tombs are modest, but there

are two huge pieces of stonework. The tomb of Mastino II della Scala, with its angel supporters, dates to 1351, while the more elaborate tomb, topped with an equestrian statue, is of Cansignorio della Scala and dates from 1375. The most famous member of the family, Cangrande I, lies beneath a less flamboyant wall-mounted tomb, above the side door of the church, which was constructed in 1330.

Back in the main square, the elegant Loggia, to the right, dates from the late 15th century, with later additions. Ahead is a statue of Dante and behind you is the Prefettura, finished off with Scaligeri fishtail battlements. To the left of Dante's statue is the Palazzo della Ragione, inside of which is a fine courtyard, the old market. The external stairway to the palazzo is magnificent. To one side of the courtyard is the Torre dei Lamberti, built in the 12th century. Be sure to climb it for a fabulous view of the city.

after an earthquake in 1117 and its façade is flanked by two round towers. Inside, the banded red and white marble adds a lightness to its austere design.

Continue up Corso Cavour to the Porta dei Borsari, the fine city gate, and turn left into Via A Diaz. Take the next right, Via F Emilei, passing the long flank of the 14th-century church of Sant'Eufemia on the left. Beyond the church, take the fourth turning on the left into Via Sant'Egidio, noting the Palazzo della Franchini, a fine 15th-century Gothic house, on the corner. Take the next turning right into Via San Mamaso. At the next junction turn left into Via Garibaldi. Go straight over at the next junction, then turn right into Strada Arcid Pacifico to return to the Piazza del Duomo and the beginning of the walk.

Juliet's house and the famous balcony; site of medieval romance

ROMEO AND JULIET

Two households, both alike in dignity,
*   In fair Verona, where we lay our scene…*

The opening lines of Shakespeare's famous tragedy are known to millions, and each year huge numbers of visitors come to Verona to see the sights mentioned in the play.

Juliet's House is the major attraction. It is to be found at No 27 Via Cappello, close to Piazza delle Erbe, and its courtyard, time-stained brick façade and tiny marble balcony are romantically correct even if the association with the Capello family is dubious. Below the balcony there is a plaque and a statue of Juliet. The courtyard throngs with visitors in summer, most discussing the feasibility of Romeo's climb to the balcony. Despite the clamour the house has enormous charm – you are left with the impression that even if it was not Juliet's House then it should have been. Romeo's House lies to the north, in Via delle Arche Scaligeri. It is one of the oldest in Verona, but is in a very poor state. There is even less evidence to suppose this to be the Montague family home and the site has little romance.

The final site is Juliet's Tomb, a red marble sarcophagus, probably dating from the 14th century, located in the crypt of an old Capuchin monastery in the south of the city, just off the Lungadige Capuleti embankment. The idea that the sarcophagus was that of Juliet is of long-standing, but again there is no evidence to support the tradition. There is a bust of Shakespeare nearby and the chapel of San Francesco, the only remnant of the monastery, houses a collection of frescos rescued from several of Verona's churches.

Map symbols

A4   Motorway - dual carriageway

A7   Motorway - single carriageway

A1   Toll motorway - dual carriageway

A6   Toll motorway - single carriageway

Motorway junction

Motorway junction restricted access

Motorway service area

Motorway under construction

Primary route

Main road

Secondary road

Other road

D600   E57   N59   Road numbers

Dual carriageway or four lanes

Road in poor condition

Under construction

TOLL   Toll road
Toll

Scenic route

)=========(Road tunnel

68   Distances (km)

10-6
970   Mountain pass (height in metres) with closure period

Gradient 14% and over. Arrow points uphill

Gradient 6% - 13%

Frontier crossing with restricted opening hours

---V---   Vehicle ferry

Airport

International boundary

Viewpoint

Motor racing circuit

2973
DIAVOLEZZA   Mountain / spot height in metres

Urban area

River, lake and canal

■ Jockfall   Place of interest

Mountain railway

Car transporter (rail)

ACCOMMODATION

Self-catering
This is likely to be the most economical choice for anyone travelling as a group of four or more. The lakes region is reasonably well supplied with farmhouses, villas and apartments for rent, but it is necessary to book up to six months in advance for the peak holiday season. Villa brochures can be obtained from travel agents specialising in Italy and they are also widely advertised in Sunday newspapers.

Hotels
Italy has an excellent system for grading hotels and fixing room prices. Hotels are inspected annually and awarded 1 to 5 stars, depending on their facilities. The grading is then used to fix the maximum price the hotel can charge for a single room (*una camera singola*), a twin-bedded room (*una camera doppia*) and a double-bedded room (*una matrimoniale*).

Most Italian hotel rates do not include breakfast (*colazione non incluso*). Breakfast will be available, at a price, but the same can be cheaper at a nearby bar. One and 2-star hotels are excellent value for the budget traveller, though they only offer basic facilities, such as a shared bathroom and toilet. Four and 5-star hotels offer comfort and luxury at a price. As well as large, well-furnished rooms with en-suite bathroom and TV, mini-bar and IDD telephone, they will usually have excellent restaurants and sports facilities, such as a swimming pool.

Most hotels fall into the 3-star category and are very reasonably priced. Standards do vary, however. Traditional city-centre hotels, constrained by the limitations of the building they occupy, may have smaller rooms and fewer facilities than rural or village hotels. Even so, clean rooms with an en-suite bathroom are standard.

Rural and village hotels are very popular with Italians themselves and are most likely to be fully booked during the main holiday season.

Tourist offices in most major towns offer a room-finding service covering the complete range of accommodation, including rooms in private houses.

ARRIVING

Documents
To enter Italy, visitors from the USA, EC and Commonwealth countries need only a valid passport. Other nationals should apply for a visa in advance from an Italian embassy. If you are driving to Italy you must carry your driving licence, car registration documents and evidence of insurance cover (an international Green Card or insurance certificate) at all times; you may be asked to produce all three at random checks.

Airports
The lakes are served by Milan's two international airports. Linate mainly handles European and domestic flights and is situated adjacent to the city's orbital autostrada, 10km due east of the city centre. The airport is connected to the city by taxi or by bus, including the official Alitalia coach that shuttles from the airport to the Central Station every half hour. Tickets must be bought inside the airport building – they are not available on the coach. City bus 73 leaves from the same place – outside and to the left of the central car rental park – and heads for San Babila. This bus is cheaper (tickets from the vending machine at the bus stop, coins only, no change given) but does stop frequently. San Babila has a Metro stop (Line 1, red) for onward travel to the Central Station (change at Duomo for Line 3, yellow or at Loreto for Line 2, green) or Cadorna.

Malpensa handles international, long-haul and European charter flights; this is situated about 50km from Milan, near the southern tip of Lake Maggiore and close to the Busto Arsizio exit of the A8 autostrada. Malpensa is connected to Milan by bus which goes to the Central Station.

Both Linate and Malpensa have excellent car rental facilities.

Flight Information for Linate and Malpensa, tel: 7485 2200.

Venice's Marco Polo airport – connected to all main European airports – could also be used, especially if Lake Garda was your main destination. Orio sul Serio, Bergamo's airport, and Villafranca, Verona's airport, are situated beside the A4 autostrada . Increasingly, these airports are being used by charter flights from British airports.

Railway
Milan's Central Station is connected to all leading European cities, mostly by overnight sleeper trains. The Information Centre at the station is open 7am to 11pm every day including Sunday. Central Station is on Metro Lines 2 (green) and 3 (yellow) and is served by a number of buses and trams.

Porta Garibaldi station is connected by motor-rail link to Paris and Boulogne. From Britain all-in tickets are available for ferry/train journeys. This service is not cheap, but it is huge adventure for children and does cut out the long drive across Europe, thus adding several days to your holiday. The trip leaves Boulogne in mid-afternoon, passes Paris in the early evening, goes through the Simplon Tunnel while you are asleep and deposits you for a free breakfast in Porta Garibaldi at about 6am.

A second motor-rail service runs through the Simplon Tunnel, cars loading and off-loading at each end of the tunnel. This service will be of interest to anyone driving down through Switzerland as it allows the car to be put on the train at Kandersteg, in the Bernese Oberland, or at Brig in the Valai. The former avoids having to drive around the Oberland ridge, but the latter is of more debateable merit, since you save little time and very few miles, while missing some fine rock-gorge scenery.

Milan is connected by rail to Lake Maggiore, to Varese (by the private Ferovia Nord as well as the state railway), to Como (by Ferrovia Nord and the state rail service) and to Bèrgamo, Brèscia and the southern tip of Lake Garda, all of which are on the line to Venice.

The eastern shore of Lake Orta, and the western shore of Lake Maggiore as far as the river Toce, are served by lines that meet at Cuzzago in the Val d'Ossola before crossing into Switzerland via the Simplon Tunnel. The remainder of Lake Maggiore's western shore has no railway, though a line runs along the eastern shore from Sesto Calende into Switzerland.

Lake Lugano is not well served by rail, though there is a line from Varese, terminating at Porto Cerésio, and another from Capolago, on Lake Como, to Lugano, by way of the lake bridge.

On Lake Como the only railway line runs from Lecco up the eastern shore, before serving the length of the Valtellina. A line runs up Lake Iseo's eastern shore and on up Val Camonica, but none of the Lake Garda towns, apart from Desenzano and Peschiera, are served by rail.

CAMPING

Camping is very popular in Italy though to many Italians this does not mean sleeping under canvas, but travelling in mobile camper vans equipped with kitchen, shower, toilet and television. There are excellent sites all over the region. Sites are graded from 1 to 3. Grade 1 sites offer only simple facilities, such as a communal washblock, whereas grade 3 sites will usually supply electricity and water to each plot, and provide a restaurant, shop, telephones and sports facilities as well as chalets for rent. Details of campsites can be obtained from local tourist offices, but the best sites are booked up in the peak season and advance reservation is advisable. For booking forms and a list of sites write to Centro Internazionale Prenotazioni

Federcampeggio, Casella Postale 23, 50041 Calenzano, Firenze (tel: 055 882 391).

CHEMISTS

Chemists (*farmacie*) are identified by a sign displaying a green cross on a white background. They are staffed by trained pharmacists who can prescribe drugs, including antibiotics, that are only available by doctor's prescription in other countries. Normal opening hours are from 9am to 1pm and from 4pm to 7pm, Monday to Friday. The address of the nearest chemist on emergency duty will be posted in the window. In rural areas, where there may be no alternative, it is acceptable to ring the doorbell out of hours in an emergency.

Drugs prescribed by a doctor or hospital are also dispensed from a *farmacia*. A small, non-recoverable tax will be charged.

CRIME

The lakes are relatively free of crime, but it always pays to be careful. Do not leave valuables in your car. It makes sense to keep photocopies of important documents separately from the originals to speed up their replacement if they are lost or stolen. Report any loss promptly at the nearest police station. The key word is *denuncia*, meaning statement, without which you will not be able to make an insurance claim.

Milan, as with all major cities, is a special case. Steer clear of the areas near the castle, Central Station and especially Parco Sempione, the main drug centre, at night. Piazza Vetra in the Ticinese area is also best avoided.

Milan has a number of beggars and gangs of small children are particularly difficult to shake off. At first they will beg and plead, but they may also start to pull at you or at your bags. If you are approached do not stop, avoid eye contact and do not enter into conversation. If you are tugged, shake yourself free, raise your arm and shout with exaggerated anger. Use of words like *Inglese* and *Polizia* will have a sobering affect, but nothing works anywhere near as well as a ferocious look and the hint of possible violence.

CUSTOMS

All items intended for your personal use can be imported duty free and there are no limitations on the import of currency. Special rules apply to the import of

hunting weapons (information from Italian embassies). EC residents aged 17 years or over can import the following duty free (non-EC residents have the same limits, except that the tobacco allowance is doubled; higher limits apply to goods purchased duty and tax paid within the EC):

Tobacco: 100 cigarettes or cigarillos or 50 cigars or 250 grammes of tobacco.

Alcohol: 1 litre of spirits or 2 litres of still, sparkling or fortified wine.

Toiletries: 50 grammes of perfume or 250 cc of toilet water.

New and more generous limits will shortly be introduced. Look for notices at your point of departure or consult a travel agent.

DISABLED VISITORS

Few concessions to the needs of disabled people are made anywhere in Italy. Churches and museums are often approached by steep flights of stairs and hotel lifts tend to be too small for a chair. One welcome concession is that free parking spaces are reserved for orange badge holders close to major tourist sites, but never enough to meet the demand. Sources of further information include the offices of the Italian State Tourist Board, whose hotel lists indicate those suitable for disabled visitors, and Radar (25 Mortimer Street, London W1M 8AB, tel: 071 637 5400).

DRIVING

Breakdown
If you break down, switch the hazard lights on immediately and place the red warning triangle 50m behind the vehicle. Find a telelphone and ring 116, the number for the Automobile Club d'Italia (ACI) which provides a free breakdown service to foreign visitors. It is well worth using this number too if you have an accident; the ACI will help with police formalities and the exchange of insurance details. If necessary they will also help to find a garage for repairs and ensure that the charges are fair.

Car Hire
Without a car it is virtually impossible to see the best that the lakes area has to offer. Bringing your own car to Italy will probably cost more than renting on arrival, and there are several travel agents offering fly-drive packages to Milan, where cars can be collected on arrival at the airport. The price should include unlimited mileage

and insurance as well as a 24-hour emergency breakdown service.

Documentation

Drivers must always carry a driving licence, the car registration documents and an insurance certificate, or international Green Card, and the owner's written permission if the vehicle is not yours. Holders of British old-style green driving licences must also carry an official Italian translation (obtainable from motoring organisations such as the AA and RAC).

Driving Conditions

Italian traffic regulations require the wearing of seat belts and the carrying of a warning triangle. Use of the car's horn is prohibited in built-up areas except in emergency; flash your lights instead as a warning. Outside towns it is customary to use the horn to warn that you are about to overtake and to warn of your presence on a blind bend. Dipped headlights must be used when driving through road tunnels.

Parking

It is vital to understand the parking rules if you do not want your vehicle towed away or to be served with a hefty fine. In some areas parking is totally banned (these are identified by a graphic sign showing a pick-up vehicle towing a car away). As a general principle, when you arrive in a town look for car park direction signs (a large square sign with the letter P painted in white on a blue

Speed limits		
Engine Capacity	Autostrada	Other Roads
Cars to 1099cc Motorcycles to 349cc	110kmh	90kmh
Cars over 1100cc Motorcycles over 350cc	130kmh	100kmh
Other Vehicles	90kmh	80kmh

In all built-up areas the speed limit is 50kmh.

background). In some streets, generally those furthest from the centre, parking is free on most days, but always look for signs detailing the one morning a week when parking is banned for street cleaning. If you are parked in the street when the cleaning wagon comes (sometime between midnight and 6am) you will be fined.

In the major towns there are meters which take 100, 200 and 500 lire coins, where you can park for up to two hours. In some squares, especially in the smaller towns, you buy a ticket from an attendant. There are also privately run multi-storey or underground car parks in most cities; you can park here for as long as you wish, but they are expensive. By far the majority of street parking, however, falls into the *zona disco* category. This means that parking is free for one hour – and sometimes two – provided that cars display a disc (purchased from petrol stations) showing the

time of arrival. Once the time is up drivers must move on and find another space; frustrating but necessary, because traffic police are very vigilant.

Petrol

Petrol stations are usually open from 7.30am to noon and 4pm to 7pm Monday to Friday. Many are closed on Saturday and all close on Sunday and public holidays, except for autostrada service stations. Some display a sign saying *Aperto 24 Ore*; this means that they have an automatic petrol pump which accepts 10,000 lire notes – but if the note is crumpled or creased the machine will either reject it or swallow it but give no petrol in exchange. Very few petrol stations accept credit cards. Two types of petrol are sold: *Super* (4 star) and *Super senza piombo* (unleaded). Diesel is sold as *gasolio*.

Petrol Coupons

Those travelling to Italy in their own cars are eligible to receive petrol coupons from ACI (Italian Automobile Club) offices at border crossings into the country. The coupon booklet contains vouchers for the lire equivalent of about 150 litres of fuel. The booklet offers a discount of about 20 per cent on pump prices and has two other advantages. Firstly a toll card is included for use on automatic autostrada booths, with a value of about 30,000 lire, and possession of the booklet makes the owner a temporary member of ACI so that its emergency services can be called upon. These include free car hire if your car breaks down and is going to be off the road for more than 12 hours. If you do need the service ring 116, or ask for ACI at the autostrada SOS columns – situated every 2km along the carriageway.

To obtain a booklet you must be driving a foreign car, not a rented Italian car, and you must show your vehicle's registration certificate.

Milanese police in ceremonial dress outshine guests at a gala fashion show

ELECTRICITY

The supply is 220 volts and the plugs are the standard continental type, with two round pins. An adaptor is needed to use three-pin appliances and a transformer if the appliances normally operate at 100-120 volts (eg US and Canadian standard).

EMERGENCY TELEPHONE NUMBERS

Police and ambulance 113
Carabinieri 112
Fire Service 115

HEALTH

For minor ailments it is best to seek the help of a pharmacist (*farmacia* – see Chemists). Every public hospital has a casualty department (*Pronto Soccorso*) where treatment is free. Call an ambulance by dialling 113. Otherwise, medical care has to be paid for. In theory, EC nationals can seek reimbursement of the costs; provided, that is, they have had the foresight to complete an official E111 form in advance of their visit. In practice, there is a lot of form-filling and bureaucracy involved, and it can be simpler to take out travel insurance, with cover for emergency medical care, in advance of your visit.

There are no special health regulations governing visitors to Italy from most countries, but adequate precautions need to be taken against sunburn.

LAKE STEAMERS

There are now very few steam-powered ferriess on the lakes but the name is still used to cover a variety of passenger boats that daily criss-cross the waters of the larger lakes – Orta, Maggiore, Lugano, Como, Iseo and Garda. Most services are provided by modern diesel-engined ferry boats. Hydrofoils (*aliscafi*) are decidedly more exciting and that reduce crossing times but cost in general, about 50 per cent more than steamers. To take advantage of their speed, hydrofoils do not call at every port, taking more direct lines between the lake ends.

Price reductions are available for those who buy 'season' tickets, valid for one day, several days, or one or two weeks. The diesel and hydrofoil ferry services, together with the car-ferries that offer limited crossings on the three major lakes, operate scheduled services every day. In addition the steamer companies run special

All aboard for a leisurely cruise by old-fashioned steamer

sightseeing services in the summer months and excellent night-time trips on light-bedecked boats with dancing to live music. Some operators use genuine 'old-fashioned' paddle steamers, offering an unforgettable outing – particularly when the boat passes close to some of the floodlit highlights of the lakes such as the Rocca d'Angera on Lake Maggiore and Malcésine's castle on Lake Garda. The boats used for these trips have restaurants and bars, full air-conditioning and the best of sound systems.

The Maggiore and Lugano steamers cross the national border between Italy and Switzerland and the services include customs and border officials; passports must be carried and dutiable goods must be declared.

On Lake Maggiore there is one car-ferry, linking Verbania-Intra with Laveno; the crossing takes around 20 minutes. Lake Como has four car ferries plying the waters near Punta Spartivento, beyond Bellágio. They link Menággio with Bellágio and with Varenna, and Cadenabbia with Bellágio and with Varenna. Each crossing takes from 15 to 30 minutes. On Lake Garda there is a single car ferry service, from Maderno to Torri del Benaco, the crossing taking about 30 minutes.

Telephone numbers for Lake Steamer Offices:
Como 031 273 342 or 260 234
Garda 030 914 1321
Iseo 035 971 483
Lugano 091 515 223
Maggiore 0322 46651 or 2352;
0323 30393, 42321 or 503 220
Orta 0322 844 862

MEDIA

The cities and bigger towns in the lakes area will have kiosks selling English-language newspapers. There are also two English-

language bookshops in Milan: the English Bookshop is at 12 Via Mascheroni (the nearest Metro station is Concilazione on Line 1, red). The American Bookshop is on the corner of Via Campero and Largo Cairoli, near the castle.

MONEY

The Italian lira (plural lire) is usually abbreviated to L or £. The lira is a relatively stable currency and the exchange rates have not fluctuated much in recent years. Many Italians would like the government to simplify the currency by knocking off three zeros (so that 1,000 lire would become 1 lira), but so far this measure has been defeated in every parliamentary vote.

Notes come in denominations of 1,000, 2,000, 5,000, 10,000, 50,000 and 100,000 lire; coins in denominations of 10, 50, 100, 200 and 500 lire. Telephone tokens (*gettoni*) are also accepted as coinage: their current value is 200 lire. The days when coins and small notes were in short supply are now over. Travellers should not normally be met with hostility if they offer a 50,000 lire note in payment – except for small items such as a cup of coffee or a postcard. 10,000 lire notes are useful for buying petrol from automatic pumps and for buying telephone cards from vending machines. A supply of 100 and 200 lire coins is useful for making local telephone calls and feeding the electricity meters in churches for illuminating frescos. They may also be useful in supermarkets for the odd few lire on the end of your bill. Supermarkets price goods to the nearest lira, despite having no coins below 10 lire – and those becoming increasingly rare. If your bill finishes with a few odd lire you are likely to receive sweets in lieu of the difference.

Banks

Banks in Italy normally open from 8.20am to 1.20pm weekdays. Some city-centre banks also open in the afternoon from 2.30pm to 3.45pm. None open at weekends, and a wise traveller in Italy also keeps an eye on the festive calendar: some banks change their opening hours just before and just after bank holidays and big festivals.

Fortunately there are several other sources of money if you run out over a weekend. Some banks in the bigger cities have hole-in-the-wall exchange machines which accept the major European currencies and US dollars and pay out lire in exchange. Instructions are given in several languages and the exchange rate is good; the machines are, though, apt to reject notes that are creased or damaged.

Equally useful are cash machines displaying the blue and red EC sign. If your credit card displays the same sign you can use these machines to draw cash, provided you feed in the correct personal identity number (check with your bank or card company before you go if you have forgotten the PIN number). If anything goes wrong, and the machine swallows your card, it can usually be retrieved by presenting your passport to the bank within three days.

The major credit cards (Visa, Mastercard/Access, American Express and Diners' Club) are accepted in most hotels and restaurants and up-market shops (look for a sign saying *Carta Si* – Card Yes – in the window). Despite the high price of petrol, however, very few garages accept cards. You will also have to pay cash for your groceries; small shops only accept cash and the out-of-town hypermarkets issue their own charge cards and only accept these.

Eurocheques are very widely accepted in Italy and are as good as money: each cheque can be cashed at a bank for up to 300,000 lire. Neither will any problem be encountered with cashing traveller's cheques, though for all bank transactions it is necessary to present your passport.

When looking for the best possible rates of exchange, it is usually more advantageous to use credit cards in payment of goods and services because the exchange calculation is carried out at the inter-bank rate, which is more favourable than the tourist rate. The same is not true of cash advances because daily interest is charged until you pay your bill. Most banks in Italy charge a small commission for a credit card advance and for changing cash or Eurocheques, though visitors should not be charged for cashing a traveller's cheque.

OPENING TIMES

Shops are usually open Monday to Saturday from 9am to 1pm and from 4pm to 7pm (8pm in summer). In cities, large stores may stay open until 9pm on Thursday or Friday, but are closed on Monday morning. In rural areas shops may close for one afternoon midweek, usually Wednesday. Flower and cake shops open in the morning on Sundays and public holidays, but very little else, although bars remain open all day six days a week. All bars and restaurants must shut at least once a week by law. The day in question will be posted outside, or on the shutters. Many businesses, including restaurants, close for two weeks in August, the traditional holiday month in Italy.

Banks are open Monday to Friday, 8.20am to 1.20pm. Some reopen from 2.30pm to 3.45pm.

Petrol stations open Monday to Friday from 7.30am to noon and 4pm to 7pm. Many are closed on Saturday and all close on Sunday and public holidays, except for autostrada service stations.

Post offices are open Monday to Saturday 8am to 1.30pm, although many bars displaying a T sign sell postage stamps.

Tourist offices follow shop opening hours, though in Milan and some other large cities they may open on Sundays in summer.

Museums are a law unto themselves. As a general guide, expect them to be closed on Mondays; on Tuesday to Saturday they should be open 9am to 1pm and 2pm to 5pm, and on Sundays 2pm to 5pm. These rules apply mainly in the summmer (April to September); in winter expect them to open later and close earlier. Hotels in the larger towns and cities can give you reasonably up-to-date information, as can tourist information centres. In rural areas, you may have to seek out a custodian, whose name should be posted on the museum door, or ring a bell to gain admittance.

Churches are usually open from 8am to 12 noon or 1pm and from 4pm to 7pm (or dusk in winter). Tourists are discouraged from wandering round the church when there is a service in progress. In rural areas, you may have to seek out a keyholder, especially in winter months.

POLICE

Italy has different police forces for different functions. Visitors are most likely to encounter the *vigili urbani*, traffic police whose main job is to prevent infringement of parking regulations and keep unauthorised vehicles out of city centres during prohibited hours. Visitors are not immune from traffic laws. If you commit an offence and fail to pay the fine on the spot, you can expect a letter to arrive on your doormat at home in due course.

Local police matters are handled by the *polizia urbana*. They also carry out random checks on vehicles, so if you are flagged down whilst travelling, do not worry. They will want to see your driving licence, car registration documents and insurance card or certificate and are generally very friendly as long as your papers are in order. If you need their help in an emergency, dial 113. If you need to report a theft, go to the police station (*questura*) and make a statement (*denuncia*) using an official multi-lingual form, keeping one stamped copy for yourself as evidence for making an insurance claim. You will also see armed police – the *carabinieri* – on duty as you travel; they are a national police force, technically a branch of the army, whose role is the handling of serious crime.

POST OFFICE

Many bars and tobacconists sell postage stamps for letters and postcards: look for a sign with the white letter T on a blue back-ground. For other transactions you will need to go to a post office: most are open Monday to Saturday 8am to 1pm though city-centre branches may open as late as 7pm.

PUBLIC HOLIDAYS

Most businesses are closed on the following national holidays:

1 January
6 January (Epiphany)
Good Friday
Easter Monday
25 April (Liberation Day)
1 May (Labour Day)
15 August (Assumption)
1 November (All Saints)
8 December (Immaculate Conception)
25 and 26 December

In addition, many businesses close for a period during August and individual towns close for big festivals. For instance there is a holiday in Milan on 7 December, Sant'Ambrogio's feast day.

PUBLIC TRANSPORT

The only city in which visitors are likely to need to use public transport is Milan, where the private car is a liability. In all the other towns and cities, the historical centre is so compact that all the sites are within comfortable walking distance. In fairness, the same is also true of Milan, but the tram, bus and Metro services are useful if you want to limit the amount of walking. There are no ticket sellers on the buses and trams: you must buy the tickets in advance from a kiosk or vending machine. When you get on the vehicle you must put your ticket in the time-punching machine. Tickets are valid for 75 minutes and you can transfer from one service to another within that time. Metro tickets can be used for one Metro ride and any number of bus and/or tram rides up to the 75-minute limit.

SENIOR CITIZENS

Some museums, but by no means the majority, offer reduced price admission to senior citizens from EC countries on production of a passport as evidence of age. More concessions may follow with EC harmonisation.

STUDENT/YOUTH TRAVEL

As with senior citizens, Italy makes few concessions to students; school children (under 18) are admitted free or at a reduced price to a few museums, but otherwise the full price is charged. Holders of student railcards can obtain discounts on the already cheap railway system.

The Italian Youth Hostels Association has limited accommodation near the lakes. For details contact: Associazone Italiana Alberghi per la Gioventi, Palazzo della Civilt' del Lavoro, Quadrato della Concordia, 00144 EUR Roma (tel: 06 591 3702)

TELEPHONES

Old-fashioned public telephones, operated by tokens (*gettoni*) are rapidly becoming part of Italian folklore as they are replaced by modern card and coin-operated phones. Coin-operated phones accept 100, 200 and 500 lire coins and can be found in many streets and squares. Insert the coins before dialling and insert more if you hear a beep while still speaking; unused coins will be refunded after a call by pushing the return button.

Phone cards are available in 5,000 and 10,000 lire values. The cards are available from kiosks and bars, and also from vending machines in airports, stations and other large centres. The vending machines take notes and coins. Once you have obtained your card tear off the top left corner, as indicated, and it is ready for use. Insert it into the slot on the card reader and wait for the current value to be indicated on the digital screen before dialling. The screen will count the value down for you as your call progresses. If the card runs out during the call you will hear the same warning tone that you hear when your money is running low, but there is a difference - when the card becomes empty of credit you cannot continue with the call by inserting coins, neither have you the time to insert another card. The call will terminate. If at the end of your call your card remains in credit, it will be returned automatically. Be patient, it only feels like the machine has eaten it out of spite.

Many bars show a telephone symbol which indicates that they have a phone that you can use. Here you will be able to dial yourself, the price being registered at the counter where you will pay after your call. Sometimes, but not always, there will be a booth and a screen to tell you how much the call is costing. The bar is entitled to add a surcharge for the service so the cost will usually be more than is registered.

Many hotel rooms also have IDD phones, but the hotel mark-up makes this an expensive way of making a call.

If the thought of using a foreign phone system is daunting go to an SIP office. SIP, the national phone company, has offices with individual booths in all major towns and cities. Tell the counter staff if you want to make an international call since some booths can only be used for local calls. When you are given your booth you dial as usual and the price is displayed on a screen in front of you. At the end of the call you pay at the counter.

To dial a number in the same province you should omit the area code; otherwise you need to dial the city or district code, then the subscriber number. If the number is engaged you will hear a series of rapid pips; the dialling tone is a series of longer notes. To make an international call dial 00, then the country code, the area code (minus the initial 0) and the subscriber number. Thus, to dial

the Italian State Tourist Office in London (tel: 071 408 1254) from Milan - or anywhere else in Italy - you dial 00 44 71 408 1254. To call Italy from another country, dial the international access code followed by 39, then the area code minus the initial 0 and the subscriber number.

TIME

Italy observes Central European Time (one hour ahead of Greenwich Mean Time) from the end of September to the end of March. Daylight Saving Time comes into effect for the summer when the Italian clocks go forward by an hour, in common with most of Europe.

TIPPING

In general, tips are not expected and are received with pleasure: a few coins for the barman, 1,000 lire for taxi drivers and porters, a little more for waiters - these will be received with smiles.

TOILETS

Railway stations, airports, bus stations, autostrada rest areas and service stations and some museums have public toilets but elsewhere they scarcely exist; restaurants provide toilets for their customers but bars do not as a rule, so if you ask to use the toilet (*bagno*, *toiletta* or *gabinetto*) in a crisis, remember that the barman is doing you a special favour if he says yes. In restaurants one toilet may serve for both sexes; if there are two they are likely to be marked *signore* or *donne* for women and *signori* or *uomini* for men.

TOURIST OFFICES

Towns, and many villages, in the lakes area have a tourist information centre, usually well signposted and often located in or near the main square. They are generally open from 9am to 1pm and 3pm to 6pm, but the hours will vary according to the season - in popular destinations in summer they may stay open through the lunch period, whereas in winter they may close earlier in the evening. The staff will help you find accommodation locally and answer questions on transport, opening times and entertainment. The emphasis is on local information; if you want more general information, contact the Italian State Tourist Office in your own country before departure.

·GLOSSARY·

Italian is a rhythmic and euphónious language that is easy to pronounce once a few basic rules are understood.

C or *cc* before *e* or *i* is pronounced *ch* (*cinque* = chinque, *cappuccino* = cappuchino). Otherwise *c*, *cc* and *ch* are pronounced *k* (*caldo* = kaldo, *piccante* = pikante, *Chianti* = Kianti).
G or *gg* before *e* or *i* is pronounced *j* (*giovedi* = jiovedi, *formaggio* = formajio). Otherwise *g*, *gg* and *gh* are prounced hard as in get. *Gli* is pronounced like the middle part of million (*Castiglione* = Castillionay). *Gn* is prounounced *ny* (*bagno* = banyo).
H is not prounounced (*hortus* = ortus).
S between vowels is pronounced *z* (*casa* = caza). *Sc* before *e* or *i* is pronounced *sh* (*scena* = shena); otherwise it is pronounced as *sc* in scampi.
Z is pronounced *ts* (*grazie* = gratsie).
The stress nearly always falls on the last but one syllable. Where it does not, you will sometimes see a stress mark over the accented syllable (Mèdici, Accadèmia, Nicolò, caffé).
Accentuation can alter the way a vowel is pronounced. *A* when stressed is like *a* in father (*andàre*); *e* when stressed is like *a* in fate (*mèle*); *i* when stressed is like *i* in machine (*primo*) and like *y* when followed by another vowel (*piove*); *o* when stressed is like *o* in rock (*notte*); *u* is pronounced like *u* in June (*uscita*) but like *w* when followed by another vowel (*uomini*).

Basic words

Even if you speak no other Italian, the following phrases will be indispensible.

Good morning **buongiorno**
Good afternoon/evening **buona sera**
Goodbye **arrivederci**
Goodnight **buona notte**
Please **per favore**
Thank you **grazie**
You are welcome **prego**
Excuse me **mi scusi/permesso**
That's fine/OK **va bene**
Yes/No **si/no**
Hot/Cold **caldo/freddo**
Open/Closed **aperto/chiuso**
Entrance **entrata**
Exit **uscita**
Ladies **signore/donne**

Gents **signori/uomini**
I don't understand **non capisco**
I don't speak Italian **non parlo Italiano**
Do you speak English? **parla Inglese?**

Hotel

Single/twin-bedded room **una camera singola/doppia**
With bathroom/shower **con bagno/doccia**
Child's bed/cot **letto di bambino/una culla**
How much per night? **quanto costa al giorno?**
Including breakfast? **colazione incluso?**
Too expensive **costa troppo**
Anything cheaper? **meno caro?**
Floor **piano**
Key **chiave**
Dining room **sala di pranzo**
What time is breakfast/dinner? **a che ora è la colazione/cena?**
Laundry service **servizio lavanderia**
Come in! **avanti!**

Restaurant

Have you a table for… **avete un tavolo per…**
 one/two/three/four? **uno/due/tre/quattro?**
Could we change tables? **potremmo spostarci?**
A quiet table? **un tavolo tranquillo**
The menu **la carta/la lista**
The bill **il conto**

Drinks

Black coffee **caffé/espresso**
White coffee cappuccino/**caffé latte**
Tea **té**
Mineral water (carbonated/still) **acqua minerale (gassata/non gassata)**
Beer (draught) **birrá (alla spina)**
Fruit juice **succo di frutta**
Orange/lemon squash **aranciata/limonata**
Red/white/rosé/sparkling wine **vino rosso/bianco/rosato/ spumante**
Dry/sweet **secco/dolce**
Another (coffee) please **un altro (caffé) per favore**

Menu terms

Aceto vinegar
Affumicato smoked
Al burro cooked in butter
Al forno baked
Alla brace charcoal grilled
Alla griglia grilled
Bianco boiled
Bruschetta garlic bread
Burro butter

Contorno vegetable side dish
Crudo raw
Diavola spicy (often hot)
Farcito stuffed
Fatto in casa homemade
Fettina a slice
Formaggio cheese
Fresco fresh
Fritto deep fried
Gelato ice cream
Pane bread
Pezzo piece (of meat or fish which is ordered by the 100 grammes)
Piatto del giorno dish of the day
Piacere cooked to your taste
Tramezzino sandwich
Uovo egg
Zucchero sugar

Meat

Agnello lamb
Bistecca beefsteak
Cervo venison
Cinghiale wild boar
Coniglio rabbit
Faggiano pheasant
Fegato liver
Lepre hare
Lingua tongue
Lumache snails
Maiale pork
Manzo beef
Piccione pigeon
Pollo chicken
Porchetta suckling pig
Prosciutto raw cured ham
Rognoni kidneys
Salsiccia sausage
Vitello veal

Numbers

1	uno
2	due
3	tre
4	quattro
5	cinque
6	sei
7	sette
8	otto
9	nove
10	dieci
11	undici
12	dodici
13	tredici
14	quattordici
15	quindici
16	sedici
17	diciasette
18	diciotto
19	diciannove
20	venti
30	trenta
40	quaranta
50	cinquanta
60	sessanta
70	settanta
80	ottanta
90	novanta
100	cento
1,000	mille

ACKNOWLEDGEMENTS

The Automobile Association wishes to thank the following
photographers and libraries for their assistance in the preparation of this
book.
PETE BENNETT was commissioned to take the photographs for this
book and his photographs appear on the following pages:
6, 7, 10a, 10b, 14, 15b, 16, 17, 20b, 21, 22, 23, 24, 26, 29a, 29b, 30, 34a,
37b, 38a, 38b, 39a, 39b, 40, 41a, 41b, 46b, 46/7, 48, 53, 55, 56a, 56b,
57, 58, 63a, 66, 73a, 74a, 74b, 75, 76, 80, 81a, 81b, 82/3, 83b, 86, 88,
89, 90a, 90b, 91, 93a, 93b, 94a, 94b, 95a, 95b, 96, 97b, 99, 100, 101,
102a, 102b, 108, 112, 114, 115
The remaining photographs are from the following libraries:
AA PHOTO LIBRARY
Adrian Baker 32b, 33   Anthony Souter 28a
J ALLAN CASH PHOTOLIBRARY 68 View over Sondrio, 69 View over
Madesimo & Skiers
LENCI DOLL MUSEUM 15a Lenci dolls
MARY EVANS PICTURE LIBRARY 8b Gregorius III, 9a Charlemagne
crosses the Alps
RICHARD SALE 8a, 12b, 18, 20a, 28b, 31, 32a, 34b, 35, 36/7, 42, 43, 44,
45a, 45b, 46a, 49b, 50a, 51a, 51b, 52a, 54, 59, 60b, 61a, 62, 63b, 65, 67,
70, 72, 73b, 77, 78a, 78b, 79a, 79b, 84a, 84/5, 85, 92, 103, 106a
SPECTRUM COLOUR LIBRARY Cover Lake Maggiore, 12a Isola Bella,
60a Performance of Aida in Verona, 104 Trobole, 106b The Arena,
Verona
ZEFA PICTURE LIBRARY 13 San Guilio Island, 105 Tremosine